The Origins of the
Great Leap Forward

Transitions: Asia and Asian America

Series Editor, *Mark Selden*

*The Origins of the Great Leap Forward:
The Case of One Chinese Province,* Jean-Luc Domenach

Privatizing Malaysia: Rents, Rhetoric, Realities, edited by Jomo K. S.

*The Politics of Democratization:
Generalizing East Asian Experiences,*
edited by Edward Friedman

Our Land Was a Forest: An Ainu Memoir, Kayano Shigeru

*The Political Economy of China's Financial Reforms:
Finance in Late Development,* Paul Bowles and Gordon White

*Reinventing Vietnamese Socialism:
Doi Moi in Comparative Perspective,*
edited by William S. Turley and Mark Selden

FORTHCOMING

*City States in the Global Economy: Industrial Restructuring in Hong Kong
and Singapore,* Stephen Chiu, Kong-Chong Ho, and Tai-lok Lui

Unofficial Histories: Chinese Reportage from the Era of Reform,
edited by Thomas Moran

Workers in the Cultural Revolution, Elizabeth Perry and Li Xun

Twentieth-Century China: An Interpretive History, Peter Zarrow

*Cooperative Innovation and Late Development:
Technological Catch-up in Japan,* Donna L. Doane

Moving Mountains: Women and Feminism in Japan, Kanai Yoshiko

*The Middle Peasant and Social Change:
The Communist Movement in the Taihang Base Area, 1937–1945,*
David Goodman

*The Chinese Triangle and the Future of the
Asia-Pacific Region,* Hsin-huang Michael Hsiao and Alvin So

Japanese Colonialism in Taiwan, Chih-ming Ka

THE ORIGINS OF THE GREAT LEAP FORWARD

The Case of One
Chinese Province

JEAN-LUC DOMENACH

Translated by A M Berrett

Westview Press
Boulder • San Francisco • Oxford

Transitions: Asia and Asian America

English-language edition copyright © 1995 by Westview Press, Inc.

Published in English in 1995 in the United States of America by Westview Press, Inc., 5500 Central Avenue, Boulder, Colorado 80301-2877, and in the United Kingdom by Westview Press, 36 Lonsdale Road, Summertown, Oxford OX2 7EW

Published in French in 1982 in France by Presses de la Fondation nationale des sciences politiques. French edition copyright © Ecole des hautes studes en sciences sociales Presses de la Fondation nationale des sciences politiques

Library of Congress Cataloging-in-Publication Data
Domenach, Jean-Luc.
    [Aux origines du Grand Bond en avant. English]
    The origins of the great leap forward : the case of one Chinese
province / Jean-Luc Domenach : translated by A.M. Berrett.
        p.   cm. — (Transitions—Asia and Asian America)
    Includes bibliographical references and index.
    ISBN 0-8133-1710-X. — ISBN 0-8133-2514-5 (if published as a paperback)
    1. Henan Province (China)—Politics and government.   I. Title.
II. Series.
DS793.H5D6513   1995
951'.18055—dc20   94-38713
                                                                                      CIP

Printed and bound in the United States of America

The paper used in this publication meets the requirements of the American National Standard for Permanence of Paper for Printed Library Materials Z39.48-1984.

10   9   8   7   6   5   4   3   2   1

Contents

Foreword
Mark Selden

Jean-Luc Domenach's *Grand Bond en Avant* was the first major study of the Great Leap Forward and its origins in any language. It remains the most probing work on the period, a seminal yet barely studied moment that set the course of mobilizational collectivism that characterized the late Mao years. Domenach suggests controversial political and social answers to a series of troubling dilemmas for students of China and of socialism: How was it possible for China's ruling party, which had come to power in the course of several decades of successful rural mobilization, to launch a movement so divorced from social reality? Above all, how are we to understand the decision to press the movement to the point of chaos and economic collapse, giving rise to arguably the greatest famine in human history and causing, depending on whose statistics one finds persuasive, 15 to 30 million or more deaths, nearly all of them in the countryside?

In this book, in contrast to other studies that focus on national politics, Domenach provides a closeup of a single critical province, Henan, the national model of the Leap, and subsequently, the leader in famine deaths. Through the close study of documentary sources, particularly provincial and local newspapers, he illuminates the dynamics of a political process that would eventually press beyond reason of humanity. Under the frenzied conditions of the Leap, what counted most in the calculus of national and provincial politics was not the fate of marginalized peasants and other working people, but overcoming political rivals and winning the support of patrons, ultimately of Mao Zedong.

In illuminating the rewards as well as the risks for models, whether local, regional, or national units or individuals, the work clarifies a distinctive feature of Chinese politics, the binary opposition between those who benefit from the favors that the state bestows and those left to survive by their wits and through such protective networks as they can create. The emergence of this relatively poor North China plains province as the national model brought Henan important symbolic and material rewards ranging from Mao's praise to featured status in the national press to the hidden economic benefits that invariably flowed to models.

Ironically, however, the very processes that gave rise to mobilizational models could produce disaster, as in Henan and many other areas singled out for praise during the Leap. This is because sustaining a front-runner position required promoting zealotry to the highest degree. As the provincial model of the Leap, Henan generated the most extreme labor-intensive and leveling policies and outstripped others in announcing impossible production figures. These policies led to famine disasters not only because they pressed alienated people beyond human endurance but also because localities claiming miraculous production results then had to make good on the highest levels of sales to the state, receiving low state prices for their grain. In the famine that followed the Leap, Henan reportedly had more deaths than any other province, ranging in the millions. Entire villages were depopulated in some of the hardest hit prefectures.

Domenach was the first scholar to recognize, in the persistent calls to establish *dashe,* or enlarged cooperatives, in the early 1950s, an important dynamic that later culminated in the Leap. Although the party sometimes spoke reassuringly of gradual voluntary cooperation, pressures for giantism, leveling, and market elimination gained momentum and led ineluctably to the formation of large state-imposed collectives of the Soviet type and the transfer of the rural surplus to state industry and the cities. From the collectivization drive that crescendoed in 1955–1956, it was but a small step to the utopianism of the communes and the Leap with their extreme leveling and the messianic belief that the millennium was at hand. This then is a critical work in searching for the roots of Communist fundamentalism in the Chinese revolution.

Re-reading Domenach's work a decade later leads me to reflect on several important issues of Chinese politics. Whereas the author presents Henan's importance as a "typical" province, I read the significance of the work in terms of the politics of models with Henan as the national exemplar. Where Domenach sees the Leap as providing grist for the mill of totalitarian politics, other frameworks seem to me more illuminating of both the powerful swings that have characterized Chinese politics and the triumph of the mobilizational collectivism in the period under study. Domenach's work will contribute to reassessment of the principal models that presently dominate understanding of the Leap, notably the "Politics at Mao's Court" approach favored by Frederick C. Teiwes and Roderick MacFarquhar and the bureaucratic politics approach advanced most forcefully by David Bachman.

This foreword pays homage not only to the pioneering work of Domenach but to the distinctive contributions of French sinology. From the superb earlier work of Etienne Balazs, Jacques Gernet, and Jean Chesneaux, to recent studies by Lucien Bianco, Pierre-Etienne Will, Marianne Bastid, Marie-Claire Bergère, and others, the small group of French China specialists has made impressive contributions toward the understanding of China's past and present. At its best, this scholarship builds on and extends the traditions of the Annales School and the work of Fernand Braudel in exploring the wellsprings of socioeconomic and political change with a keen eye to the *longue durée.*

Domenach's study highlights the fact that further study at the provincial and local levels will pay dividends to researchers who can now look to abundant new sources, from mainland archives and the local press to interviewing, and including a wealth of published and unpublished memoirs that were preciously unavailable. For the present, Domenach's contribution sets a high standard for understanding how socialist egalitarianism, carried to irrational lengths in the mobilizational frenzy of the Leap, could end so tragically.

Preface to the English-Language Edition

The work that Mark Selden suggested I make available to the American scholarly world was originally published in Paris in 1982. I am grateful to Lucien Bianco, Marie-Claire Bergère, and Annie Kriegel for their help at that time.

The aims of my study and the case-study method that I use are set out in the Introduction, but I feel that the book's publication in the United States more than ten years after its appearance in France calls for some clarification, particularly of the atmosphere that prevailed in French intellectual circles in the 1970s. That decade, which has been dubbed "the years of utopia",[1] was wholly overshadowed by the consequences of the events of May 1968, which proved to be confused and contradictory. Initially, commitment to utopia was universal and indiscriminate: *all* utopias were on the agenda again—whether cultural, social, or political; Communist, socialist, or anarchist. It was only gradually that this miasma of utopia dissipated and an increasingly radical critique of totalitarianism emerged. In that shift, the publication in 1974 of a French translation of Aleksandr Solzhenitsyn's *Gulag Archipelago* marked a turning point.

As happened in other comebacks of utopian thought in French intellectual life in this century (and indeed as in neighbouring European countries), this period saw an extreme fascination with "models" inspired by certain foreign countries. Along with the Cuban myth and the Vietnamese myth, the Chinese myth aroused enormous enthusiasm for reasons that have not yet been fully analysed. One reason for this public appeal could be that in spite of its stereotyped propaganda language, the myth responded to a traditional French intellectual fascination with the Middle Kingdom and at the same time to the quest for identity of two categories of activists: Christians whom Vatican II had committed to political life and some Communists who had been left bereft by the de-Stalinisation of the Soviet Union.

French China specialists, few in number but effectively grouped around the "China Centre" of the Ecole des Hautes Etudes en Sciences Sociales, thus found themselves in a very delicate professional and intellectual situation. On the one hand, they were the focus of a demand that was clearly ideological in nature from the media and also from some leading academic and political figures. Unmet, this demand could easily turn into a boycott. At the time, for example, the newspaper *Le Monde* explicitly refused to carry "anti-Chinese" items. But on the other hand, especially at the beginning of the decade, it was difficult for these experts to build up an autonomous body of knowledge for the simple reason that available information on the situation in China was both exceedingly sparse and difficult of access.[2]

In these circumstances, two factors enabled some French specialists on the People's Republic of China (PRC) to resist the fever of utopianism. The first was what might be called the historian's reflex. In France there is a well-established school of history (thanks particularly to the work of Fernand Braudel) that stresses the long-term trends of the economy, society, and culture. On China, this school inspired the writings of Etienne Balazs, Jacques Gernet, Jacques Guillermaz, and later Lucien Bianco and Marie-Claire Bergère.[3] The writings of these authors made it impossible to understand Chinese Communism as a totally new beginning and forced people to take account in their analyses of the domestic and international constraints deriving from the past.

Second, U.S. research on the PRC had an enormous influence. For despite its frequent ideological assumptions and the diversity of its conclusions, it shared a real methodological professionalism and a great respect for facts. It provided a body of knowledge about the Communist regime set up in 1949 that was, it is true, incomplete, but was exact and concrete and certainly invalidated the claims of both the activists and the utopians. It provided a sort of technical model, especially the research that was by definition the most specialised: case-studies of a particular phenomenon, or more important, of a locality or a province.

All this meant that a deliberately historical, case-study method could not avoid the questions arising at the time from the intellectual atmosphere in France. That is an original feature and one of the weaknesses of the book. On rereading it gives the impression of paying very great, perhaps excessive attention to simple questions that today appear to be settled, especially ones about the more or less dictatorial nature of the Communist regime or the support of the popular masses—this book spends a lot of time, sometimes too much time, on phenomena or analyses that are common currency today.

Yet this shortcoming may have some advantages. The fact that I did not simply take up specialised issues explains why I endeavoured to draw the most comprehensive possible social and political portrait of a Chinese province after a few years of Communist rule, taking into account the questions facing a population newly caught up in a revolutionary process: How much change has there been? How far have living conditions improved? How widely accepted is the new regime? Has hope been met or betrayed? These very simple questions still seem to be the true questions for the time. Second, I also sought to answer another question, one that was particularly tangible in Henan, but essential for the history of the PRC—one that the histories of several revolutions unfortunately pose: How, concretely, do utopian frenzies come into being? In a utopian frenzy, how are manipulation and dream, error and murder articulated? Obviously, this book does not provide a complete answer to such vast questions. But it does provide the first elements that I later extended and revised in the course of research on repression and incarceration in the PRC.[4]

In the years that have passed since this book was published, knowledge of China has strikingly improved. Many new sources have become available, in particular eyewitness accounts of the years that preceded the Communists' coming to power, and a variety of accounts and documents published in the last decade. Outside China, many detailed works have appeared making use of the new abundance of sources and the possibility of conducting interviews. For example, the writings of Frederick C. Teiwes throw light on the mechanics of the purges that have occurred among the top Chinese leadership. An important book by David Bachman puts forward an interesting hypothesis on the institutional origins of the Great Leap Forward in the centre: the idea of an alliance between the planning and heavy industry coalition and the more moderate leaders. Major research has also been done on the rural policy of the Chinese Communist Party (CCP).[5]

But I feel that these works do not entirely deprive the two main approaches used in this research of their interest: the idea that there is a strong but complex relationship between the policies applied by the leaders of a totalitarian regime at various levels and the reactions of various categories of the population; and the idea that it is necessary to examine the link—which varies greatly from case to case and time to time—between the political space of the provinces and the different impetuses coming from the centre. The text here offered to the U.S. public is thus the 1982 one, with only minor amendments. Most of these have to do with the form. A few passages have been scaled down because they were too influenced by the climate of the 1970s. The few additions (mainly in the notes) take into account subsequent publications and the recent publication of statistical series in China.

Jean-Luc Domenach
Paris

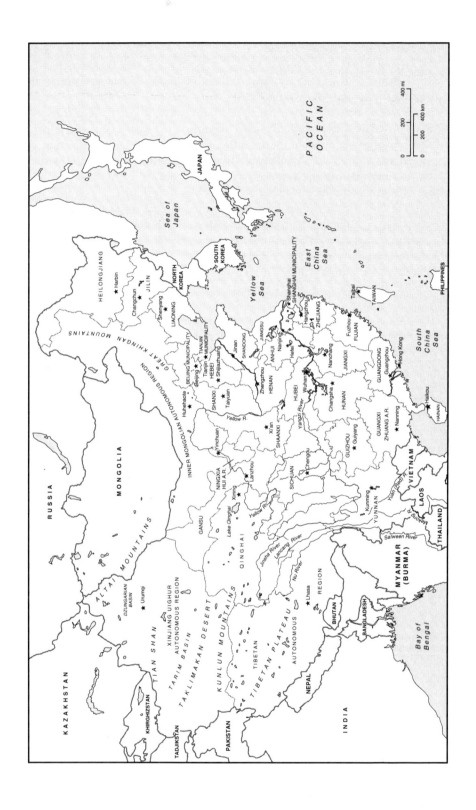

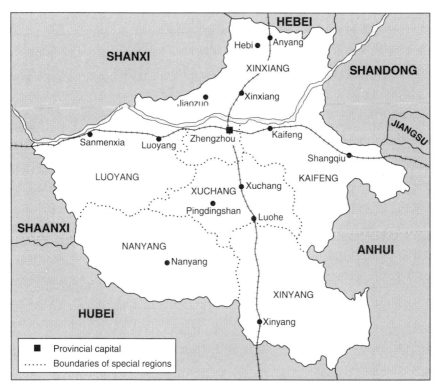

HEBEI

Hebi ● Anyang

SHANXI

XINXIANG

SHANDONG

Xinxiang

Jiaozuo

JIANGSU

Sanmenxia   Luoyang   Zhengzhou   Kaifeng

Shangqiu ●

LUOYANG   KAIFENG

XUCHANG ● Xuchang

Pingdingshan ●   Luohe

SHAANXI

NANYANG

● Nanyang

ANHUI

XINYANG

HUBEI   ● Xinyang

■ Provincial capital
······ Boundaries of special regions

Administrative map of Henan in 1959

Introduction

The history of the People's Republic of China revolves around three events inter-related by an implacable logic: the Great Leap Forward, the Cultural Revolution, and the succession of Mao Zedong. Of these events, the last two are today the better known, but their primary cause lies in the Great Leap Forward. Because it failed to draw the whole Chinese people into a "victorious war on nature", Mao was forced, starting in 1966, to break his opponents and impose his undivided rule on the masses, thus making their final disaffection inevitable. The Great Leap Forward thus constitutes both the first serious setback to communism in China and the starting point of a series of political upheavals.

The Great Leap Forward confronts the historian with at least two problems. The first involves the precise, as it were, technical, reasons for the disaster. The second problem concerns its origins. Why in autumn 1957 did leaders who a few years previously had embarked on what was a rather conventional and effective programme of industrialisation rush into one of the most original and irrational economic policies this century has seen? How did it happen that this frenzy fol-lowed abruptly on the economic relaxation and political liberalisation of the Hundred Flowers period of 1956–1957? In short, what is the guiding thread link-ing the apparently contradictory events that unfolded between 1955, when the movement to generalise cooperatives got under way, and the formation of the first people's communes in 1958?

If the first aim of this work is historical, the second has more to do with politi-cal science and the functioning of the Chinese Communist regime in the 1950s. The first question is to discover where within the Chinese Communist Party real decisionmaking power lay in each period in its history. Is it possible to detect marked changes in the functioning of power that coincide with changes of polit-ical line? If the answer is yes, how did these changes affect the relations between the various instances? Did changes of political line show up true political fault lines in the Party?

The second question—which is even more important for anyone aiming to de-fine the nature of the Chinese political regime—concerns its relations with the

popular masses.[1] Although it is clear that the Chinese masses resigned themselves, with more or less good grace, to being deprived of power by the very
people who claimed to represent them, the circumstances and effects of that dis-
possession call for assessment. Above all we need to ask what direct or indirect
influence the popular masses were able to retain, at different times, on the decisionmaking process in China. We need to look beyond the claims, and behind
the incapacities, of the Chinese political regime to see how it is defined by the
type of interaction that may occur, varying from period to period, between those
in power and the masses.

   Finally, a third question is prompted by concerns of political science in France
and by developments in the situation in China. Advancing in the wake of history
and sociology, some political scientists have asked whether even—or especially—
in a dictatorial regime, political activity is reduced to its public, that is, official,
manifestations and its expression in the single party; is it not expressed also in an
at least partly autonomous manner? Furthermore, since the "two deaths" of Mao
Zedong in 1976,[2] (one political and the other physical), events in China have
considerably altered the image of China, in Beijing as well as in Hong Kong and
Paris. The China that we now see—still from too great a distance—is no longer a
triumphant China, but a suffering one, a China in crisis, where power and society
are no longer looking in the same direction. In such a situation new questions
arise about the past: When did the crisis of confidence that we are witnessing
today start? What are the roots of the current protest movement in the history of
the People's Republic of China? Did opposition have a causal influence on the
unfolding of events, particularly at the time of the Hundred Flowers?

A Provincial Case-Study

To answer these questions, I opted to use the most empirical, most modest of
research methods: the case-study, which in the light of the available sources, con-
centrates the study in a narrowly defined framework. This method has produced
excellent results in the other social sciences. In addition, work carried out in
the United States on Soviet, and more recently, Chinese politics[3] has demonstrated its value, at least in the collection of facts and the location of real political
mechanisms.

   When this research was undertaken, in 1971, studies carried out in France on
the People's Republic of China had to overcome at least two hurdles before they
could make any progress: the dream and the propaganda. The public statements
of a number of clear-minded individuals, some of them sinologists, and above all
the succession of disappointments inflicted by Beijing on its supporters[4] removed the first of these hurdles. But the second is only slightly less challenging:
The Chinese government now gives out, or allows to come out, much more information, but that information is still just as slanted, if in a different direction,

and it only rarely throws any light on history. If we are to understand why the Great Leap Forward occurred and analyse the nature of the Chinese political regime in the second half of the 1950s, I thus feel almost as strongly as was the case ten years ago the need to turn to a method that above all offers a shorter route to the facts.

There are three reasons why I felt that the provincial framework would allow me to carry out an effective piece of case-study research. First, there is a very active provincial press in China, which is both much richer in concrete information than the press in the centre and less specialised than professional publications: It thus provides interesting material. Second, in China the province has long constituted a major political subdivision. It is in many ways only an intermediary level, because unitary traditions are very strong, but its administrative and sometimes its political position have been strengthened by periods of fragmentation; a degree of geographical, cultural, and human homogeneity; and now the appearance of the modern economy. The province is a framework suited to both a historical study and a political science analysis. Unlike other possible frameworks for a case-study—a biography, the study of one aspect of a political or social system, or even the study of a locality—the province provides a research unit all but complete in itself. Of course, in a period of effective unification, it is the least self-contained unit in the political sphere, since the central government by definition is external to it. But this research area enables the observation of relations between the centre and the various provincial and local levels of political power. And there was a further reason: the example of U.S. scholars. Since the late 1960s, they have shown concretely the historical and political interest of provincial case-studies. Their works represent essential contributions to knowledge about the People's Republic of China.[5] It would be interesting to test the validity of the method for wider questions.

Henan:
A Representative Province

The first reason for choosing Henan has to do with the availability of documentation: The leading U.S. and Japanese research centres possess significant runs of the Henan press, especially the *Henan Daily*.[6] I was also influenced by existing work: Most of the case-studies already published relate to the southern provinces or the great Chinese cities, whereas the research of Parris II. Chang has brought out the severe crisis experienced in Henan in 1956–1957 and the vanguard role that Henan played in the launching of the Great Leap Forward.[7]

But the deciding factor was the fact that the historical, geographical, and economic situation of Henan in the mid-twentieth century made it a representative province. History had made Henan one of the oldest centres of Chinese civilisation, but had on the whole abandoned it during the second millennium of the common era. Since the mid-nineteenth century, the great revolutionary impulses have emerged from coastal and southern China, which was the area first and most affected by the enterprises and influences of the West. Henan suffered only the side-effects of these successive impulses (though sometimes those effects were violent, as under the Taiping[8]). Thus, although the rural areas of Henan were the scene of violent revolutionary agitation until the defeat of 1927, subsequent Communist guerilla activity was isolated and confined to the borders with Anhui and Hubei.[9] It was only towards the end of the war against Japan and above all during the last civil war that Communist influence spread and Red bases in neighbouring provinces (Shanxi, Hebei) expanded into the rural areas of Henan.[10] Already, however, in the majority of counties, Communist power had been installed upon the departure of Nationalist troops and the victory of the Red army elsewhere. It is tempting to write of a change of dynasty, for in most parts of Henan, Communism was in a way an outside force, and this played a part in future developments. Among the first Communist leaders in Henan, only a few were natives, the majority coming from other provinces of North China.[11] This circumstance explains too the very particular situation of counties liberated early by neighbouring Red bases (for example Linxian, Huixian, and Jiyuan in the northwest) or by a local guerilla unit (Lushan). Their cadres would be tempted when faced with a provincial leadership made up largely of outsiders to adopt the mantle of an authentically indigenous Henan vanguard. Thus, the belated occupation of Henan by Communist forces is symbolic of a wider reality. Recent history has transformed Henan like many other provinces into a testing ground for ideas coming from elsewhere.

This fact of history is largely explained by geography.[12] Henan is part of continental and agrarian North China. To the south, a series of mountains makes communications with Hubei difficult; to the west, high mountainous massifs and the rocky barrier of the Taihangshan hinder access to Shaanxi and Shanxi. At the same time, topography opens Henan completely to Hebei to the north and Shandong and Anhui to the east. Instead of joining the Yellow River, which crosses the province from west to east, most of the water courses of Henan flow either northwards or southeastwards. Henan is thus cut off from western China, but the coastal areas and their big urban centres are quite far away. In 1950 even the fastest train took a day to get from Zhengzhou to Shanghai (and hardly less to reach the capital). The province was too remote from the most dynamic coastal areas to participate directly in their expansion. It was open to them, but as a remote agricultural dependency.

Agriculture is in fact the traditional base of the economy of Henan. In the plain, the soil, often covered with a layer of loess, lends itself well to wheat. From earliest times Henan was one of the empire's major granaries. Industrial crops, notably cotton (around Xinxiang) and tobacco (around Xuchang) have spread in recent decades. Conversely, the province seemed ill endowed for industry: Capital, skills, and contacts with the outside world were lacking; most mineral resources are scattered and difficult to extract. Its sole advantages were rail links with the rest of the country and the presence of large coal deposits. In 1949 the province possessed neither a steel industry (its coal went elsewhere) nor engineering industries. Only a few agriculture-related sectors were developed to any extent: food industries, cigarettes, and above all textiles. The share of industry in the value of agricultural and industrial production had hovered around 3 percent since the mid-1930s. Urbanisation thus remained limited. Including the agricultural and administrative small towns, in 1949 there were only a million city-dwellers, 2.6 percent of the population. Only three towns even partially fulfilled the functions of modern cities: Luoyang and Kaifeng, old imperial capitals, and Zhengzhou, favoured by its situation at the crossing of the two main Chinese railways, the Beijing-Canton line and the Lanzhou railway. These were simply islands of civilisation lost in an ocean of villages. In 1949, 85 percent of the people of Henan were illiterate and the province had only 49,310 secondary school pupils and four cinemas.[13]

Henan is representative not only in the predominance of agriculture but also in its variety of geographical environments, which almost make it a microcosm of China. The fact is that the conventional image of a Henan that is entirely flat is false. The province comprises two very different natural environments. Of its 167,000 square km, almost 45 percent is taken up by the mountains in the west and the hills in the south. The climate there is harsher (often more than 160 days a year below freezing), the relief broken, the soil eroded, agriculture more precarious and more and more patchy. It is in the flat regions that the bulk of the cultivated area is to be found—80,000 square km, which is a lot—and over 80 percent of the population live. But these regions are themselves diverse: The rich and overpopulated wheat lands in the north often suffer from drought, those in the east are at the mercy of flooding by tributaries of the Huai and the rice fields of Xinyang region—truly a piece of central China—are very sensitive to any variation in rainfall.

In fact, as in the rest of North China, as so often described by geographers,[14] there is a high level of dependence on meteorological conditions. Rainfall is sufficient in overall amount (600 mm around Anyang in the north, 1,000 mm on the Huai) but irregular; two-thirds fall in summer, sometimes in a few storms, and the rest of the time, drought looms. There is never a year without local droughts or flooding, never a decade without several climatic calamities. According to historical chronicles, in 2,100 years Henan suffered 982 natural calamities. Floods and droughts overwhelmed the province during the first half of the twentieth century.[15] In general, droughts have been the more deadly, especially as in 1949 the irrigated area accounted for less than 5 percent of the cultivated area.[16] Floods are aggravated by two related phenomena: the change of slope at the outlet of watercourses in the plain and the raising of their bed as a result of the mud that they carry down from eroded regions. Floods destroy the soil by increasing salt levels and depositing pebbles over thousands of square kilometres. Freezing snaps and grasshopper invasions, to which, for more than a century, were added the ravages of banditry and destruction by armies on campaign, further aggravated these disasters. Around 1949, four Chinese characters commonly served to summarise the calamities suffered by the peasantry of Henan: *shui, han, huang, tang* (floods, drought, grasshoppers, and Tang Enbo, a local potentate).

Other causes, just as tragically banal, explain the misery of the rural areas of Henan before 1949. The technological backwardness of agriculture (notably the use of low-yielding crop varieties and the absence of fertilisers and machinery) largely accounted for the low yields: 0.65–0.69 metric ton per hectare for grains and 0.13 for cotton.[17] The injustice of the land tenure situation, albeit less than in southern China,[18] forced the vast majority of peasants to produce in order to survive.

But in Henan as elsewhere, it is above all the population explosion that explains the deterioration of the food situation during the first half of the twentieth century. The population of the province was approaching perhaps 20 million in the eighteenth century and barely exceeded this figure at the beginning of the twentieth; it seems to have risen from 30 million around 1923 to 33 million in 1936 and 38 million at liberation, despite wars and calamities.[19] But cereal production seems to have fallen between 1936 and 1949—a bad year if ever there was one, although production may have been underestimated by Communist sources— from 10.25–9.2 million metric tons to 7.85–7.5 million metric tons.[20] The theoretical ration of an individual in Henan thus fell from the comparatively satisfactory level of 279–310.5 kg around 1936[21] to 170–180 kg in 1949.

History and geography as well as the food situation combined to make conditions in Henan in 1949 much like those in the rest of the 18 provinces that are generally considered to make up China proper. The province certainly included no cities like Canton or Shanghai, where the country's innovativeness and energy have been concentrated at different times.[22] But it was indirectly dependent on them and found itself in a situation very different from the outlying provinces. Its economy was chiefly agricultural and it had little industry, but that was the situation of all the noncoastal provinces and it was not immutable. The standard of living, or rather survival, of its population had recently deteriorated, as it had elsewhere.

The characteristics of Henan in 1949 also placed it in an average and representative situation in regard to the new government. By its size, geographical situation, and symbolic importance, it belonged amongst the provinces of North China that the new regime absolutely had to control. Its economic underdevelopment and the impoverishment of its population required the CCP to ensure that reconstruction and planning measures succeeded. Henan thus forms an interesting setting to study the ambitions of the Communist authorities—and discover their errors.

Prologue
1949–1955: Years of Reason?

If the Great Leap Forward marks a break in the history of the People's Republic of China, the question remains: A break in relation to what? Does this break represent a contrast between reason and folly, coherence and incoherence, cause and effect? The question is not simply historical but political. It concerns as much the present as the past, and it is at the centre of the main debates that have emerged abroad and on the fringes of and even within the Chinese Communist regime since 1976. For this question touches on the relations that that regime maintains, fundamentally, with Maoism. Study of the years from 1949 to 1955 forms an essential prologue to any study of the first Maoist upsurges in Chinese politics.

My research shows that the years 1949–1955 in Henan can be assessed in two different ways. If they are seen in the context of the history of the People's Republic of China with its numerous conflicts, uncertainties, and setbacks, these years stand out as the period when the Chinese Communist regime conducted the most decisive and effective political and economic action. But if this period is isolated and looked at from, say, 1955, then the analysis must be much more reserved. The shortcomings of the development effort and the negative effects of Communist Party rule then stand out as much as the results obtained. By 1955, on top of the problems deriving from the old society, there were those deriving from the action to promote economic and political transformation undertaken by the new regime.

In the economic sphere, which is the most striking, by about 1955 what was apparent was not only the speed of industrialisation, but also its limits, and above all the difficulties of agriculture and the emergence of new social problems.

Industrialisation, Urbanisation, Modernisation

In Henan, the first years of the Communist regime undeniably represented a period of unparalleled economic growth during which the foundations were laid of a modern economy and society. Until about 1952, the principal objective pursued was the raising of production through the restoration of order and the great "democratic reforms". But the new regime lost no time in equipping itself with the means to carry out a policy of industrialisation. By 1952, through confiscations and new building of factories, the public sector controlled 75.9 percent of the value of the province's industrial production.[1] Starting in 1953–1954, the whole of China entered a phase of planned industrialisation, and Henan, previously disadvantaged by its geographical situation, benefited from Beijing's strategy to ensure that all parts of the country enjoyed economic progress.[2] Twenty-six "above-norm projects" were assigned to Henan between 1953 and 1957, with investments totalling 654 million yuan. The building and transplanting of numerous factories strengthened and extended the industrial base. The food industries sector and above all textiles were strengthened; six cotton factories were brought into service one after the other in Zhengzhou between 1953 and 1959; other textile enterprises were set up in Kaifeng, Xinxiang, and Anyang. In the coal sector, the mines at Jiaozuo were rehabilitated, enlarged, and modernised; at Hebi in 1952 and Pingdingshan in 1954 exploitation of promising deposits was begun. The most spectacular aspect of this effort was the establishment in the province of wholly new activities: thermal electric industry, chemical industries (such as the insecticides factory at Zhengzhou), and above all engineering industries such as the famous tractor factory at Luoyang, the first of its type in the country. These factories, generally developed with Soviet or East German aid, were usually built on the same massive and vast model as those in eastern Europe. In Zhengzhou and Luoyang industrialisation involved the building of new districts, the construction of imposing bridges, and the opening of broad avenues.

The strategy of the First Five-Year Plan decidedly favoured the industrial sector, but it did not neglect the rural areas, although direct aid to agriculture was low. Agricultural loans seem to have been of minor importance and were concentrated in a small number of model units and in disaster areas. Initially, to disseminate mechanisation, reliance was put on the example set by the state farms in the province; in 1954, 6 enormous ones were run from Beijing, and 131, some of them tiny, came under local authorities, usually counties. Henan also had six agricultural machinery stations.[3] Indirect aid to agriculture received more attention. Thus, a notable effort was made in communications, as shown in Table P.1. Despite shortcomings (in 1956 it was acknowledged that 95 percent of roads remained passable only with difficulty during the rainy season), the development of the road network opened up some isolated rural areas to progress. ·

The most spectacular projects of benefit to agriculture were in irrigation. During the first two years, action was limited to raising dykes and maintaining existing reservoirs and canals. In 1951 the state began to commit large sums to works on the two great rivers that had ravaged the province for centuries: the Huai and the Yellow River. Reservoirs were constructed at Baisha and Panjiao on tributaries

TABLE P.1 Communications in Henan, 1949–1957

Year	Roads (km)	Motorable Roads (km)	Navigable Waterways (km)
1949	–	420	–
1952	7,972	5,700	2,600
1956	13,000	10,600	–
1957	15,069	–	3,800

SOURCES: Zhengzhou shifan xueyuan dilixi (Department of Geography of the Zhengzhou Teacher Training School), *Henan dili* (Geography of Henan), Beijing, Shangwu yinshuguan (Commercial Publishing House), 1959, pp. 122–126; *Henan ribao* (Henan Daily), 29 September 1956.

of the Huai. Between 1951 and 1953 Soviet aid made possible the digging of the People's Victory Canal between the Yellow River and the Wei River.[4] The cost in both financial and human terms (7.26 million yuan expended and 100,000 peasants displaced) was indeed considerable, in addition to fearsome problems of silting up and rising salt levels in the soil that soon became apparent. Yet the canal made it possible to irrigate 51,000 new hectares in the Xinxiang area and improve communications by water with Hebei. When it was subsequently completed, the People's Victory Canal certainly played a major role in the agricultural takeoff of the Xinxiang region. But the regime's most ambitious undertaking, to which it pinned its highest hopes, was the hydroelectric complex at Sanmen, situated where Henan, Shanxi, and Shaanxi meet.

The political and engineering history of this project, from the first studies carried out in the 1930s to the admissions made in 1974, would certainly be worth lingering over, typical as it is.[5] Suffice it to say here that with the dam at Liujiaxia in Gansu, it was one of the two main elements in the initial fifteen-year phase of a giant programme to control and develop the Yellow River that the National People's Congress adopted in July 1955. A great earth dam below Mangshan, near Zhengzhou, was proposed by Chinese experts all but paralysed by their awareness of their bad origins, but equipped with a minimum sense of realities and would have been much less costly financially and socially. Ignoring their preliminary studies and reservations, Soviet missions headed by an engineer named Korokovski began in 1952 to draw up plans and then in autumn 1954 obtained approval for a multipurpose dam inspired by illustrious Ukrainian examples. Ninety metres high, with a holding capacity of 36 billion cubic metres, the dam was to make it possible to regulate outflows at twice the normal annual maximum (17,500 cubic metres per second) and guarantee a flow of 500 cubic metres per second at its lowest rate of flow (200 cubic metres per second). When completed in 1961, the dam was to irrigate a further 1.4 million hectares. Its electrical production capacity would reach a million kilowatts. Ships of 3,000 metric tons would be able to travel upriver as far as Zhengzhou. What matter the financial cost of the operation (1,220 million yuan, more than four times the total expenditure of the provincial government in 1955 and almost eight times the sum devoted since 1949 to works on the Henan tributaries of the river)? What matter its social cost (600,000 people would be displaced, 215,000 of them in the first phase)? What matter the risks of silting up the reservoir from inadequate soil control measures on the upper tributaries of the river? What matter, finally, the omission of less spectacular but indispensable irrigation works on secondary waterways? The Sanmen project was started in 1955 in Shaanxian county and the first villages were evacuated in spring 1956.

Today such hopes may appear derisory. Yet at the time, they were the most brilliant symbol of the ambitious strategy pursued by the regime and its first successes. For, by concentrating investments in a few key sectors, the regime could by 1955 point to spectacular and unprecedented results. First, industrial production had rapidly increased and enlarged its share in the provincial economy, as Table P.2 shows. Growth affected all branches of industry. Already by 1952, coal production, at 1.6 million metric tons, had come close to the best prewar level.[6] In textiles, the advance was striking: Production of cotton goods in 1955 was twenty times higher than in 1949; Henan was now processing 60 percent of its cotton as against 20 percent.[7] Luoyang and Zhengzhou (where twenty new factories had been built since liberation) were among the fastest-growing industrial cities in the whole of China.

Urbanisation was the sign and consequence of industrial development.[8] According to my calculations, the population of cities grew less than contemporary sources suggest and did not match that of other provinces in North China. Nevertheless, it rose from 1 million in 1949 to 2.6 million in 1957 (5.8 percent of the population of the province), an increase of 180 percent in eight years.[9] Most of this increase occurred between 1949 and 1954; by the latter year the urban population of Henan was already 2.2 million. The increase was all but universal, for in Henan as elsewhere, the city was now the vector and symbol of progress. But there were inequalities in development, flowing from the industrial choices made by the central government. Kaifeng, the administrative and university city of

TABLE P.2   Industrial Production in Henan, 1949–1954

Year	Industrial Production (million yuan)	Share of Total Agricultural and Industrial Production (%)
1949	50	2.8
1952	306	9.3
1954	1,227	14.7

SOURCES: Zhengzhou shifan xueyuan dilixi (Department of Geography of the Zhengzhou Teacher Training School), *Henan dili* (Geography of Henan), Beijing, Shangwu yinshuguan (Commercial Publishing House), 1959, p. 104; *Renmin ribao* (People's Daily), 15 April 1955; and above all, Frederick C. Teiwes, "Provincial Politics in China", in John Lindbeck (ed.), China: *Mismanagement of a Revolutionary Society*, Seattle, University of Washington Press, 1971, p. 180.

Guomindang times, is an exception. It was disadvantaged by the First Five-Year Plan, and its population stagnated at the already high figure of 300,000. Some small towns situated in the heart of important agricultural regions but lacking modern industry grew only slightly; the population of Xuchang rose from 40,000 to 58,000 in 1953, and that of Xinyang from 50,000 to 80,000. The towns most favoured by the industrialisation strategy grew fastest. Between 1949 and 1957 Zhengzhou rose from 171,000 to 700,000 inhabitants (including 160,000 workers) and Luoyang from 60,000 to 450,000 (including 65,000 workers). Three as yet relatively small but vigorous urban centres were created from scratch (Pingdingshan, Hebi, and Sanmen), and Jiaozuo, although very old, reached 200,000 inhabitants in 1958.

Overall, the geographical distribution of urbanisation, traditionally concentrated close to major communication routes, was hardly modified. But the definition of a city was being transformed. Without totally disappearing, its traditional roles as an administrative centre, commercial centre, and rural market were giving way to more modern functions, such as its role in transport and above all industry. This explains why in autumn 1954, Kaifeng yielded the position of provincial capital to Zhengzhou, much more representative of modern times.

Progress spread out from the cities. In the area of health, the results were remarkable, although much remained to be done. By 1956 Henan had 13,572 practitioners of Western medicine (which, by the way, was markedly favoured by the authorities) and 29,084 practitioners of traditional medicine. By March 1957 the province had 172 hospitals with 10,200 beds.[10] At least as significant an effort was devoted to education (see Table P.3).[11]

The order in which progress was made stands out clearly. Initially the effort was put on primary education, then on secondary, then on technical and higher education. There too the results were more limited than it appears. University development marked time. Specialised technical education and secondary schools were concentrated in the towns and to a lesser extent in the richest rural counties; they could absorb only some of the graduates of primary schools. The

TABLE P.3　Education in Henan, 1949–1957

Year	Institutions of Higher Education	Technical Institutions	Students	Secondary School Students	Primary School Students
1949	1	–	550	49,310	1,600,000
1952	5	–	–	170,000	4,200,000
1955	5	15	–	240,000	4,400,000
1956	7	28	5,300	320,000	4,760,000
1957	7	–	9,500	381,000	4,950,000

SOURCES: *Henan ribao* (Henan Daily), 24 August, 4 and 5 September 1957; *Renmin jiaoyu* (Popular education), 4, 1958, p. 12.

costs of schooling and student support constituted a burden for poor families that was often more than they could bear. In Zhengzhou, despite the standard of living being much higher than the provincial average, the children of workers and poor peasants constituted 44.5 percent of the total number of pupils in the lower-level secondary schools, 34.8 percent in the higher level, and only 17.5 percent of university students. In 1957, 1.11 million children were still not attending primary school. In a county impoverished by floods like Huaibin, the school enrolment ratio was still only 46.9 percent.[12]

Yet given the initial backwardness, these results appear remarkable. They were supplemented by the first attempts at adult literacy programmes and the dissemination of culture.[13] By 1956, 52 percent of townships were regularly linked to the postal network, 63 percent had at least one telephone (every township in 30 counties), and 87 counties and cities had a radio broadcasting station. Between 1953 and 1956 the Henan People's Publishing House published 243 works; in August 1957 it had 279 sales outlets. At the same time, almost every county distributed a newspaper, often twice weekly, and the *Henan Daily*, mainly distributed by subscription, had a run of 130,000 copies. All that explains why, as the cultural level rose, there began to appear in the villages, particularly among basic-level cadres, a new sense of belonging to a wider community. The ending of cultural isolation would facilitate the modernisation of agriculture; from this angle too Henan was entering the modern world.

The Limits
of Industrialisation

Today, it is tempting to present these successes as the chief aspect of the period. For it was indeed in the years 1949–1957, and especially 1949–1955, that the bases of Chinese economic development were laid. But around 1955, many of the people of Henan were less sensitive to the trumpeting of propaganda than to the limits and shortcomings of a development enterprise that had raised so many hopes.

First, industrialisation was limited and costly. Investment had been concentrated in a small number of branches and geographical zones, and the others often continued to lag very seriously. Despite coal deposits, some iron, and a good rail network, the province had not been provided with any steel-making capacity; coal was taken to the big industrial centres outside the province, in particular Wuhan. The inadequacy of light and consumer goods industries meant that the necessary goods often had to be bought elsewhere. The big-equipment factories set up in the province by the state, such as the Luoyang tractor factory, made products intended for the national market and not the needs of the province. This situation was aggravated by the weakness of enterprises controlled by localities (provinces or counties). With inadequate equipment and little support from public funds (particularly as many enterprises remained in the hands of private capital), they provided insufficient quantities of mediocre goods that in 1955 still accounted for only 14.4 percent of the value of provincial production.[14] Handicraft continued to be practised only in a few traditional sectors (for example, jade working in the area about Anyang). There was an enormous gap between the big textile and engineering industries and light industry or handicrafts. This dualism also manifested geographically, since the most modern enterprises were set up in a small number of "key cities", themselves concentrated in northern Henan. In short, a cleavage was appearing in urban and industrial Henan between zones very differently affected by economic progress.

In addition, the methods of industrialisation adopted were extremely costly.[15] Transfers to Henan of factories from other provinces posed serious social problems. Construction costs were high and often exorbitant. Hundreds of hectares of high-yielding land were taken over, often unwisely, in the suburbs of Zhengzhou and Luoyang, and despite peasant protests. The dogmatism and incompetence of both Chinese and Soviet engineers led to misallocation, waste, and construction defects that ended up making the lives of the inhabitants of the suburbs of Zhengzhou and Luoyang unbearable. Some errors were on too great a scale to be hidden indefinitely. Thus, in June 1955 it was necessary to convene nothing less than a meeting of provincial Party delegates to criticise publicly the megalomania in urban construction.[16] For example, the diameter of the water pipes of the new city of Luoyang was greater than anywhere in the Soviet Union at the time. In Zhengzhou it had been thought a good idea to demolish whole swathes of the old city to build a new industrial area and provincial offices. But even before construction was completed, it was realised with horror that the site was sandy, with a very shallow water-table, and altogether unsuited to the construction of modern buildings. The initial plans had to be hastily revised and what had been intended to be put in one place was separated, with the office buildings, which were already too far advanced to alter, left where they were and the industrial establishments moved elsewhere. Indeed, as a provincial planning official admitted, the desire to plan everywhere came up against the lack of qualified personnel and the administration's penchant for red tape.[17]

The Problem of Agriculture

The most serious shortcoming of the development strategy in the First Five-Year Plan was that it disadvantaged the nonindustrial sectors from which the vast majority of the population of Henan derived its living. Unfortunately we do not know the exact distribution of government funds between the various sectors of the provincial economy, but we do have some information about the Henan government's expenditures in budget years 1955, 1956, and 1957.[18] First, it would appear that the government had too few resources and too little decisionmaking autonomy to make much impact on the choices made by the centre—not that local officials would even have thought of doing so. Of successive revenues of 663, 693, and 711 million yuan, the provincial government could only spend 342, 431, and 450 million yuan, respectively, on its own projects, the difference going into the coffers of the central government. And even this budget had to bear very heavy administrative (successively 27.3 percent, 24.1 percent, and 24.2 percent) and sociocultural costs (mainly education: 44.2 percent, 40 percent, and 47.1 percent) that the centre delegated to the province. Thus the provincial government could only devote modest amounts to economic construction: 78 million yuan in 1955 (26 percent of expenditure), 153.6 million in 1956 (35.8 percent), and 119 million in 1957 (26.4 percent). The sums devoted to nonindustrial sectors were even smaller. Thus, in 1957 (the sole year for which detailed sectoral figures are available) 12 million yuan were invested in transport and communications, 45.5 million in irrigation (9 percent of total expenditure), and only 20.5 million in agriculture and forests (4.5 percent). It is likely that the share of agriculture and forests had been even lower in previous budgets.[19]

In any case, in January 1955, an article by the vice-chairman of the provincial government's Communications Office pointed out that the poor quality of roads and the lack of modern means of transport made it impossible to transport more than 14,700 metric tons of the 22,600 metric tons that according to the Plan had to move each month between Xuchang and Nanyang; modern methods would have to be supplemented by traditional means of transport (beasts of burden, porters, etc.).[20]

It was mainly agriculture that bore the cost of the First Five-Year Plan's economic strategy. In Henan, agriculture meant first and foremost production of food grains. Table P.4 shows the change in production between 1949 and 1955. This series is broadly confirmed by the development of the production and yield of wheat and "miscellaneous grains" (*zaliang*), which are the main components of production (Table P.5). We also know the development of grain production in three special regions and five countries (see Table P.6).

What do these figures show? Those relating to 1949 seem arbitrary. We may well wonder how it was possible, just a few months after the end of hostilities, to estimate the production of tens of thousands of villages under varying degrees of government control. The value of these figures is as much political as economic: They were probably underestimated so as to play up the scale of destruction caused by the war and exaggerate subsequent progress. Conversely, the figures for 1952–1955 seem fairly reliable, especially as they are mutually consistent. By then, political and statistical control of the rural areas had been considerably strengthened.

There is unfortunately no better course than to accept, very hypothetically, the cereal production figures given for 1949. Those for 1955 then show a remarkable advance of 66 percent (low hypothesis) to 79.8 percent (high hypothesis). This advance stems from an extension of the area under cultivation (+12.5 percent) and above all an improvement in yields (47.6 percent to 62.3 percent). Increases

TABLE P.4   Cereal Production, Yield, and Availability in Henan, 1949–1955

Year	Cultivatd Area (million ha)	Production (million mt)	Yield (mt/ha)	Availability per Capita (kg/cap)
1949	9.92	6.65	0.655	170
		6.85	0.690	180
1952	10.8	9.21	0.852	212.9
		10.25	0.849	236.8
1953	11.16	9.95	0.891	225.1
		10.25	0.918	231.9
1954	11.36	10.87	0.956	240.6
1955	11.16	11.37	1.018	246.5
		11.69	1.047	253.3

SOURCES: Sun Jingzhi, *Huabei jingji dili* (Economic geography of North China), Beijing, Kexue chubanshe (Scientific Publishing House), 1957, p. 158; *Zhongguo nongbao* (Journal of Chinese agriculture), 8 August 1957; Zhengzhou shifan xueyuan dilixi (Department of Geography of the Zhengzhou Teacher Training School), *Henan dili* (Geography of Henan), Beijing, Shangwu yinshuguan (Commercial Publishing House), 1959, p. 88; *Henan ribao* (Henan Daily), 27 November and 31 December 1957. The cultivated area naturally includes double-cropped areas. Guojia tongji ju zonghe si (State Statistical Bureau General Company), *Quanguo gesheng, zizhiqu, zhihaishi lishi tongji ziliao huibian (1949–1989)* (Collection of historical statistical materials in all the provinces, autonomous regions, and directly administered cities), Beijing, Zhongguo tongji chubanshe (China Statistical Publishing House), 1990, does indeed show a slightly higher production figure for 1949, 7.13 million metric tons, and often slightly higher figures for the following years: 10 million metric tons in 1952, 10.9 million in 1953, 11.4 million in 1954, 12.5 million in 1955. These figures are not necessarily accurate and do not significantly alter the analysis.

affected wheat (+46 percent) but also miscellaneous grains (+50.4 percent). Local examples confirm this overall impression, though with marked variations. Luoyang special region, which is very mountainous, gained only 37.7 percent between 1947 and 1955; in more favoured counties such as Changyuan and Yanshi cereal production rose 68.7 percent and 87.2 percent, respectively, between 1949 and 1955.

But the speed of progress slowed after 1952. To measure this slowdown, the two figures given by the available sources for 1952 pose a difficult problem. Using the high figure of 10.25 million metric tons provided by a 1959 source,[21] output growth reached 52.3–57.6 percent in the first three years of the regime as against only 10.9–14 percent in the following three years (and the increase in yields would have been even lower). The example of Luoyang special region tends to confirm this figure. On the other hand, the growth percentages for wheat and miscellaneous grains between 1949 and 1952 (25.8 percent and 24.6 percent, respectively, for a total rise of 46 percent and 50.4 percent by 1955) are consistent with the low figure of 9.21 million metric tons in 1952. However, even with this latter figure, the slowdown in the rate of increase is marked, falling from 34.5–41.7 percent between 1949 and 1952 to only 23.4–26.9 percent between 1952 and 1955.

It is true that, as regards cereals, the years 1949–1955 were amongst the best in

TABLE P.5.   Wheat and Miscellaneous Grains Production and Yield in Henan, 1949–1955

	Cultivated Area (million ha)		Production (million mt)		Yield (mt/ha)	
Year	Wheat	Miscellaneous Grains	Wheat	Miscellaneous Grains	Wheat	Miscellaneous Grains
1949	3.98	4.44	2.39	3.06	0.59	0.68
1950	4.08	–	2.49	–	0.61	–
1951	4.13	–	3.16	–	0.76	–
1952	4.63	4.83	3.01	3.81	0.64	0.78
1953	4.88	4.98	2.98	4.5	0.60	0.90
1954	5.11	4.8	3.75	3.83	0.73	0.79
1955	4.95	4.8	3.52	4.69	0.71	0.95

SOURCES: Sun Jingzhi, *Huabei jingji dili* (Economic geography of North China), Beijing, Kexue chubanshe (Scientific Publishing House), 1957, p. 158; *Zhongguo nongbao* (Journal of Chinese agriculture), 6 July 1957; *Heilongjiang ribao* (Heilongjiang Daily), 13 October 1954; *Henan ribao* (Henan Daily), 21 July 1954, 27 September, 21 December 1957. Guojia tongji ju zonghe si (State Statistical Bureau General Company), *Quanguo gesheng, zizhiqu, zhihaishi lishi tongji ziliao huibian (1949–1989)* (Collection of historical statistical materials in all the provinces, autonomous regions, and directly administered cities), Beijing, Zhongguo tongji chubanshe (China Statistical Publishing House), 1990, provides figures for wheat production of the same order for 1949 (2.5 million metric tons), 1952 (3.06 million metric tons), and 1953 (2.00 million metric tons), but higher ones for 1954 (4.2 million metric tons) and 1955 (4.26 million metric tons); these figures do not significantly alter the analysis.

the whole history of the regime. Even the less brilliant (but more reliably reported) results for 1952–1955 show a rapid growth rate that agriculture in Henan was not to see again until 1969.[22] At the time the central government considered the province a grain surplus area; it was not to be so again until 1974.[23]

It is also true that the concentration of efforts on cereals did not prevent the achievement of remarkable advances in other sectors of agriculture, notably cotton and livestock (see Table P.7). Thanks to striking increases in cultivated area and also to an enormous improvement in yield, cotton production rose by 133.7 percent between 1949 and 1955, easily passing the best prewar level. In livestock, pigs declined dramatically before 1950, and then increased. For cattle, growth was less rapid from a level that was still high in 1950.

Yet, despite these undeniable achievements, it was in the agricultural sector that the most dangerous weakness lay in the development strategy pursued by the regime. To begin with a banal observation: Generally, the rises recorded between 1949 and 1952 simply marked a return to the prewar production level. That is the case, as we have seen, with provincewide (not per capita) cereal production. Another commonplace is that these advances derived largely from political, not economic, action by the regime. Thus, the increase in the area sown to grains (9 percent between 1949 and 1952) cannot be understood without the restoration of order and the end of the civil war. More generally, the agrarian reform and the resumption of small family farming are the most likely explanation for the peas-

TABLE P.6   Grain Production in Three Special Regions and Five Counties, 1947–1955 (thousand mt)

Year	Luoyang Special Region	Xuchang Special Region	Nanyang Special Region
	Three Special Regions		
1947	742.5	–	–
1949	–	–	–
1952	–	1,348	–
1953	945	1,480	1,477.5
1954	991.5	1,655	1,842
1955	1,022.5	1,670	1,916

Year	Changge	Changyuan	Neihuang	Wenxian	Yanshi
	Five Counties				
1947	–	–	–	–	55
1949	–	60	–	31.5	–
1952	91	99.5	75	39	70
1953	120	–	–	–	85
1954	–	–	–	–	50
1955	127.5	101	90	55	103

SOURCES: For the Luoyang special region, *Henan ribao* (Henan Daily), 5 September 1957; for the Xuchang special region, Henan ribao (Henan Daily), 1 September 1957; for the Nanyang special region, ibid.; for Changge, Zhonggong henansheng changgexian weijuanhui (Changge County CCP Committee), *Changge shuili jianshe* (Irrigation construction in Changge), Beijing, Nongye chubanshe (Agricultural Publishing House), 1958, p. 11, and Nongye liangshi zuowu shengchanju (Cereal Production Bureau of the Ministry of Agriculture), Yijiuwubanian xiaomai fengchan jingyan huibian (Collection of reports on the excellent 1958 wheat harvest), Beijing, Nongye chubanshe (Agricultural Publishing House), 1958, p. 198; for Changyuan, *Henan ribao* (Henan Daily), 11 September 1957; for Neihuang, ibid.; for Wenxian, *Renmin ribao* (People's Daily), 19 January 1956; for Yanshi, Zhonghua renmin gongheguo nongye bangongting (General Bureau of the Ministry of Agriculture of the PRC), *Zuzhi nongye shengchan dayuejin de dianxing jingyan* (Model experiences in the organisation of the Great Leap Forward of agricultural production), Beijing, Caizheng jingji chubanshe (Financial and Economic Publishing House), 1958, p. 172, and *Quanmian dayuejin zhongde liangshi gongzuo* (Grain work during the total Great Leap Forward), Zhengzhou, Henan renmin chubanshe (Henan People's Publishing House), 1958, p. 40.

antry's new will to work and the increase in yields in the early years. And both these factors began to change after 1952. On the one hand, the maximum extent of cropping possible with the available technology had almost been reached. Increases of cultivated land declined considerably and became less stable. On the other hand, the encouragement given by the authorities to "mutual aid and cooperation", and more important, as will be seen, the imposition of state control over the grain trade led to a deterioration in the social atmosphere.

The necessary growth of yields per hectare would have required the introduction of new technology on a massive scale. It is here that the strategy of the First Plan proved to be inadequate and perhaps even harmful. The fact is that direct

TABLE P.7   Cotton and Stock-Raising in Henan, 1930–1955

	Cotton			Livestock	
Year	Area (thousand ha)	Production (thousand mt)	Yield (mt/ha)	Cattle (million head)	Pigs (million head)
1930	–	–	–	–	–
1936	400	110	0.276	2.99	3.56
1949	450	63	0.139	–	–
1950	–	–	–	3.87	1.48
1952	–	137	–	–	–
1953	670	120	0.178	–	4.17
1954	756	150	0.198	5.04	–
1955	733	170	0.231	–	–

SOURCES: For cotton, Sun Jingzhi, *Huabei jingji dili* (Economic geography of North China), Beijing, Kexue chubanshe (Scientific Publishing House), 1957, pp. 159–160; *Renmin ribao* (People's Daily) 29 October 1954, 5 October 1955, 11 September 1956; *Henan ribao* (Henan Daily), 12 January, 29 and 31 December 1957. For stock-raising, *Henan ribao* (Henan Daily), 27 November 1956; Zhongnan qu ji yi jie jinchukou huiyi dahui mishuchu (Secretariat of the first session of the Association for Promoting the External Trade of the Central-South Region), *Zhongnan qu tutechan tongji ziliao* (Statistical materials on local production of the Central-South Region), n.p., n.d., p. 9.

aid was slight and concentrated on a few model farms. Agricultural machinery was nonexistent, inefficient, or unusable. Seed selection remained at the experimental stage and chemical fertilisers were practically unknown. These factors explain the fall in the cereal output growth rate, from 18–39.1 percent in 1949–1952 to 7.5–22.7 percent in 1952–1955. And even then the growth was partly due to exceptionally good climatic conditions in 1955, which made possible some substantial rises in production (4.6–7.5 percent) and yield (6.5–9.4 percent) compared to 1954. Again, the increase in yields was indeed remarkable; what is worrying is that it was slowing down and threatening to slow down even further as time went on if new technology was not brought into play.

Population growth was at least equally threatening, as shown in Table P.8. It was particularly rapid between 1949 and 1952, probably because of the rise in births and the numbers of persons (primarily soldiers) returning to the province from elsewhere. Subsequently, growth stabilised at a high level, 2.16 percent per annum, or a million extra inhabitants. Population rose by 8 million up to 1955 and 10 million up to 1957.

It is not at all surprising that population growth should consume much of the extra cereals being produced. Per capita grain availability rose less rapidly than production: 33–44 percent as against 66–79.8 percent. Between 1952 and 1955 Henan ranked fourth or fifth amongst cereal-producing provinces, but only nineteenth or twenty-first for per capita availability; from this perspective, in North China, only the inhabitants of Shandong were less well provided for than those of Henan.[24]

TABLE P.8   Population Growth in Henan, 1949–1957 (million inhabitants)

1949	38
1952	43.28
1953	44.21
1954	45.17
1955	46.14
1957	48.16

SOURCES: Figures are available for the population increase in four counties between 1949 and 1956–1958: Linxian (from 400,000 to 526,000), Lushan (from 380,000 to 420,000), Mengjin (from 140,000 to 241,000), and Nanyang (from 400,000 to 528,000). See *Henan ribao* (Henan Daily), 29 December 1957, and *Pékin Information*, 11 December 1972; *Xinhua yuebao* (Xinhua Monthly), 18, 1952, p. 15, and *Henan ribao* (Henan Daily), 8 April 1958; Zhengzhou shifan xueyuan dilixi (Department of Geography of the Zhengzhou Teacher Training School), *Henan dili* (Geography of Henan), Beijing, Shangwu yinshuguan (Commercial Publishing House), 1959, p. 79; *Xinhua yuebao* (Xinhua Monthly), 5, 1950, p. 87, and *Henan ribao* (Henan Daily), 18 June 1958.

In addition, production continued to vary from season to season and region to region. In the province as a whole, growth was less rapid in 1952–1954 than in the previous years and 1955. Wheat production had two peaks, in 1951 and 1954, followed by periods of stagnation or even a slight fall. For miscellaneous grains the poor year was 1954. In the same year, cotton recorded a marked decline. Furthermore, although cotton production overall greatly increased, it rarely reached the norms set by the plan, which sometimes forced cotton factories to operate below capacity.

The annual variations were even more marked in individual localities. The year 1954 was good for the hilly and mountainous areas, such as Luoyang, Nanyang, and Xuchang special regions, but mediocre or bad elsewhere. In general the 1955 harvest, good and sometimes excellent in the plains, was mediocre in the mountains of Luoyang and the hills around Xuchang. Striking inequalities in production levels thus persisted. In 1955, although the wheat yield reached or approached 1.5 metric ton per hectare in favoured counties like Mengxian or Yanshi, it was no more than .0525 metric ton per hectare in Yuanyang. Between 1951 and 1959 wheat production did not rise in seventeen counties.[25]

What was surely most serious was that these variations and inequalities originated in a factor that had scarcely varied for six years: the vagaries of the climate. Yet the weather had in fact been rather good between 1949 and 1955, and the province had not suffered any of the age-old calamities that strike every ten years or so. The period 1950–1952 seems even to have been particularly good. And yet on average 15 percent of the cultivated area was devastated each year.[26] Natural calamities largely explain the variations and in part the slowdown in cereal growth. The year 1953 saw a deadly freeze, in 1954 there were floods around the Huai River and especially the Yellow River, and in 1955 localised droughts occurred in mountainous areas. The alternation of droughts and floods aggravated the backwardness of some areas. Thus Yuanyang county, on the northern bank of the Yellow River, experienced a flood in 1951, a harsh drought in 1952 (only 140 mm of rain for the whole year) and again in 1953, and devastating floods in 1954 and 1955.[27]

If nature remained threatening, it was largely because the efforts undertaken in that area were inadequate and inappropriate. In 1955 the Sanmen dam only existed on paper; the irrigated area had more than doubled but was still only 10 percent of the cultivated area. That explains why the area sown to rice (which, as is well known, has higher yields) scarcely increased between 1952 and 1955.[28]

By 1955 the advances in agricultural production thus appeared both striking and fragile. Without more sustained and more appropriate efforts, further weakening threatened to compromise the expensively won advances that had been recorded in industry.

The Difficulties of Social Change

On top of all else, both the results and the failings of economic growth were giving rise to social problems about which unfortunately too little is known.[29]

To begin with, industrialisation precipitated considerable social upheaval. The local "bourgeois class", at whose expense the process was in part carried through, found itself bit by bit deprived of property and status, often impoverished. Moreover, in an overwhelmingly rural province like Henan it was necessary to forge a working class. The number of "workers and employees" reportedly rose from 170,000 to 910,000 between 1949 and 1955,[30] including skilled workers transferred from the coastal areas and mixed in with young recruits from the surrounding countryside. The immigrants often found it hard to adapt, especially as they were frequently separated from their family. They were accused of working unenthusiastically and unsmilingly, like officials. As for the local people, they long formed an undisciplined, low-skilled labour force. In addition, in enterprises that dated from before the war it took months, and sometimes years, to eliminate the personnel and bad practices inherited from the previous period. A firedamp explosion precipitated by carelessness caused 174 deaths in the mine at Yiluo, in western Henan, on 27 February 1950. On that occasion problems were uncovered that were sufficiently serious and widespread for the central press to take notice and for Wu Zhipu, the governor of Henan, to make a self-criticism. The miners, mostly taken on before liberation, continued to be just as undisciplined. Venal and brutal petty supervisors, protected by the trade union that controlled hiring and accepted only supervisors and surface workers as members, beat the miners and locked them in cells.[31]

Urbanisation also posed difficult technical and social problems. The modern housing that was hastily put up on the Soviet model often proved to be defective and uncomfortable. Nor were there enough housing units to meet the demand, thousands of families remained crowded into unhealthy hovels. There were long delays in getting public transport going and the commercial, administrative, and cultural infrastructure built in the new cities.[32] The diffusion of primary education initially aroused a widespread desire for learning and upward social mobility, but became one more reason to criticise the often-defective equipment, the cost of courses, the inadequate number of places in secondary schools, and the irrational assignment of graduates.[33]

Finally, although wages were generally much higher in the cities, they were also unequal. Alongside the new aristocracy of cadres, who sometimes threw themselves into the delights of corruption,[34] and the cossetted stratum of workers in large-scale industry, there existed a whole world of temporary workers, small artisans on the edge of failure, young unemployed people, and peasants seeking clandestine work whose living conditions were poor, and often appalling. But even the most favoured had something to complain about; they too found their housing too small, the cost of living too high, the supply of foodstuffs and consumer goods inadequate.[35]

In the countryside, after a few years of euphoria, the social atmosphere began to deteriorate. Amongst those who profited from the economic recovery some, even Party members, deplored that grants were begrudged them, even after natural calamities, and that their income was rising more slowly than that of city-dwellers. Propaganda did not conceal the fact that priority was given to industrialisation.[36] The future lay in the cities. So, people who could not worm their way into the city sought to get a son admitted into a secondary school or an apprenticeship there. New inequalities began to appear or old ones deepened. In the suburbs or on the sites of the big irrigation works, tens of thousands of expelled peasants were purely and simply sacrificed to progress. Elsewhere, in the mountains, representatives of government were seen only when time came for taxes or compulsory deliveries to be collected. In some well-situated areas, peasants could sell their excess production in local markets for good prices, but whole regions depended to get through the lean spring period before the next harvest on such supplies as the authorities would or could allocate to them.[37]

In the villages, life was particularly hard for the elderly and families with a large number of small children (up to 10 percent of the population), who experienced difficulties in getting enough to eat.[38] More and more often peasant families were forced to sell their land and hire out as labourers. Conversely, a small number of other families—perhaps 5–10 percent of the village population, most frequently those that included a cadre—managed to turn the new conditions to advantage, buying land or a van or starting a small business or the like.[39]

The picture was certainly not one of universal misery, even less of despair, but rather of a society undergoing change. The difficulties were a direct result of the movement sweeping society. But the fact remains that there were few traces to be found of the militant enthusiasm that the new regime would have liked to inspire. At best there were the advantages of office and gumption; at worst, recriminations, or more often, silence from the poor. Change is of course painful for any social organism. The changes the society of Henan experienced after 1949 were all the more so because they were *suffered*.

*   *   *

It was in the political sphere that the new regime manifested both its greatest effectiveness and its most ominous defects. Of course, the crisis of 1956–1957 cannot be understood without taking into account the initial backwardness and the shortcomings of economic strategy. But leaving aside the fact that these derived largely from deliberate choices of direction made by the regime, the excesses as well as the hesitations of the Party gave rise to a peculiarly political malaise and lay the ground for the serious mistakes of 1955–1958.

Available sources[40] make it possible to pinpoint three main characteristics of the political evolution of Henan between 1949 and 1955. The determining factor was the establishment of the active domination of the Communist Party over the economic, political, and social life of the province, provoking reactions that were a mixture of passivity and defiance. The growing monopolisation of power by the Party and popular reactions aggravated the effects of personal conflicts that had arisen at the top of the provincial Party apparatus.

Party Rule

After 1949 the new regime pursued two main political objectives in Henan: to set up an effective administration and to ensure the power of the Communist Party. A first and often little noticed indicator of the strengthening of the provincial administration is alterations to territorial administrative boundaries.[41] In the PRC any strengthening of administrative power is reflected in a concentration of administrative units, that is, a reduction in their number and an increase in their size. During the early period, from 1949 to 1952, the various Chinese administrative units continued to be scattered under the authority of six large military-administrative regions, doubtless because of the scarcity of administrative skills and the paramount need to ensure military control. At that time Henan was divided into two provinces: Pingyuan in the area north of the Yellow River, and in the south, Henan proper. Pingyuan fell under the authority of the North China region; Henan proper, that of the Central-South region. In addition each of these two provinces included a relatively high number of special regions (*zhuanshu*)— three in Pingyuan and ten in Henan—each covering several counties. A process of concentration at the national and provincial level got under way in 1952. In October Pingyuan was reabsorbed into Henan. In 1954 the six national regions were dissolved. In Henan, four special regions were abolished in late 1952 and another in December 1954, which reduced their number to eight until the end of 1957. The number of counties remained stationary overall: 109 remained at the end of 1956.[42] At the same time, the increase in the number of municipalities strengthened the power of the *zhuanshu* at the expense of that of the counties. Four (Zhengzhou, Kaifeng, Xinxiang, and Luoyang) were under the direct authority of the provincial government, but the other nine came under various different special regions.

The strengthening of the administrative apparatus[43] made it possible to enlarge the responsibilities of the province and the special regions. Statistics are lacking on administrative personnel strictly defined, but the data show that the total number of cadres in the province (probably from the township level upwards) rose from 40,153 in 1949 to 241,000 in June 1956. Within the provincial government, in 1956–1957 there were some thirty bureaus (*ting* or *ju*), themselves divided into directorates (*ke*) and subdirectorates (*chu*). The greatest proliferation was in financial and commercial administration, which by 1958 included 300,000 employees and cadres. Even at the highest level, management personnel increased. Thus whereas in 1940 there were four vice-governors in the two provinces of Henan and Pingyuan, by February 1955 there were six, and by November 1956 thirteen.

At that time, administrative office had both weight and prestige. At the provincial level the functions of Party head and government were usually in separate hands. This was the case in Pingyuan between 1949 and 1952, and formally at least, in Henan between 1953 and 1958. Differences between Wu Zhipu, the governor of the province, and Pan Fusheng, the first secretary—who was to be absent from summer 1954 to spring 1957—led Wu to upgrade the importance of his office. Having these two posts in separate hands seems to have been commonly the case in the cities and special regions and almost always the rule in the counties.[44]

The United Front line officially applied since 1949 contributed to strengthening the administration. In specialist positions use was made of many engineers and technicians from the previous regime, since their talents proved to be indispensable. They could feel themselves represented at the highest level by men such as Zhang Zhonglu, a former high official and member of the Guomindang, who was successively head of the provincial Industry Bureau and then the Transport Bureau.[45] The survival of the small "democratic" parties and associations contributed to the regime's moderate image and the representativeness of its administration.[46] In the provincial capital, the cities, and the county seats of traditionally commercial counties as well as in secondary schools and higher institutions, the Guomindang Revolutionary Committee, the Democratic League, the Democratic Construction Party, the 3 September Society, the Federation of Industrialists and Businesspersons, and the Workers' and Peasants' Party held official meetings in due form. In thirty-one localities their delegates, along with a number of respectable figures belonging to no party, formed representative bodies, the committees of the Chinese People's Political Consultative Conference, the activities of which, closely harmonised with those of their national committee, were given a great deal of publicity.

In reality of course all these organisations were languishing. Recruitment to them was arbitrarily limited to certain professional categories in the urban areas (teachers, doctors, engineers, "national capitalists") and subject to quotas. The United Front departments of Party committees carefully regulated organisation activities and even ceremonial. Communist cadres (officially or otherwise) usually headed the secretariat. The organisations were allowed no resources of their own. During the Hundred Flowers there would even be complaints of lacking funds to offer tea at meetings. The regime kept all these mini-organisations just short of collapse and most of their leaders under threat of being totally cast out in the cold. Thus, to conserve their sinecures, all the vice-chairmen of something or other outdid each other in obsequiousness at official ceremonies.

In fact, the Party allowed these bodies to survive above all because they elected leaders whose nominal collaboration legitimised government bodies. Subtle balancing gave the government bodies the appearance of being United Front coalitions. In each city, at least one assistant mayor was a non-Communist. Indeed, some of these government democrats did not lack either popularity or capacity, such as the two non-Communists who held posts as vice-governor after 1949: Ji Wenfu, a progressive historian who had been twice imprisoned by the Guomindang and devoted his acknowledged skill to school and university problems, and Jia Xinzhai, an old Henan democrat who spent his time on the most delicate social problems, such as displaced persons.[47]

In culture and education, "democratic personalities" held influential and sometimes even dominant positions. Su Jinsan, vice-president of the Provincial Writers' Union, was a writer who had been closely associated with Hu Feng but knew how to manipulate adeptly the official orthodoxy. He retained sufficient power to block the publication of manuscripts by "amateur young writers" nurtured on socialist realism or to exhaust them with criticism. Non-Communist teachers headed some secondary schools and held important positions in higher education. Luo Shengwu, appointed head of the Kaifeng Teacher Training School in 1949, succeeded in securing the removal of successive Party secretaries. These academics sometimes found enough time to continue old quarrels. Thus, at the University of Henan, fierce rivalry pitted Wang Yizhai, a famous teacher who headed the establishment secretariat, against the rector, Ji Wenfu.[48]

Although owing their position to the Party, these figures were also maintained by the fiction of power promulgated by the press: The public believed them powerful. After calamities it was they who were sent to "comfort" the victims and listen to their complaints. They could believe themselves popular and at least closer to the masses than many Party functionaries.[49] In addition, even their geriatric committees did not totally lack importance. Rather than risk private conversations that would inevitably be denounced as plots, they preferred to meet quite legally in those committees to make their customary praise of the "justice of the principles", and then go on to express timid reservations about "errors of application". These organisations were places where old friendships could be kept up or still-heated quarrels continued. The personalities best regarded by the regime would build up a clientele in these bodies. Some individuals who had not yet given up all ambition could believe themselves on stand-by for service to the People's Republic.

Above all the extension of the power of the Communist Party made strengthening the administration possible. The number of CCP members in Henan rose from 170,000 in 1949 to 457,000 in July 1955, 680,000 in November 1956, and 730,000 in December 1957.[50] The rural component of the Party increased. In 1956, 70 percent of CCP members worked in the rural areas and 80 percent were of rural birth. Alongside the now-classic profiles of Communists come up through the guerilla movement, the People's Liberation Army, or the administrations of liberated areas, a new type of cadre emerged in the villages. Still only semiliterate, but capable of running a meeting, and more important, of leading from the front and so attracting others to work, the new cadres got where they were more because of qualities of character than because of their political training. Nevertheless, the Youth League and the army provided the most appreciated education. The league selected 119,784 future Communists between 1953 and 1956; 64,000 soldiers of the 310,000 demobilised in Henan between 1950 and 1957 were accepted into the ranks of the Party (and a larger number into the administration). The most highly rated of these recruits could follow training courses in the various Party schools and become eligible for founding the first cooperatives or holding management positions at the township and county level. In short, whatever their training, Party members were becoming more and more the social and political elite in the countryside.

But this remarkable strengthening did not give the Party all the means it needed, and the Party ranks included only a small percentage of the provincial population—around 0.45 percent in 1949, 1 percent in July 1955, and 1.5 percent in December 1957. The growth in membership was remarkable, more rapid even than in the rest of the country, since Henan caught up with the national average in 1956–1957. But still Henan lagged far behind the other provinces in North China,[51] and as elsewhere, the Communist Party was very unevenly established. Despite significant variations, in general the countryside was much less penetrated than the cities; in 1955 numerous townships and a great many villages still lacked a Party branch.[52] The CCP's rural base was not deep enough to enable it to know everything that was going on, far less control matters. The cities were better covered, although there were exceptions.[53] In Luoyang, for example, 5.5 percent (7.3 percent counting trainees) of the population were members of the Communist Party in May 1957. The fact is that the cities were where industrialisation was taking place, and the regime attached supreme importance to political control of the working class. The proportion of Party members among mine workers for example, was 12 percent; it was not accidental that one of the most frequently cited models in the press was the miner Liu Jiuxue, who had gone down into the mines at the age of nine, then become a foreman, and under the new regime a team leader in the mine at Jiaozuo as well as member for Henan in the National Assembly. Cities were increasingly the seats of administration and decision-making. They were where political leaders were, ever more absorbed in their office tasks, and obscure pen-pushers found that frequenting the corridors of power opened up possibilities for making a career within the Party.

Rural cadres followed the same path, rapidly becoming caught up in a process of bureaucratisation. Once the agrarian reform was carried through and production under way, they found themselves more and more overwhelmed with administrative tasks and ended up taking refuge in the headquarters of the township (*xiang*), the district (*qu*), or the county (*xian*). In Huixian, in 1949, of the 500 cadres at the township level and above, 300 were still directly engaged in production. By December 1956 their total number had risen to 1,800 (900 of them in the powerful "commercial and financial system"), but only a hundred or so were still working with their hands.[54]

The technical quality of this supervisory apparatus was often most unsatisfactory. The "agrarian reform cadres" were tough, and often popular in the village despite their roughness, but they lacked training. As for the ex–secondary school students from the cities who had been unable to avoid being assigned to the countryside, they knew how to write reports but were sometimes totally ignorant of agriculture. Good accountants were in short supply everywhere. In December 1955, at the time of the cooperatives movement, the press acknowledged that only 57 of the 136 township secretaries in Qixian county were capable of accurately checking the production goods delivered by peasants to the new collective bodies.[55] What is more, some cadres lacked the necessary moral qualities. The big "affairs" revealed by the central press in 1953–1954 and the complaints expressed in 1956–1957 in provincial papers brought out abuses of power and misappropriation that had sometimes been going on for many years.[56] The fact is that in the countryside as in the cities cadres (paid by the state from the township level upwards) enjoyed the considerable advantages of a regular salary, facilities of all sorts, and above all power without any real checks. In addition, the Party's internal control bodies acted only sporadically and then indulgently. Until 1957 the campaigns to purge the ranks of the CCP were small-scale affairs. The Party was more concerned with "rectifying" certain social categories and strengthening itself than in putting its own house in order.

These weaknesses and defects help to explain two contradictory temptations for those in the Party apparatus. Their numerical weakness, technical shortcomings, and growing social distance from the mass of the population led cadres either to lie low, let things slide, and enjoy their advantages in peace, or on the contrary, when they wanted to or had to put their heads above the parapet and carry out instructions to be firm, to impose by dictatorial means measures that they had been incapable of making popular.

Weaknesses and defects hindered the Party's action but did not stop it. The absence of any organised resistance; the servility, prudence, or passivity of the population; and finally, the growing strength of the Party apparatus enabled the CCP, acting vigorously to repress and reform, to extend its power over the main areas of economic and social life. This was particularly true in the cities where the successive repressive campaigns that followed the agrarian reform rendered Guomindang officers and functionaries, "bureaucratic capitalists", and even the boldest of the liberal intellectuals incapable of causing any harm. It was also in the cities that, as has been seen, the regime's economic action was most concentrated.

Conversely, in the rural areas, establishing the Party's power proved to be more difficult. It was not enough for the Communist apparatus to be set up everywhere; it was still necessary to transform social structures. As in the rest of the country, this policy developed in two phases.[57] The first was the agrarian reform. Begun vigorously in 1949 in the liberated areas, reform was completed in 1951 throughout the province in at least a toned-down version. Each peasant was allocated 0.25 hectare. Then, in a second phase, an attempt to limit the development of "spontaneous capitalist tendencies" was made through "mutual aid and cooperation". By 1952 40 percent of the province's rural population was engaged in mutual aid teams (mostly seasonal). "Semisocialist cooperatives" took hold much more slowly. The province had only 159 at the end of 1952, and despite a stepping up of the movement in 1954, only 12.8 percent of rural households were cooperativised by the spring of 1955, which put Henan only twelfth among Chinese provinces.

In fact the most important step taken towards ensuring control of the countryside was the establishment in autumn 1953 of the "unified purchase and supply system for cereals". By reserving to itself the monopoly of the trade in the bulk of grain production, this measure gave the state the pretext and the means to exercise much tighter control of agriculture, delivering a severe blow to all the "new well-off middle peasants" who had previously been profiting from the freedom of rural trade. Despite all these efforts, in 1955 the rural areas were generally less tightly controlled than the cities. The Party reigned unchallenged, but it did not rule everything.

On the Social Effects
of Party Rule

It would be satisfying to be able to define precisely the social effects of Party rule up to 1955 and thus answer the vital question: At what point did the Chinese begin to see the Communist regime as tyrannical? The poverty of the sources unfortunately enables no more than two likely hypotheses: Everywhere that it was close and active, especially in the cities, the rule of the CCP led to fear, passivity, and resentment; but the reactions of the rural population were more mixed.

In the cities, the harshness and uneven intensity of the first waves of repression in 1951 and 1952, coming after a short period of quiescence, led to a general atmosphere of fear, the memory of which was very much alive in 1957. What family did not have a former collaborator or a member who in order to survive had engaged in a little trafficking in salt or grains? People kept to themselves, fearing that an imprudent remark or a neighbour's accusation might bring down a visit from the police. Fear was kept alive by the impossibility of knowing precisely when a new repressive campaign might occur or how far it might reach. Campaigns could strike even "democratic figures" well in with the regime.[58]

After a few years the new conditions came to seem normal, and life went on. "Counterrevolutionaries" were released with mere warnings, although it was best not to ask for information about those who had been condemned to "labour reform" (*laogai*). You could live in peace so long as you minded your p's and q's. Extreme attention had to be paid to the external appearances of conformity: going to political meetings, "participating actively" in mass meetings, even accepting positions of responsibility that were entrusted to you, and above all, not talking politics to your friends. If you took these precautions, you might even benefit from the new situation: get around cadres to get your family better housing, ask a workshop head for an easier and better paid job, get the enterprise offices to write a letter of recommendation to get your eldest son taken on or secure his admission into a secondary school. Behind the fear and passive obedience, a network of exchanges of favours and fiddles was organised: Life was resuming.

In this dominated society, the hierarchy was based less on income than on proximity to power. At the top, cadres received material advantages and general respect. Entering the army seemed the best means of receiving the political training that could lead to a position of authority. Or you could seek admission to the Party. Those the Party most freely welcomed into its ranks were workers and employees of state enterprises, who benefited in addition from much higher than average wages and social benefits. Lower down the hierarchy were to be found the employees of locally managed public enterprises, those in mixed enterprises, and finally handicraft workers and small traders, who might have substantial incomes, but lacked guarantees for the future. Finally, at the very bottom were the outsiders of all sorts: Moslems, universally scorned; ruined small business owners; families of "counterrevolutionaries" reduced to a hand-to-mouth existence; and a whole army of people whose situation was more or less irregular. Yet this situation could—and did—endure, although in 1957 people were to learn what deep resentment fear, make-believe, and humiliation had nurtured amongst those least resigned to the new regime, particularly the youngest ones.

Until 1955, the situation seems to have been somewhat different in the countryside. The repression that accompanied the agrarian reform seems to have been relatively restrained in the beginning, perhaps from being applied belatedly to the whole province and in a toned-down version. The victims were almost all landlords. Often, of course, the arrest and execution of small landlords provoked astonishment in the peasants as well as anger in the victims' families. The agrarian reform also removed the reservations many had felt. Available sources confirm that in 1950–1952 the social climate was excellent. Later, the regime's rule grew more burdensome. Taxes were ill received. The collection and transport of "public" grain raised general hostility. Already in winter 1949, a grain convoy in Pingyuan had lost four men and a hundred draught animals when they starved to death because of poor organisation and even more the hostility of the population: The foodstuffs and forage provided by the peasants had frozen.[59] In the absence of obvious economic advantages, people only entered mutual aid teams to avoid trouble, and then they would try to group themselves by family or economic ties. The establishment at the end of 1953 of the "unified purchase and supply system for cereals" raised everybody's hackles, touching as it did every single peasant.[60] People began to hide what they could of the harvest. The cooperatives were never popular, even in their "semisocialist" version. In short, the authorities met hostility and deception whenever they attempted to strengthen their grip.

But these tensions remained localised, and all in all, not very acute. At least in the earliest years, the Party apparatus seems to have been reasonably close to the people—who indeed supplied the Party with recruits. Difficulties in implementing the marriage law show that in the villages life had changed little.[61] The cooperatives remained few and far between, except in a few vanguard counties and townships. On that point the regime's short-term intentions remained unclear. In any event, the peasants possessed boundless resources of passivity.

One cannot therefore but be sceptical in the face of those who idealise the early years of the People's Republic of China. By 1955 the negative effects of Party rule were not insignificant. With the discontent engendered by the speed and unevenness of economic progress, the situation was producing a malaise that promised to worsen. Even if the social situation showed no immediate danger of exploding, two serious threats loomed: First, although in the countryside relations with the regime were not bad, it was clear that the peasantry did not fully support the official goals of collectivisation. In addition, the hostility, reserve, or even indifference of the people could not fail sooner or later to penetrate the Party and fuel and aggravate its internal divisions.

The Party Divided

As far as can be known, the same divisions did not appear with regard to the industrialisation strategy or the campaigns of repression decided on by the centre—even though this or that leader might show himself individually more accommodating than others.[62] Henan leaders split over how to implement the rural policy adopted by the centre. It seems that the origins of their disagreements lay in the debates that had arisen in the liberated areas as a result of the

oscillations in rural policy in the years 1946–1949. That at any rate is what is suggested by remarks in speeches made by Pan Fusheng in 1947 in support of a radical agrarian policy and his violent criticisms of cadres in the Hebei-Shandong-
Henan region for their "pacifism" in preventing "the masses" from "liberating
themselves".[63] From 1949 to 1951 the agrarian reform was implemented with more
flexibility.[64] Economic recovery required handling rich peasants gently and taking a positive attitude towards the middle peasantry. It was not enough to criticise the errors committed earlier: In some of the areas first liberated, land redistribution had to be reviewed. Even in former guerilla areas the mutual aid teams
were introduced only gingerly. According to later revelations, in Pingyuan province Pan Fusheng energetically applied this moderate policy with which he was to
become identified. He is said to have summarised the principle of it in 1951: "The
rural areas are 'middle-peasantised'. The main contradiction today is: Do the
peasants dare to produce?"[65] Pan does not seem to have been found guilty of
earlier errors. Although he was later accused of having implemented a "peaceful
agrarian reform", his future rival Wu Zhipu does not seem to have pursued a very
different policy in Henan province. Whether they liked it or not, both men implemented the new lines of rural policy, which were popular.

In fact, serious conflicts only became apparent after 1952 when the problem of
collectivisation began to be posed, and above all, when personal and bureaucratic rivalries surfaced. The debates over collectivisation gave a political content
to preexisting conflicts over prerogatives and power. The immediate origin of
these conflicts probably goes back to the formation in 1949–1950 of two distinct
leading groups in Henan and Pingyuan. Wu Zhipu, aged about forty-three, from
the Henan-Anhui-Shandong border area, was put in charge of both the Party
(with Zhang Xi, an experienced cadre, as his deputy) and the government in
Henan. In Pingyuan, the situation was more complicated: Leadership of the Party
went to Wu De and of the government to Chao Zhefu. Pan Fusheng, a forty-
three-year-old leader from the Hebei-Shandong-Henan border area, held the
post of assistant secretary of the Party committee (where Yang Jue and Wang
Tingdong, two cadres whom we shall come across later, were also working).
When Pingyuan was abolished in autumn 1952 the two apparatuses were amalgamated. Wu Zhipu retained the leadership of the government of Henan but had
to give up that of the Party—and thus preeminence—to Pan Fusheng (whom
Yang and Wang followed). This promotion of a little-known leader from an apparently lower rank and not a native of the province provoked murmurings and
perhaps partly explains Zhang Xi's departure for Beijing. Everything suggests that
Wu Zhipu, already firmly installed in command of three-quarters of the newly
formed province and benefiting too from something of a national reputation,
only reluctantly accepted having to give way to a representative of the minuscule
Pingyuan.[66] Two factions seem to have come into being at this time within the
provincial committee of the Party, as the leaders of some special regions apparently also accepted the advent of Pan Fusheng with ill grace.

In any event, Pan set out at once to impose his authority. To do this, he put to use a recent shift in the centre's rural policy away from its overall moderate course.[67] After the "laisser-faire" of 1950–1951, policy veered to the left in 1952. There had been a real development of mutual aid teams and cooperatives, but after the beginning of 1953, the stress was on "consolidation". "Bureaucratic" and "commandist" errors of the previous period were criticised. Pan Fusheng seized this occasion to assert his authority over a provincial apparatus that had inevitably been compromised in the implementation of the 1952 policy. In the *Ten Proclamations,* which he published after his arrival, he gave guarantees for the development of private agriculture, and to encourage production, authorised (under conditions that cannot now be ascertained) the sale of land, the hiring of labour, and private loans. Amongst the slogans that were later attributed to him, some ring true, and moreover simply summarise frankly what was at the time the policy of the centre: "Protect the results of the agrarian reform", "Stability, unity, production" (*anding, tuanjie, shengchan*), "Consolidate private property", "For the time being relax the mutual aid and cooperation movement". At the same time, the new Party boss came down heavily on the "political work" accomplished in the province before his arrival and "rectified the illegalities" committed by some local cadres in 1952.

As often in China in this sort of situation, an "affair" was publicly unveiled as a warning and model of disciplinary settlement. In this case it was the Wen Xianglan affair, which was picked up by the central press in February 1953.[68] Here it will suffice to outline the main features of the incident and its political significance. In spring 1952, Wen Xianglan, a young peasant from Lushan county (Xuchang special region), already a member of the Youth League and elected a model worker, was chosen by her superiors to found one of the first seventy-two county cooperatives. In June, to demonstrate her success she announced a record wheat harvest (with a unit yield of 0.58 metric ton per hectare on 0.20 hectare). In fact, the record was false: The yield had been no more than 0.30 metric ton per hectare on an actual area of 0.22 hectare. Everybody on the spot thought the figures fraudulent, including the local authorities. This is what was discovered by a journalist, Lü Jianzhong, called in to do a report. But the leaders of Lushan and Xuchang, anxious to assert themselves and to cover up for their subordinates, initially succeeded in preventing the truth from coming out and secured a large bonus for Wen Xianglan. It was only in January 1953, after Beijing launched a national campaign against false reports and premature cooperatives, that the provincial government got to know the truth and required self-criticisms from Wen Xianglan as well as the leaders of Lushan county and Xuchang special region.

The political significance of this affair was clear. On the one hand, it illustrated the centre's new line: Collectivisation carried out too fast and to order was bound to end in failure and lies (a good proportion of the seventy-two cooperatives in Lushan had collapsed). On the other hand, and more important for Pan Fusheng, it was a matter of bringing a local party apparatus into line, not only to make an example, but also because of the political threat that it represented.

In fact, Xuchang special region had played and would continue to play a major role in Henan politics. Many members of the Xuchang Party apparatus held posts remarkably long or experienced an exceptional rise.[69] Zhao Tianxi and Ma Jinming held the posts of assistant secretary and then first secretary of the Party committee of the special region from 1952 to 1958 and 1960 at least. Wang Yantai, secretary of Lushan county in 1951–1953 and assistant head of the special region in 1958, was still heading it in 1975. In addition, it was in this special region that two leaders who were later to be given major promotions served their apprenticeship: Qi Wenjian, secretary of the special region until June 1952, served as vice-governor of Henan from 1955 to 1958. Ji Dengkui, secretary of the region in 1952–1954, later became provincial secretary, and after the Cultural Revolution, entered the CCP's Political Bureau and counted as one of the most important central leaders until his removal in February 1980.

There are a few other examples in Henan of this sort of longevity and political ascension. What makes the case of the Xuchang leaders significant is that their special region (and in particular the pilot county of Lushan) continually distinguished itself between 1949 and 1958 for its "vanguard" implementation of the centre's rural policy. Liberated in 1947, Xuchang implemented the agrarian reform (in radical form, apparently) in seven counties by the winter of 1949, before the rest of the province.[70] Xuchang was always ahead in the cooperative movement and was held up as a model at certain points in the Great Leap Forward.

As for Pan Fusheng, it was not long before the Centre's rural policy changed again and began to hurt him and give comfort to his enemies. A first leftward slide appeared in autumn 1953 with the establishment of the "unified purchase and supply system for cereals". Pan apparently vainly asked Beijing to postpone implementation in Henan for a year. He also had to deal with "leftist" interpretations of this policy, as shown in two internal documents made public in 1958.[71] The first, which is complete, is a report by Liu Ping, one of the leaders of Xuchang special region, about the general meeting of Party delegates from Xiangxian county, dated 17 November 1953. This report stresses not only the economic but also the political importance of controlling grains. What was required, according to Liu Ping, was to combat "spontaneous capitalist tendencies" in the peasantry and even in local Party apparatuses and reassert the inevitable socialisation of agriculture. The second document is an incomplete but evocative account of two speeches by Pan Fusheng, dated 16 and 24 December 1953, criticising Liu Ping's report before the provincial committee. Pan brutally attacks the "leftist" tendencies that had surfaced at the previous month's general assembly of provincial Party delegates, and more important, in "a fair number" of special region committees, which have "advanced and used the general line in order to go through our work with a fine-toothed comb". He strongly reasserts the continuity of rural policy since the agrarian reform: "You must not blame the small peasantry. . . . We must not go too fast, we must not do too much. . . . Policy towards rich peasants is to limit and reform them, not wipe them out. . . . The four great freedoms are still legally in force." In short, unlike Liu, Pan felt that a measure that was simply an economic one should not be politicised.

It appears that radical cadres, especially those in Xuchang, did not give up. Most of the figures compromised in the Lushan affair, first and foremost Wen Xianglan herself, publicly supported by Ji Dengkui,[72] retained their posts or were soon promoted. So Pan Fusheng tried to involve them in another compromising situation, the Wang Chaojun affair.[73] At the time of the "Three Antis" movement, in January 1952, Wang Chaojun, the head of the Organisation Department of the Party committee of Yancheng county in Xuchang special region, brought accusations to his superiors of waste and abuses by Zhou Gang and Jiao Guangliang, respectively secretary and assistant secretary of the county Party committee. These latter got word and succeeded in turning the tables. By false reports about Wang's past, Zhou and Jiao got Wang imprisoned in May 1952, then expelled from the Party by the Xuchang authorities. Through the intervention of the provincial committee, Wang Chaojun was freed in January 1953, but the indolence of the authorities of the special region and deliberate obstruction by those of Yancheng for eighteen months delayed his rehabilitation and the punishment of those responsible. In July 1954, Zhou and Jiao were expelled from the Party, and more important, Liu Ping, Ji Dengkui, and Zhao Tianxi received a disciplinary warning from the provincial committee.

This affair may have spurred Pan Fusheng's opponents to organise a counteroffensive about which we know nothing. In any event, time was working with them. With the publication in January 1954 of its "Decision on the Development of Production Cooperatives", the centre in effect encouraged the spread of cooperatives more firmly than it had in the past and disavowed the moderate policy that Pan had espoused. Deprived of the political legitimacy of the centre, Pan became the butt of hostility from a sizeable fraction of the provincial apparatus and faced growing difficulty in exercising his authority. He withdrew in late summer 1954, citing health reasons. It is true that he spent some time in a hospital in Beijing, but it is an odd invalid who receives numerous delegations of local cadres in his bed and visits local tourist spots with his wife, accompanied by the hospital manager, a nurse, and a secretary.[74] Furthermore, the speed of his return to power and the vigour of his action in spring 1957 when the political situation had changed confirm that his physical health was less troublesome to Pan Fusheng than his political health. By withdrawing he effectively put himself on the Henan reserve team.

Meanwhile, Wu Zhipu, who took over the de facto leadership of the Party in the province, at once found himself in a difficult situation. Although the central press several times published indications that he was appreciated in Beijing, his political preeminence in Henan was not officially recognised. At best, Wu was referred to as second secretary of the provincial committee,[75] and Pan retained the title of first secretary.

In addition, the political problems that had led to Pan Fusheng's departure had not vanished. After a period of acceleration during which numerous cooperatives were set up—by December 1954 the province had 27,632 cooperatives and a total of 50,000 was expected to be reached by the end of spring 1955—it became neces-

sary, on Beijing's directives, to change direction and focus on strengthening existing cooperatives and above all generalising mutual aid teams. These shifts[76] kept
alive disagreements in the Party apparatus. Cadres in some localities were still
hesitating to abandon their individual holdings, whereas in other counties the
activism of leaders had to be restrained. Thus in November 1954 Lü Jianzhong,
the same journalist who had revealed the Wen Xianglan affair, wrote an article in
the *People's Daily* denouncing excessively rapid establishment of cooperatives
in Kaifeng county.[77] Once again, Xuchang special region was in the vanguard: In
winter 1954–1955, the number of its cooperatives "leaped" from 2,117 to 7,900 (for
over a quarter of the cooperatives but with only about one-eighth of the rural
population of the province).[78] By December, the cooperatives enrolled 16.3 percent of peasant households, a proportion already higher than that achieved for
the whole of Henan in summer 1955. In Lushan county, jewel in the crown of
the special region, 30.8 percent of families had joined cooperatives and 51.2 percent mutual aid teams by summer 1955. So as not to deviate from the centre's
newly moderate line Wu Zhipu himself reined in this "commandist" ardour. The
Lushan cadres were once again obliged to publish their self-criticism, this time
because of losses of cattle (10 percent of herds) precipitated by hasty cooperativisation. Shortly before Mao Zedong made his famous speech on accelerating collectivisation in the countryside in July 1955, these cadres were still criticising
themselves publicly for having neglected to develop the mutual aid teams before
spreading cooperatives.

In sum, Pan Fusheng's "government in exile", shifts in central policy, and the
persistence of divergences inside the Henan Party apparatus placed Wu Zhipu in
an uncomfortable position. Challenged both inside and out, Wu needed to
strengthen his authority. The solution he adopted proved similar to that Pan
Fusheng had used against him at the beginning of 1953: to place his province
square in the line of central policy and to make it a national model and thus
receive extra legitimacy. The difference comes from the fact that instead of placing himself "on the right" Wu placed himself "on the left", taking advantage of
much wider and more radical political changes than the modest rightwards rectification of 1953: the cooperatives movement of 1955–1956 and the Great Leap Forward of 1957–1958. In short, alongside major economic and social factors in
Henan radicalism, others of a less wholesome sort were already apparent before
1955: personal ambition, factional rivalries, and the like.

The years 1949–1955 are years of "reason" only in an ahistorical conception of
the past, a view that takes into account only tangible results—the undeniable
economic growth and the establishment of a strong, indeed very strong, regime—but not specific causes, the way in which these causes were experienced,
and above all their consequences. Both the errors of economic planning and the
serious pathologies of the political system carried within them, in Henan, the
seeds of the "unreason" of later years.

PART ONE

The Economic and Social Crisis in Henan in 1956–1957

Starting in 1955, a new stage began in the history of the Chinese Communist regime. With the cooperative movement, there was a change in both the nature and the scale of official ambitions. The results too were no longer the same: Agricultural failure obliged the regime to beat a retreat for the first time as early as summer 1956 and engendered a serious social crisis. This series of unparalleled events raises two questions. The first has to do with the historical definition of the 1955–1956 mobilisation movement in relation to the strategy of the First Five-Year Plan—did it mark a real break and if so what sort of break?—and in relation to the Great Leap Forward—was it simply a forerunner or a full-dress rehearsal? The second question touches on what constitutes a social crisis in a totalitarian regime such as the People's Republic of China, and more important, how such a crisis might develop: Under what conditions does it appear? Can it modify the relationship between power and the social sphere?

1

The First Leftist Excesses and Their Consequences (Summer 1955–Winter 1956)

Observers often wonder why the cooperativisation movement of 1955–1956 had such significant consequences, since surely it was, at least as initially defined, a conventional—indeed predictable—movement designed to transform the structure of rural property ownership but not the character of the regime or its fundamental direction. Has there not long been seen a clear distinction between the flexible but effective methods adopted by the CCP in 1955 and 1956 and the terror that the Soviet big brother resorted to?

One solution might be to relativise this famous difference between the Chinese experience and the Soviet precedent: The great wave of social mobilisation unleashed in China in summer 1956 was preceded and accompanied by a police operation, the "movement to exterminate hidden counterrevolutionaries" (in short, the Sufan), which extended the purge of Gao Gang and Rao Shushi and the political and literary "criticise Hu Feng" movement.

The Sufan

According to the sources the police repression explanation appears to be inadequate. The anti–Hu Feng campaign had already been quite severe in Henan,[1] and the Sufan seems more important for the bad memories it left behind in certain urban circles than for its immediate effects, for it turns out to have been less violent than previous campaigns of repression. If we are to credit later—and thus perhaps underestimated—official figures there were no more than 5,770 arrests due to the Sufan for the whole province.[2] A large proportion of the individuals arrested—former Guomindang cadres or officers in the Nationalist army, leaders of secret societies, landlords who had actively engaged in counterguerilla activities—lacked a base in the new society. Additionally, there were a few spies, real and false, who had remained where they were or returned to the country with groups of overseas Chinese. Thus, in Fangcheng county, with a population of some 200,000, 3,800 denunciation letters forced 1,555 individuals to confess "historical problems", that is, errors dating from before 1949, but led to the arrest of only 39 "counterrevolutionaries", including 20 former members of "reactionary parties", 5 former officers, 5 "spies", 4 authors of "counterrevolutionary crimes", 3 former bandits and 2 "bad elements". To justify the repression, the press emphasised the number of weapons seized, including kitchen knives.

The movement began violently, but it soon became less so. By spring 1956, the authorities were warning public security agencies against false denunciations and the extortion of confessions under duress.[3] They also promised leniency to "counterrevolutionaries" who voluntarily turned themselves in to the police. Of the 37,000 individuals who responded to this appeal, only 14 percent were prosecuted and 1.7 percent sentenced to punishments, often minor ones.[4] Finally, in the second half of 1956 the authorities called for review of overhasty verdicts delivered in the previous months. In the province as a whole, 7 percent of sentences were reduced or cancelled. In short, the repression would seem to have been relatively moderate.[5]

Why then, in Henan as in the rest of China, was there such an outcry against the Sufan at the time of the Hundred Flowers? Of course, the campaign was still fresh in people's minds. But also the Sufan had particularly hurt urban intellectuals. It had dashed their hopes, raised by the 1954 constitution, for legalisation of the regime. For the fact is that although few were actually arrested, there was a great deal of searching and questioning and "criticising". In many administrative units, the conventional figure of 5 percent was arbitrarily maintained for the proportion of "counterrevolutionaries and bad elements". According to later sources, 600,000 people took part in the movement, 200,000 wrote letters of denunciation, and 80,000 were required to confess some error.[6] The importance of these figures becomes apparent in comparison to the population of the cities and towns where the movement was most intense: about 3 million inhabitants. And in what was the biggest disappointment of all, violent attacks were made on the very people who were putting most hope in a liberalisation of the regime, intellectuals and "democratic figures".

Practically every citizen who had a bad social origin or "historical problem" was harassed.[7] For example, Li Qing, a journalist on the *Zhengzhou Daily,* had been collaborating with the CCP since 1949, but his father had been a county head under the Guomindang and he himself had professed anarchist ideas at the time. Some cadres in the Youth League and even in the Party fell into this category, the Youth secretary at the Nanyang press, because he was the son of a landlord, and Luan Xing, an official in Cultural Affairs and a Party member, because he had shown insufficient enthusiasm for the new literary orthodoxy. Struggle meetings, interrogations, and searches were carried out ruthlessly. The police sacked the library of Ma Bingyu, a young "amateur writer" who had shown admiration for Hu Feng; a woman student at the Kaifeng Teacher Training School threw herself down a well in despair. These were dark days for "democratic figures"; once again they had to contritely suffer the insults of their "activist" colleagues, or to avoid attack, confess in advance and denounce their friends. In short, at the time, the Sufan sounded a death knell for hopes of reintegration into society by all those marked by original sin, be it of a family or a personal nature. Even as the Sufan further stifled any signs of opposition, it was deepening the malaise in the cities, leaving behind tenacious resentments that surfaced in spring 1957. The Sufan thus contributed to the crisis of confidence that further degenerated in autumn 1957, but the campaign does not seem in itself to have exercised any decisive influence on the events of 1955–1956, especially as it was confined to the cities.

The Cooperative Movement
and the First Leap

Like the Sufan, the assumption of partial control of the 498 private industrial enterprises that survived in Henan does not seem to have posed serious problems.[8] Pressured by the tax authorities and deprived of all real authority by the constant interventions of the Party and the trade union, "national capitalists" sometimes seemed relieved to have half the burden of their enterprise lifted from their shoulders. In addition the new mixed companies kept a job for them and a share of the profits. It is of course true that in Henan as elsewhere the process of "mixing" involved serious technical, personal, and social problems. From the very beginning, relations were at best distant between the old and the new cadres in mixed enterprises, and especially between the "private part" and the "public part" that held the real power. On many occasions, the efforts to achieve technical and administrative reorganisation were carried out incompetently and brutally. The workers in these enterprises, hitherto disadvantaged vis-à-vis their colleagues in the publicly managed sector, were often disappointed not to receive pay rises at once. But all in all, these were second-order problems that affected only a small part of the urban population. Only later did people dare to raise these problems. Similarly, although it upset people, the absorption of handicraft workers into cooperatives did not at the time provoke any significant resistance.

In the rural areas, matters were different. There the cooperativisation movement launched by Mao Zedong's famous speech of 31 July 1955 developed in a series of abrupt accelerations.[9] In October 1955 Henan still had 54,000 lower cooperatives and it was planned to raise their number only to 120,000 (embracing only 40 percent of rural households) by the following spring. But by March 1956,

45 percent of rural households had "joined" higher cooperatives. The most important acceleration occurred in the following two months, since by May 1956, 95.7 percent of rural households had joined the 25,665 higher cooperatives in the province. By August, there were 26,211 higher cooperatives, with an average of 358 households and in total 97.2 percent of the rural population. This proportion put Henan fifth among Chinese provinces, whereas up till then it had been rather behind in this regard.

As in the rest of the country, cooperativisation involved an upheaval in rural society through the transformations it brought in and the way it was carried through. The whole peasantry suddenly found itself caught up in a collective and guided economy. The most abrupt changes—the elimination of payments for land and instruments of production, the ban for some months on all private activity in most cooperatives—hit peasants all the harder because they now belonged to bodies embracing several hundred households, often including several villages, perhaps with unfamiliar leaders.

The innovations that were most applauded by the press—and were the least popular with the people—concerned the size of the new cooperatives. It was not uncommon for these cooperatives, now more generally known as *dashe* (big cooperatives) or *jiti nongzhuang* (collective farms), to reach previously unheard-of size. Wu Zhipu later reported that in summer 1956 the province had 808 cooperatives with more than a thousand households each,[10] a figure I do not believe exaggerated. The press at the time often mentioned such "big cooperatives", both in the relatively favoured plains and in traditionally left-leaning counties. In the first category mention may be made of Xinxiang special region, for example in Xiuwu, Mengxian, and Xinxiang county itself, which included five "*xiang* collective farms" (including the one at Qiliying with 1,036 households). In the second category are of course to be found several counties in Xuchang special region, including Lushan, where seven cooperatives had more than 3,000 households each.[11] By their size, as well as attempts to take on nonagricultural activities such as handicrafts and to equalise the incomes of members, these "big cooperatives" represent the peak of the movement. In the light of later events, they look like the buds of the people's communes within the cooperative movement.

How cooperatives were founded is a subject about which little is known,[12] but it seems that the cooperative movement lacked neither preparation nor organisation.[13] The spread of the CCP apparatus in the countryside had preceded and accompanied the "high tide of socialism". During the movement, 80,000 new Party members were recruited, the vast majority to fill leadership positions in these new collective bodies. In addition, tried and tested organisational techniques were used on a much larger scale than previously. The movement unfolded in two stages in each township: First, available resources were concentrated on the establishment of one or several model cooperatives. These examples were then disseminated through propaganda and the despatch of "work teams". To strengthen administrative authority and free up a sufficient number of cadres, the number of districts (*qu*), an intermediate level between the counties and the townships, was cut by 43 percent. The townships, which were in principle to retain only three cadres "seconded from production", were enlarged and reduced in a like proportion. Their total number fell from 13,513 to 7,650 between November 1954 and July 1956. These organisational preparations largely explain the speed with which the changes were carried out.

Yet the movement still encountered opposition. In summer 1957 it was learned that some cadres at the provincial level had criticised not only the speed of cooperativisation, something that was not at all uncommon, but even the very principle of higher cooperatives.[14] Conversely, it is true, many small rural cadres seem to have welcomed a movement that enhanced their power. In the ranks of the peasantry, a strong minority (often 10 percent of heads of family) felt what the press at the time delicately described as "reservations".[15] As elsewhere, these reservations led peasants to down trees and slaughter cattle. On this subject, at the time only sporadic pieces of information filtered out, but the reports were confirmed by the diminution and weakening of livestock in 1956. Collapses of cooperatives, and more generally the rural crisis that occurred between autumn 1956 and late summer 1957, leave no doubt about the character of the alleged spontaneity of peasant membership of cooperatives. In short, T. P. Bernstein's assertion that it was the consequences of cooperativisation and not the manner of its introduction that provoked difficulties needs to be modified.[16]

This interpretation seems all the more true because in Henan, as in the rest of China, cooperativisation was accompanied by a campaign to raise production that for the first time required the regimentation of the population—the "first leap", in Roderick MacFarquhar's words.[17] Without daring or wishing openly to go back on the principles of its planning strategy, the national leadership of the CCP decided to step up the tempo of economic development. In 1956 Henan industry experienced exceptional growth, with production rising 20 percent compared to the previous year. The main effort was focused on big urban infrastructure works, which enjoyed twice as much investment as in 1955.[18]

But it was in the rural areas that the production campaign was most intense. After a first draft agricultural development programme had been adopted by the centre in January 1956, the provincial and local levels of the Party and government formulated very ambitious short- and long-term targets. The first outbreak of statistical fever that Henan, like other provinces, experienced dates from winter and spring 1956—not winter 1957. The "Draft Twelve-Year Agricultural Development Programme" adopted by the provincial committee proposed in particular a doubling of cereal production by 1962 (with an average yield of 37.5 quintals per hectare) and a doubling of cotton production by 1958.[19] These targets in turn were "outdone" by lower-level officials. Those in Xinxiang special region, for example, proposed yields of 1.35 metric tons per hectare for cereals (as against 0.99 in 1955) and 0.41 metric tons per hectare for cotton (as against 0.22 by 1956. And county leaders frequently went completely over the top with their targets: Lushan opted for a 50 percent rise in cereal production in one year; Neixiang, which had just harvested 2.66 metric tons per hectare (already a very fine achievement) proposed 4.3 metric tons by 1956.[20] To meet these targets, vast rural development plans were put together for the first time, combining technical improvements and intense mobilisation of peasant labour. The first attempts at the accelerated dissemination of certain "model" agronomic methods date from this time; they were often the same ones that would later be more widely disseminated, and in a more authoritarian way, at the time of the Great Leap Forward. The one most trumpeted in Henan was "close sowing". Its introduction into cotton cultivation, following "advanced experiments" carried out in Xinjiang by Soviet advisers, had such poor results that it precipitated a muted polemic in the central and provincial press that went on until autumn 1957.[21] At the same time, the higher cooperatives had barely been founded before they were being used to mobilise labour with a previously unknown intensity for countless water projects.[22] Over a million new wells were dug, half of which later proved to be unusable. The (theoretically) irrigated area more than doubled in a year.

Research is needed, with the help of new and more representative material, to study the analogies beyond the obvious and well-known differences between the "first" and the "great" leap forward: the preparatory police work, the planning megalomania, and the combination of technical reforms and total labour mobilisation as well as the immediate failure, a failure that the authorities blamed on natural disasters.

The Failure in Agriculture

The net result of all the changes and efforts was extremely disappointing. Total grain production for 1956 proved in the end, according to official figures, to be virtually no higher than it had been in 1955: 11.94 million metric tons, an increase of only 2.1 percent, wiped out by the increase in population and easily overtaken by the rise in grain consumption (10.6 percent).[23]

Care must be taken not to overdramatise a situation that varied from crop to crop and place to place. The average grain yield rose very slightly: 1.08 metric tons per hectare as against 1.04. There was a marked rise in wheat production and yield, from 3.52 to 4.27 million metric tons and from 0.71 to 0.88 metric tons per hectare.[24] Even if it did not prove to be immediately profitable, the increase in the area sown to rice (555,000 hectares as against 458,000 in 1955) and maize prepared the ground for later advances.[25] In the areas least vulnerable to flooding, notably in the west and southwest, the 1956 harvest showed a slight rise over that of 1955. Some counties situated in low-lying areas recorded increases in grain harvests.[26]

Yet overall, 1956 was bad and sometimes catastrophic. The tiny increase in grain production was a poor reward for all the effort invested. Almost a third of the area sown to wheat still had a yield lower than 0.45 metric tons per hectare.[27]

More important, almost every other crop recorded a loss, most notably industrial crops. Tobacco production fell from 90,000 to 76,500 metric tons, and cotton, from which so much was expected, from 170,000 to 150,000, although the cultivated area had been increased. Cattle-raising fell back to the 1954 level (5 million head). Depending on the source, following the spread of cooperatives, the number of pigs collapsed to 2.85 or 1.35 million head (as against 4.17 million in 1954). In addition the livestock was in a bad state.[28]

Alongside these failures affecting the main categories of production, there were other, less visible losses. The concentration of efforts on the major grain and industrial crops, the neglect of handicraft cooperatives, and the suppression of private activities led to the disappearance or weakening of the "secondary activities" in which peasants had engaged since time immemorial. Thus, in Qingfeng county, the production of straw hats, which had flourished before the civil war and took off again in the first years of the Communist regime, practically disappeared in 1956.[29]

The social effects amplified the agricultural failure. The new cooperatives had invested considerable sums in the purchase of agricultural equipment, and therefore had to limit the distribution of cash and even grain even more than planned. But the virtual disappearance of secondary activities prevented the peasants from compensating for this shortfall in order to buy essentials such as oil, salt, or cloth. Money ceased to circulate, traditional markets disappeared, and everyday goods became impossible to find. In short, peasants found themselves worn out and impoverished just as the state and the new collective organs had been strengthened and embarked on ambitious projects.

The official press blamed the agricultural failure on climatic causes, piling on dramatic details. It is true that in 1956 Henan suffered particularly serious flooding. The first series of summer storms struck the province at the beginning of June, several weeks earlier than normal, at a time when the wheat harvest was not all in. From 2 to 11 June, 163 mm of rain fell at Nanyang and 290 at Xinxiang. In many areas, the harvest was destroyed in the fields or rotted in granaries, ruined by the humidity.[30] Then even more rain fell. Three more series of storms fell on Henan, the most violent striking at the beginning of August. In the regions of Anyang (229 mm of rain at Linxian) and Xinyang all the rivers burst their banks.[31]

Overall, two-thirds of counties were affected and 4.1 million hectares flooded. 14.9 million peasants and over 6,000 cooperatives were classified as disaster victims. Almost 2 million dwellings were destroyed or damaged by the water, and 640,000 people had to be temporarily evacuated.[32] Because of flooding, 550,000 metric tons of grain were lost. Only the mountain and hilly regions were relatively spared. In Anyang special region, 1,427 villages were flooded, 809 cooperatives out of 2,000 damaged, 110,000 houses destroyed, and 251,000 peasants had to be evacuated (out of some 4 million); the disasters led to a 37 percent drop in grain production and 40 percent for cotton. The situation was serious in counties through which the Wei River flowed. In Xinxiang special region, water covered half the cultivated area and the city of Xinxiang itself was cut off by floods three times. But the most devastated regions were Shangqiu and Xinyang, through which the tributaries of the Huai River flow. In Shangqiu only 1,500 cooperatives out of more than 4,000 increased their production in 1956. Xinyang special region received 1,200–1,400 mm of rain between June and August 1956: 280,000 homes were destroyed and 3.2 million peasants (out of a total of almost 6 million) were left homeless. In the most affected county in the special region and the province, Huaibin, 60 percent of the total surface area was covered by floods and 230,000 out of 440,000 inhabitants left homeless; grain production fell by 66 percent in 1956 and the authorities had to send large amounts of relief. In short, the 1956 floods caused heavy losses and some local catastrophes in about one-third of the province.

But climatic reasons are not enough to explain the agricultural setback of 1956. Over most of the territory natural disasters were no worse than normal. The Huai and its tributaries had recorded extraordinary flows in 1954. In 1957 and 1958 the Yellow River would reach higher levels.[33] Very often the disaster had more to do with human error than the scale of natural phenomena. The big projects carried out since autumn 1955 had aimed more at achieving a statistical increase in the irrigated area than enhancing flood control capacity, as some technicians were to regret during the Hundred Flowers campaign.[34] Many recent projects failed to withstand the floods. In addition, work on the large projects had exhausted much of the population. The fact is that it is difficult to blame the poor physical state of much of the population simply on the immediate consequence of the floods. By the beginning of September 1956, 83 counties were affected by meningitis epidemics. In Nanyang special region (relatively unscathed by the waters) 13,000 people were suffering from meningitis and malaria.[35]

The demoralising effect of the establishment of cooperatives and the mistakes made are the most likely fundamental explanations for the agricultural failure. This is suggested by two examples from Xiuwu county and the Xuliang "collective farm" in Boai county.[36] Cooperatives meant first and foremost domination over the peasant collectivity by leaders with little experience who needed to impress both their superiors and those under them in the shortest possible time. The production targets set by Xiuwu county were extremely ambitious (0.51 metric tons per hectare for cotton as against 0.16 produced in 1955 and 0.3 metric tons per hectare of grain as against 0.16). Cadres in some cooperatives thought it a good thing to sow cotton in wheat fields and then wheat in cotton fields. They caused many useless or excessively fragile wells to be dug (1,000 collapsed during the subsequent summer storms). In the small town (*zhen*) of Xuliang, which had 923 households and 3,500 inhabitants for only 133 cultivated hectares and 67 hectares of bamboo fields, growing and working bamboo traditionally occupied 1,600 peasants and provided more than 70 percent of income. But when a collective farm was started there, the cadres sought to encourage cereal growing; they underestimated the working day for bamboo and set a very tight scale of remuneration. Consequently, the number of peasants working the bamboo fell to 300, production fell by three-quarters, and rural income collapsed. In the middle of the summer harvest, 80 workers left to take seasonal work on the farm of the neighbouring county to earn some cash. For what most demoralised the peasants was the effective decline in visible, that is, cash, income. Rightly or wrongly, they found it hard to accept that, as in Xiuwu, the money due to them for grain sold outside the state quota should be unilaterally assigned to the purchase of agricultural equipment for the collectivity. The peasants did not feel sufficiently involved in the new cooperative institutions to work in them zealously or defend them against the wrath of heaven. In China, especially in Henan, every natural disaster is also a political one.

The best proof that the first leap and the higher cooperatives were largely responsible for the agricultural setback was to be given in short order by the regime itself. Not content with providing relief to the affected areas, the regime also softened its economic and social policy throughout the country. This retreat doubtless limited the losses, but it did not prevent the slump from persisting in agriculture and even spreading into industry.

Relief

The first task was to head off the worst in the disaster areas. The fight against natural disasters that took up the summer months of 1956 had two successive phases. The initial focus was on avoiding deaths and limiting material losses by mobilising the province's entire administrative apparatus and even units of the army. People and cattle marooned by the floods were evacuated and then returned home. Emergency food, clothing, and medicine were distributed. Potential outbreaks of panic among the population, as people began to react as they always had by fleeing and begging, were mostly prevented or diverted. For example, the authorities had to authorise the departure of 356 families from a Moslem village in Wuzhi county. All along the Jinghan line, starving peasants took over trains to travel to Wuhan to beg.[37] Where the situation was exceptionally serious, the authorities acted skilfully. Instead of banning emigration, they channelled it into new colonisation in Gansu and Qinghai in the west and Heilongjiang in the northwest. By September 1956, 163,000 inhabitants of Henan had emigrated, including, it is true, at least 100,000 displaced by irrigation works. Disaster-affected people continued to be moved, but the movements were given less publicity; suggesting the relocations were less voluntary and less easily controlled. There were references in the press to the return of peasants who had been unable to adapt to the arid conditions in the west.[38]

From late August the affected counties had to be helped to provide their populations with food and to repair the damage. The means available were limited, obliging provincial leaders to concentrate aid on getting production restarted. A meeting called in September 1956 by the people's government of Henan called on the population to "produce to escape disasters" and to resume as many as possible of the activities hitherto banned or neglected; the provincial authorities would directly relieve only the worst-affected areas.[39] The provision of food, clothing, and fuel was limited to the bare minimum, as were tax exemptions.[40] Moreover, as construction of the large urban projects was behind schedule, temporary workers were recruited from the disaster areas. In September and October 1956, 84,062 peasants were assigned to these projects. More important, the amount of loans to agriculture was raised (in all 24.6 million yuan) and much of the relief (28.7 million yuan) was allocated to the development of subsidiary activities and handicrafts.[41]

Despite the poor state of communication routes and many blunders, relief efforts produced real results. The incompetence and devotion to red tape displayed by some cadres delayed the movement of emergency relief. A frequent cause of delay lay in the fact that deliveries had to follow proper procedures. Often it took "emergency orders" and calling provincial officials on the carpet to get relief effectively distributed to disaster victims. Some cadres diverted funds. In Xiangcheng county much of the relief went to the cadres' social fund, and in one township in Xiancheng, 96 rural families were forced to repay relief with interest.[42]

Nevertheless, major catastrophes were averted. There were very few deaths. Local food shortages occurred, to which the press made veiled allusion, but nothing on the scale that precipitated the purge of major provincial leaders in Guangxi.[43] A real effort was made to adapt relief and credits to local needs. To that end, every level of the provincial apparatus of the Party sent missions of "inquiry" or "sympathy" to those at the basic levels. That winter, extra cadres were sent to areas facing problems (for example, 1,490 county-level cadres to Xinyang region).[44] Subsidiary activities rapidly got under way. According to available sources, Anyang special region, where 61 percent of labour continued to be assigned between October and December 1956, produced an extra income of 23.2 million yuan. By January 1957, 41.6 percent of affected cooperatives in the province had all but returned to a normal life.[45] The situation remained serious, but the worst had been averted.

The Swing to the Right

The development of secondary activities was encouraged outside the affected areas as well. It was in fact part and parcel of a shift to the right of the regime's political line. This change of direction began several weeks before the onset of the first disastrous rains, which suggests that at least some central leaders were already foreseeing the agricultural failure. A joint directive of the CCP Central Committee and the State Council dated 4 April 1956 denounced the waste of property and labour and stressed the importance of secondary activities. Starting in May, the provincial press published frequent appeals to "revitalise the rural economy" by assigning extra credits to cooperatives and relaunching trade as well as restoring cattle-raising and subsidiary activities. Cooperatives were advised to trim their investments, with the result that 65 percent of the summer harvest was effectively distributed to the peasants.[46]

The mediocrity of the summer harvest in the country as a whole led to a speeding up of this process of rightist rectification. On 15 June 1956, following a Central Committee meeting at Beidaihe, Li Xiannian made a speech before the National People's Congress that altered political priorities: The fight against "adventurism" now became the principal task. Until the end of 1956 the complicated and confused political debates that unfolded in the centre, notably at the Eighth Congress of the CCP (August–September 1956), saw supporters of a considerable softening of the official line in social matters and a controlled relaxation in the cultural and political domains generally getting the upper hand.[47]

This rightwards shift of the centre's line posed a particular problem to the leadership in Henan. By placing their province among the good students of the cooperative movement and increasing the number of "advanced experiments", Wu Zhipu and the majority of his colleagues had dangerously compromised themselves. Now that the political line was all but reversed, they risked being criticised and seeing their authority over the local apparatus diminished. The danger was that much greater because in his Beijing retreat, Pan Fusheng continued to concern himself with provincial affairs, talking to those close to him (such as Yang Jue, who would soon join the secretariat of the provincial committee) in very harsh terms about the "errors" committed in Henan during the cooperativisation movement. Furthermore, Pan had not lost all support in the centre. Wu Zhipu received a remarked-upon promotion in being directly elected a full member of the Central Committee at the Eighth Congress, but Pan Fusheng became an alternate member. Subsequently, Wu was no longer referred to by the press as second secretary, but rather as "secretary of the secretariat" of the provincial committee of the Party. His manoeuvring room thus became increasingly limited. To avoid sanctions from the centre he had to apply the new softer line. At the same time, to eliminate any excuse for Pan Fusheng to return to Henan affairs, Wu had not only to consult him long-distance but also more generally give the impression that there had been no fundamental change in the political line since summer 1955. This skilful and ambiguous behaviour was only possible so long as the national line remained confused in its principles and only half-heartedly enforced.

In any case, what we see in the second half of 1956 is a marked contrast between the centrist character of the officially declared line in Henan and the adoption in accordance with directives from Beijing of rightist concrete measures. A good example of this is the first provincial Congress of the Party, which met from 9 to 17 July.[48] This Congress, which was intended to draw up a balance-sheet of several years of political and economic transformation in the province, in fact heard sharp criticism of the recent errors of the provincial leadership and some local committees. But Wu Zhipu cleverly forestalled the complaints in his progress report and drew their sting in a closing speech in which he asserted the continuity of the political line and the need to fight against both "adventurist tendencies" and "rightist conservatism". Moreover, the accounts of the Congress carried by the provincial press placed much less stress than the account in the *People's Daily* on the criticisms of the provincial leadership. Before the Eighth Party Congress, Wu Zhipu defended his position with even more care. In a speech on 20 September he stressed the successes achieved thanks to the cooperatives and then went on at length on the side of advocates of concrete improvements in peasant incomes. He thus skilfully combined a discreet defence of the previous line with apparently total political conformism.[49]

In Henan, Wu could act more freely. The summary that appeared in the *Henan Daily* of an eight-hour speech he gave to an important meeting of local leaders in October 1956 designed to "disseminate the spirit of the Eighth Congress", glossed over the political slide to the right in very general considerations that would be incomprehensible to the uninitiated.[50] Almost a month later, when the fifth plenum of the first provincial assembly closed its doors, Wu was more decisive. After endorsing the more liberal measures that had just been approved, he established a political limit:

> We must absolutely recognise the successes honestly and taking an overall view. . . . Naturally, excessively rapid advances must be opposed, but so too must backwards-looking conservatism, and while criticising and correcting adventurist feelings, we must absolutely prevent the occurrence of errors that consist in underestimating the results of our labours and the level of consciousness of the masses and overestimating the inadequacies, errors, and difficulties and thereby harming our enthusiastic forwards march.[51]

The Hundred Flowers Under the Control of the Gardener

The cultural and political liberalisation advocated by some of the highest leaders in the centre was strictly limited in Henan. It is tempting to see its manifestations as a forewarning. In July 1956, in Xinxiang, delegates of the small democratic parties denounced the authoritarianism of the United Front's municipal department. In two personal interventions in the *Henan Daily*, Ji Wenfu, vice-governor of the province, encouraged the struggle against "dogmatism" and the opening up of a free debate, judging that these practices would not lead to disorder. A meeting of members of the Democratic League serving in higher education attacked "brutal attitudes in the scientific domain" and suggested that Marxism-Leninism might well be only an "ultimate critical standard" and not a "guiding ideology". Other specialist meetings and press articles expressed veiled criticisms and desires for reform in the area of the arts and literature, science and medicine, education and the running of schools.[52] A look at what was said and written shows that many of the topics that were to be much in vogue in spring 1957 (except the most dangerous ones, such as complaints against the advantages enjoyed by the bureaucracy, the repressive nature of the political system, and rural poverty) were already present in summer 1956. The troublesome *Henan Daily* thought the right time had come to publish its self-criticism: Henceforth, it was promised, the editors would no longer be satisfied with explaining the policy of the Party and glorifying the results achieved, but would present divergent opinions and take an interest in far-off regions that did not have the good fortune to pass for models—in short the editors would fulfil their duty to inform.[53]

In fact, these more or less sincere gestures lacked political punch or social impact. The reactivation of the small democratic parties was limited and largely channelled into the national campaign to win over Taiwan. The future blossoms of spring 1957 maintained a prudent silence. Was Ji Wenfu, the liberal of the hour, anything more than a fellow-traveller? One has the impression that in organising discussion meetings that were neither too frank nor too numerous, the various departments of the United Front were simply seeking to obey, but without doing too much about it, higher directives that were themselves ambiguous. The provincial leaders devoted themselves to tasks that they saw as more important, such as the fight against disasters. The topic of the Hundred Flowers is not mentioned in any of Wu Zhipu's big speeches mentioned above. One single act of political liberalism was later to take on some importance: the election in November 1956 of three non-Communists among seven new vice-governors of the province. One was Hou Lianying, the chairman of the provincial committee of the Revolutionary Guomindang, an inoffensive old man. But another was Zhang Zhen, the political and military boss of Henan in the last days of the old regime who had distinguished himself by his ferocity before switching sides and surrendering the province in 1948. And still another was Wang Yizhai, a liberal academic who did not lack fire. Promoted now to respectable status, these two, especially Wang, would be able to speak up the following spring.

And yet—and this is what gave the Party's calls for discussion so little credibility—the Party renounced none of its power. A few more non-Communist vice-governors or bureau chiefs counted for little in a system of power that remained wholly dominated by the same apparatus—an apparatus that published no self-criticism for faults that any and everybody could see. It did acknowledge a few "shortcomings", but since the political line had remained unshakeably "correct" since the summer of 1955, these could only be more or less accidental phenomena due to local errors in the interpretation or concrete application of official thinking. In Henan, the authorities did not instigate any of those "affairs" that signal a true political change in China. The press at the time did not mention any purge among county leaders. The serious lapses that led to a sharp fall in maize production in Luanchuan county earned some pointed criticism for those responsible, but no serious punishments. The *Henan Daily* blamed Shi Shaoju, the Party secretary in Huaibin, for the serious mistakes made in delivering relief, but that did not prevent him staying in his job and subsequently being praised as exemplary.[54]

The Social Climate Begins to Improve

Although Wu Zhipu could take advantage of the ambiguity of central directives to restrain political liberalisation, he did not possess the same freedom of action in the social sphere, where the orders were crystal clear. Whether Wu liked it or not, he had to implement a policy of detente. In the cities, a number of hasty verdicts dating from the Sufan were reviewed. Even more important, efforts began to be made to improve the living standards and conditions of urban-dwellers. The wage reform carried through between April and August 1956 favoured cadres and technicians, but it also led to a general rise in wages that for example amounted to 23 percent in locally managed enterprises and 10 percent in the city of Luoyang.[55] At the same time the leadership began to show a new concern for problems of supply. A cut in the official price of some food items, including vegetables, and consumer goods was announced. Complaints about housing conditions were now listened to and sometimes given a positive response. In secondary schools less authoritarian teaching methods were called for, designed to encourage individual development.[56]

This softening of social policy had an economic aim, for industrial production was rarely reaching the technical norms laid down in the plan. In May 1956 a directive from the provincial Industry Bureau called for an improvement in production quality. The press went on to advocate improving working conditions and raising the social benefits of employees. Particular efforts were made to improve the working atmosphere in enterprises. The suppression of the "one-man management" system that originally served to extend the power of Party committees in enterprises was now portrayed as a measure intended to correct the authoritarianism of cadres. To encourage workers to work more actively and suggest "rationalisation proposals", the authorities were even prepared to go so far as to defend them from some abuses of power.[57] Two "affairs" were highlighted to serve as a warning. In June 1956 the *Henan Daily* revealed the oppression of a worker in the Xuchang press between 1952 and 1955 by the director of the enterprise and the chairman of the municipal trade union committee for "proposing improvements" (and thus criticising their actions). The Guo Ziqiang affair, revealed in September, is even more significant. The worker, Guo Ziqiang, who was criticised by a mass meeting of the Zhengzhou Number 3 cotton factory and received a disciplinary warning for having "created incidents and harmed production", seems indeed to have been a hothead. To get him off, it had to be admitted that the authoritarianism of the factory managers, the fact that the machinery was very old, and the unsuitability of some regulations constituted the true causes of his bad behaviour. This affair marked a distinct advance in the softening of social policy.[58]

The New Rural Policy

In the countryside, the softening was both more spectacular and more consequential. Inspired by the centre, a new rural policy was set out at the provincial congress of the CCP in July 1956 and spelled out by the "financial and economic meeting" of 6–17 August 1956 and a "Draft Programme of Political Work by the Party in Agricultural Production Cooperatives" published on 15 August. A "meeting on work in mountain areas" brought the first concrete interpretation of the new policy with the decision to reduce the size of townships and cooperatives in hilly areas.[59] In September, the Central Committee and State Council directive on cooperatives, which firmly reined in the ambitions of the previous spring, was widely disseminated. Subsequently, the Henan authorities endeavoured to deal with the difficulties that were arising in some sectors. Thus, on 25 October, the provincial committee published a directive aimed at speeding up the work of purchasing grain from peasants and ensuring better monitoring of deliveries to the state. In the same month, a meeting was convened to study the problems of keeping and feeding cattle. On 14 December, the provincial government distributed a directive from the State Council aimed at limiting the effects of the re-opening of private markets.[60]

The excesses that followed the sudden and vigorous modification of rural policy helped precipitate a tightening of central policy early in 1957.[61] The institution of cooperatives and the power of the Party had to be protected. The provincial committee denounced the widespread dismantling of cooperatives, and in January 1957, launched a "propaganda movement" (sometimes called a "socialist education movement") to convince peasants that the difficulties of the moment were not due to cooperatives but to natural disasters, and above all, that the regime would not accept the overstepping of certain limits.[62] In February the provincial committee called a "meeting on rural work" aimed at giving rural cadres back confidence in their authority and in the possibility of raising production in 1957.[63] But these were all simply belated initiatives intended to hold back the effects of a policy that in its broad lines remained unchanged.

The host of directives and decisions from all corners that rained down on cadres after summer 1956 in fact formed a new and coherent rural policy. Its principle was simple, even if difficult to turn into reality: Loosen institutional, social, and economic constraints as far as possible without weakening the political power of the Party and the economic control of the state, that is, the cooperatives and the unified purchase and supply system. Major alterations were made in the

size and internal organisation of cooperatives. Autumn 1956 saw the start of
a process of breaking up cooperatives into smaller units that continued until
winter 1957–1958. It is difficult to assess the speed with which the breakups progressed, since on this politically sensitive problem available sources are both unreliable and contradictory. Accounts from 1958 reveal a rapid evolution from
summer 1956 to spring 1957, but sources at the time put the main change later, in
autumn 1957; local examples reveal a great variety of experiences.[64] In any event,
there can be no argument about the upshot of this process. In the space of a year,
the number of cooperatives in Henan about doubled, rising from 26,211 in summer 1956 to 51,000–54,000 in autumn 1957. The average number of households
per cooperative fell from 358 to under 200.[65]

It is equally certain that the *dashe* were the first cooperatives to be broken up.
In Anyang special region alone, in spring 1957, 896 cooperatives thought to be too
large were divided. In Xiuwu county the 35 largest higher cooperatives formed in
winter 1955–1956 continued to exist on paper, but their main tasks were transferred to 245 autonomous brigades, each with 550 inhabitants.[66] The dismantling
of the most famous *dashe,* such as the large one at Lushan, constituted a resounding victory for the moderates. In addition, within the cooperatives, the number
of production teams rose, almost doubling in Anyang and Xinxiang special regions.[67] Their power was strengthened to such a degree that in two counties at
least cooperatives were now simply called "management zones".[68] Not only
did the teams now generally serve as accounting units, but they received enhanced powers in the financial domain, notably for the purchase of agricultural
equipment.

The transformation of the role of production teams was probably of more importance than the reduction in the size of cooperatives. For the moment, the
main activities of peasant life unfolded once again, as in the time of the first lower
cooperatives, in small units that were part of a village or a hamlet (35 families per
production team in Anyang special region in January 1957; 17 in August of the
same year in Xinxiang). In units of this size, people could know the team leaders,
sort problems out with them, even complain to them. Above all, people could
feel really involved in the collective economy.

Human-scale social units were being reconstituted in the cooperatives because
economic policy was now directed less at the collectivity than at the individual
and based on incentives and material inducements rather than on mobilisation
and coercion. In distribution, "egalitarianist" errors were a thing of the past; now
only work actually done counted. The various deductions for the benefit of the
collectivity were limited to 35 percent of income. Ninety percent, and then eighty
percent, of members of cooperatives unaffected by disasters had to be guaranteed
increased income.[69] The autumn harvest was initially counted on to achieve this
result, but it was too small, and resort was had to activities hitherto neglected or
abandoned. To reestablish cattle-raising, cooperatives' cattle-keepers were promised allowances, and to restore handicrafts, loans and assistance were made available.[70] Commercial departments were called upon to supply raw materials and

outlets to subsidiary activities. So as to give peasants time for these activities, regulations granted one or two days a week off agricultural work. At the beginning of 1957, on almost two-thirds of the land area of the province, over half the rural labour was devoted to subsidiary activities.[71]

At the same time, the subject of private plots was reopened. Between July and September, some county newspapers followed by the *Henan Daily* published a discussion forum on this subject.[72] The interest of this forum lies in the fact that genuinely opposing views were presented in the first weeks. Several basic-level cadres stated frankly that allowing private plots would mean not only a backwards step politically but also, for them, a serious loss of prestige and power. Other correspondents, portrayed as simple peasants, replied with a simple fact: Without the private plots, there was a risk of famine, and the new rural policy would lose all credibility. The press ended up agreeing with the peasants, but not without some good words for their opponents. The explanation for this apparent impartiality lies in the scale of the resentment felt by the basic-level cadres (a resentment that was well understood higher up) and also in the concern to ensure their acceptance of the new decisions as being in accordance with the wishes of the majority of the population. In any event, whether convinced or not, cooperative leaders had to distribute or enlarge private plots. In May 1957 Pan Fusheng estimated the annual production of food grains on private plots at 800,000 metric tons, 6.7 percent of provincial production.[73] In other sectors—vegetables, fruits, pig-raising and the like—the share was probably much larger.

The most enticing material incentive for the peasants was obviously the reopening of free markets where they could sell the harvest from their private plots as well as some of their production beyond quotas. But this vital measure was also the most dangerous. The fact is that it was difficult for the administration to control all the countless points of sale and tempting for the peasants to sell privately, at prices that bore no relation to the official ones, products that could theoretically only be sold through the public system. In short, generalising private markets threatened to endanger the unified purchase and supply system, and hence, the state's control over the rural economy. Yet, despite opposition from numerous cadres, it was decided to go ahead at the "financial and economic meeting" of August 1956. Prices allowed under the new regulations were only slightly higher than the rates for official sales.[74] In fact prices fluctuated considerably. By the beginning of October 1956 the province had 2,500 private markets for cereals alone. By 20 September, 75,000 metric tons had been marketed in this way.[75] The private markets flourished until autumn 1957, despite a few attempts to rein them in.

The Economic Slump Spreads

The increase in the number of private transactions, which the press took good care not to put into precise figures after September 1956, was both the sign and the means of an undeniable economic recovery. The worst had been avoided and something better was becoming visible. However, it soon became apparent that a real recovery would be delayed. The peasantry was still exhausted by the trials of 1956. Spring 1957 was difficult in the countryside of Henan. In many places, famine loomed, and the people depended on food supplies from the state. The rigours of the climate, moderate though they were, hit hard. A drought in autumn 1956 had prevented 333,000 ha being sown to wheat. The following spring, 1.3 million ha were struck by various disasters: drought, tornadoes, insects, hail.[76] The summer harvest was expected to be very poor indeed. The present looked bleak and the future was hardly bright. The recovery proved to be particularly slow for livestock-raising. Despite repeated prohibitions, the lure of profit (or the need for cash) and the lack of forage and grain drove cooperatives to slaughter their flocks and herds. Inadequate care increased losses. In April 1957 pigs were hit by epidemics in 55 counties.[77]

At the same time the economic situation was deteriorating in the cities. Two essential sectors had suffered early from the agricultural crisis. In winter 1956–1957 activity in the food and textile industries slowed, and sometimes even halted completely (notably in the many small local oil presses), because of stagnating or falling cotton, tobacco, and oilseed harvests, and even more, from the slowness and disorder of purchasing operations for these products in the countryside.[78] The year 1957 was marked by a contrast between the rise in the purchasing power of the urban population after the wage reform and the disappearance of manufactured consumer items, such as clothes.

Second, the cut in public investment led to a slump in basic construction. Government revenues stagnated because of the poor results of 1956 and the funds withheld by the centre. In addition, the need to come to the help of disaster-struck areas and agriculture limited the funds available for "economic construction". In the provincial budget this category fell from 153.6 million yuan (35.8 percent of expenditure) in 1956 to 119.5 million (27.1 percent) in 1957. And it is likely that within this expenditure head, the share of industry fell and that of agriculture and water projects rose.[79] The most direct effect of the credit restrictions was a slowdown in construction that mainly hit social and educational projects.[80] It seems that the big building sites directly financed by the state were less affected.

The slump that appeared in the food and textile industries as well as in construction was also transmitted to other industrial sectors. Thus, in Luoyang, the Songda cement works was able to meet only 47.5 percent of its monthly plan in January 1957. After being unavailable for many months, bricks were suddenly surplus everywhere as demand fell. Local enterprises were the first affected by the slump, then it was the turn of larger units. For example, in the first months of 1957 the Kaifeng engineering factory had to lay off 400 workers.[81]

The employment situation deteriorated in turn. Employers stopped taking on temporary workers and attempts were made to better control immigration from the rural areas. It became more and more difficult for young city-dwellers, thrown onto the labour market in increasing numbers by the inadequate number of secondary school places, to find a job in the cities. In a mainly rural province like Henan, these problems naturally were not as serious as in the coastal provinces, but they constituted an important aspect of the social crisis that the cities of Henan began to experience in autumn 1956 and of the political agitation of the following spring.

*   *   *

It is impossible to overestimate the importance of events in Henan between summer 1955 and early 1957. Whatever the difficulties previously encountered by the new regime, it is with the first leap that those in power for the first time revealed the scale of their ambitions, and it is at the end of the first leap that they suffered their first serious setback. The setback was economic, but it also involved social consequences. The peasants, who had only engaged in collectivisation half-heartedly, saw incomes stagnate for the first time since 1949.

The response of the authorities—the rightwards shift of the political line—averted disaster. But the hesitation shown was bound to weaken confidence. The average Henan citizen knew nothing at all of the personal conflicts within the provincial leadership. But he or she could not be unaware of the reservations provoked by the new line and the precautions with which it was hedged about. The first leap had lasted barely a year: How long would the new policy last?

The contradictions inherent in the policy reinforced doubt. Could it seriously be imagined that workshop or cooperative committee secretaries would rigorously apply a policy that impinged on their prerogatives? To calm the worries of the cadres, liberalisation had deliberately been limited to the economic and social spheres. But was it possible both to urge the peasants to earn money and to refuse to abolish the cooperatives and purchasing and supply system without upsetting both cadres and peasants? Could social constraints be relaxed to any real degree without seriously modifying the structures of control and the distribution of power?

With the failure of the first leap the Chinese Communist regime began to sow doubt about itself. The hesitant retreat following a broken-off offensive provoked two contrary but equally harmful behaviours in the population. By not providing sufficient guarantees of good intentions and by refusing to call into question the power position of the Party, the authorities encouraged the masses to adopt a position of prudent political passivity, while taking advantage of the small freedoms that were graciously left to them. But by also giving the impression of yielding ground, of weakening, the authorities gave heart to the minority of stubborn and bold individuals who would attempt to gain a few additional smidgens of freedom.

2

A Social Crisis in China: Henan Society from Summer 1956 to Summer 1957

What constitutes a social crisis in Communist China?[1] The sources provoke this question in showing quite clearly not only that the material situation of the people of Henan stagnated or worsened between summer 1956 and summer 1957, but also—and more important—that awareness of this deterioration combined with the temporary weakening of authority led to discontent and social agitation. Pan Fusheng himself declared in the spring of 1957: "We are sitting on a volcano".[2]

It was through the countryside that the social crisis of 1956–1957 reached Henan, but it was also in the rural areas that the crisis was least serious, though to this day least well known. The regime claimed to derive its original legitimacy from the countryside, but the voice of the peasantry was scarcely heard. What is true for the *People's Daily* is equally so for the *Henan Daily* and even the *Miyang Journal*:[3] There is not a single concrete eyewitness account of peasant life and its pains and joys and sorrows to be found in the press, not a single report that was not written by a cadre or dictated by the imperatives of propaganda. That is why subsequent knowledge of the social situation in the countryside remains indirect and imprecise.

Poverty Again?

At the root of the rural crisis was the agricultural failure of 1956, which can be summed up in the stagnation of the theoretical per capita availability of food-grains: 253.35 kg as against 253.25 in 1955. But this measure is misleading. First, it does not show the real impoverishment of the population. To buy equipment, cooperatives reduced the amounts of cash and even grain that they distributed.[4]

The recovery of secondary activities and private trading in autumn and winter 1956 did not make up for the losses throughout the province in the summer. Second, half the province had become a disaster area as the parts most affected by floods also saw the reappearance of the famines, panics, and epidemics that were supposed to have been a thing of the past.

It is difficult to give an exact or complete picture of the peasantry's material difficulties. The available sources simply allude to a situation that everyone was aware of. But it is quite certain that in the disaster-hit areas the population continued in places to lack basics until the autumn harvest in 1957. In Yuanyang, 17,000 families out of 70,000 were without grain in the spring. By the beginning of June the food situation was still difficult over 15–20 percent of the province. At the end of the same month, in 92 townships in Xinyang special region most cooperatives only had one month's food reserves. Similar difficulties were reported in the north of the province in July and August 1957.[5] Driven by hunger, peasants in eastern Henan sought to sell their daughters. In some places competition between humans and cattle for food made a reappearance—a sure sign of *xiahuang* (summer famine), which led to new slaughtering, for example in Fengqiu, where the price of pork on the free market fell by 60 percent. During winter 1956–1957 the peasants sometimes suffered more from the shortage of clothes than of grain. By December, many were selling food rations to be able to buy clothes. Although the provincial government had distributed 600,000 items of clothing in autumn 1956, many localities were still short at the end of November. Many houses were rebuilt only slowly.

There is even less information about the conditions of the peasants in the areas untouched by disaster. Despite wide local variations, in 1956 the standard of living stagnated or progressed less than in previous years. The softening of the Party's rural policy made possible a gradual recovery in 1957, but this recovery produced an unexpected psychological effect in confirming many peasants in the feeling that the fact that incomes were stagnating or falling was not due to natural disasters alone, but more to the cooperatives, the errors of cadres, and government policy generally. As some peasants in Yanshi declared ironically: "In socialism, all is well, even if there is nothing to eat."[6] Contrary to the promises made by the Party and the hopes of the early years, socialism now signified the impoverishment of one and all. Were people once again to fall into poverty because of obeying the follies of a few?

What transformed the impoverishment of some and the stagnation of the standard of living of many into a social crisis was the way this concern was expressed in withdrawals from cooperatives, attacks on cadres, and more generally, economic disobedience.

Cooperatives in Danger

In the eyes of the peasants, the cooperatives bore the greatest responsibility for the failure. The best way of getting rid of them was, obviously, to leave them.[7] To that end, an official request could be made, for the authorities, although still not genuinely respecting the principle of voluntary membership, did now allow withdrawals under certain conditions. Another solution, the one most commonly adopted, was to come together with others to get back property that had been collectivised, hoping thereby to face the cadres with a fait accompli.

Withdrawals occurred in many counties (at least nineteen are documented),[8] beginning late in 1956 and continuing into summer 1957. Contrary to official accusations, those involved were not only from "counterrevolutionary" social categories. In Xinxiang, Linxian, Linru, and Yingyang counties, people banded together to leave the cooperatives. Several cases are documented of withdrawal by the leader of the production team. The effects of these withdrawals must not be minimised. In Xinyang special region, the withdrawals helped precipitate the collapse of 492 cooperatives and elsewhere hastened the breakup into smaller units.

Yet in the end, only a tiny percentage of the rural population was affected: 10,000 families in Xinyang special region, which had a population of over a million; 8,400 out of 100,000 in Xixian county. The official number of applicants was not much higher: 200 families in one particularly affected township in Linru, and 743 families in that whole county; 5,800 out of about 50,000 in Tangyin county. In addition, many withdrawals proved to be only temporary. According to the official figures of 40,000 "individual households" in November 1957 as against 5,572 in November 1956, only some 35,000 families left the cooperatives in a year.[9] One explanation for the low level of withdrawals lies in the deliberate softening of official policy, notably as regards the division of cooperatives and the revival of private activities, as well as in the purely nominal survival of many cooperatives whose equipment was stolen and granaries sacked.

Disturbances or Incidents?

The crisis threatened not only the new institutions. In summer 1957 the provincial press suddenly began asserting that "class enemies" had taken advantage of the agitation in the cities to foment counterrevolutionary disturbances in the countryside, publishing specific examples to back up this accusation.[10] In spring 1957, near Zhengzhou, several illicit Buddhist societies continued to survive as did the Equality Party, about which nothing is known. The Human Species Party was recruiting among secondary school students in Shaanxian and the Universe Party near Jiaozuo. Two subversive organisations were crushed in a glare of publicity. The Prostraters' Society, already dissolved in 1953, still had 120 members, some of whom were local cadres of the Communist Party and the administration, who continued activities in five counties (Mengxian, Gongxian, Yingyang, Kaifeng, and Tongxu). They had 10 guns, 270 bullets, and US$291. The New China Young Catholics' Party, founded in spring 1956, had a hundred or so members scattered about the mountainous areas of the two administrative regions of Nanyang and Xiangyang (Hubei). Although accused of planning the use of force, their activity was almost certainly mainly political. Only one gun and three re-volvers were seized from party members, together with many membership cards and documents denouncing the regime's rural policy.

These examples are a reminder that the new regime had not been able to crush the secret societies in one stroke, nor especially after poor harvests, fully control some areas where small groups of opponents kept up sporadic activities. But these are not enough to prove the existence of genuine political disturbances. The subversion these groups were accused of was mainly of an ideological kind; none of them had the means or probably even the intention of moving over to action.

In general, the rural crisis gave rise to localised and sporadic incidents rather than to genuine political disturbances.[11] These incidents frequently pitted peas-ants against basic-level cadres. Sometimes the peasants were content simply to ridicule and mock their leaders. But attack sometimes followed gibes. At the time of the sharing out of the summer harvest the accountant of a cooperative in Yanshi county no longer dared to return home for fear of being torn to pieces. In a village in Shangcheng, three children of cadres were murdered.

The press later wanted it believed that these incidents had been most danger-ous in July and August, that is, just when the provincial leadership was most di-vided over what response to make to the accusations of the rightists. Thus "a thousand reactionary slogans" were alleged to have appeared on the wall of a co-operative in Xinyang county during the night of 31 July–1 August 1957; and in Yingyang, a former landlord declared at this time that "there would be a revolt in August". The timing is not implausible since July and August were the months when an often-disappointing summer harvest was distributed. Thus the dis-orders in Yanshi, which went on for twenty days, were precipitated by a fall in wheat production. But other sources give the incidents as occurring before and not after the wheat harvest.[12] Whatever the case, the 1957 harvest rarely proved to be catastrophic; in fact it often improved the food situation. My impression is that the agitation was endemic, with a peak perhaps in summer 1957.

Conversely, assigning responsibility for the incidents to "landlords, rich peas-ants, bad elements, and well-off middle peasants" alone is highly questionable, although it is true that some such cases did occur. In one township in Minquan, seven former brigands and thirteen members of secret societies apparently led the agitation.[13] Some former landlords and rich peasants were said to have re-sorted to force to recover some of their cattle or lands.[14] In the province as a whole, 3,000 people belonging to these social categories were tried in September and October 1957. But one may well ask how the other categories of the rural population, who were equally involved in withdrawals from cooperatives, and as will be seen, in economic offences, failed to engage in such crimes. In September and October 1957 the press itself several times stressed the low morale of many poor peasants. According to Pan Fusheng, the proportion of "backwards ele-ments" (i.e., malcontents) in six cooperatives at the beginning of autumn 1957 was 8 percent among "former middle-poor peasants", 5.3 percent among "middle-poor" and 4.2 percent among poor peasants. The proportion of "centrists" (i.e., undecided) was 40 percent, 28 percent, and 23 percent, respectively. Of the 124 families guilty of "serious capitalist tendencies" (8.9 percent of the population of the six cooperatives), 64 belonged to these three categories.[15]

In total, available information requires one to be cautious. The rural areas in Henan did not actually experience a rebellion, but incidents of a variety of sorts that all in all were not very serious. These incidents are, however, evidence of widespread hostility towards cadres.

Problems with Cadres

The peasants responded to official exhortations to denounce the excesses of their local leaders. Officially encouraged "assemblies of representatives of members of cooperatives", could not always be totally manipulated and controlled by authorities.[16] On occasion serious criticisms were voiced in these assemblies. Most had to do with the authoritarianism and privileges of cadres.[17] Thus, for example, it was learned that the 473 members of a cooperative in Changge had been fined at the distribution of grain in July 1956; fifteen of the ninety-six basic-level cadres in a cooperative in Guangshan were criticised for abusing the peasants and ten for beating them. And the head of the Propaganda Department of the Party committee in the suburbs of Luoyang calmly acknowledged in May 1957 that until very recently he still thought the best method of government was to administer a few slaps. The peasants protested against the privileges enjoyed by their leaders: 1,131 days off work in a year for meetings allowed to cadres of a cooperative in Lingbao, official bicycles, low-interest loans that were never repaid, and the like.

The cadres, objects of mistrust and hostility from the population, found that they were no longer backed up by their superiors as in the past, but held responsible for "errors" that until very recently had been "advanced experiments". The power of the cadres had been considerably increased in 1955–1956, but now was reduced by the division of cooperatives, the redistribution of plots of land, and the reopening of private markets. Rural policy had changed to their disadvantage and without their having been consulted. Thus, from fear or conviction, they now hesitated to put into practice the instructions that set the bounds of liberalisation. Many articles in the newspapers deplored the weakening of the authority of rural cadres.[18] Sometimes, their disillusionment was less passive. In Fudian township in Yanshi, 47 cadres publicly dissociated themselves from the political objectives of the regime. In Jiyuan 8.6 percent of cadres were carrying on "capitalist activities"; in the four counties of Linru, Yingyang, Xinxiang, and Linxian, 20 percent were noncommittal. Of the 11,121 cadres in Linxian county, 1,409 were classified as "rightist opportunists", 741 were demonstrating "capitalist ideology and activities", 1,040 had committed "localist" errors, and 555 had shown "individualism"—all of which meant that a considerable proportion of cadres felt that a permanent halt had to be called to the process of collectivisation and were themselves either indulging in various sorts of trafficking or turning a blind eye to it.[19]

Economic Disobedience

Whatever be the case, the weakening of the cadres' authority and their frequent compromising opened the way to what was the most widespread manifestation of the social crisis in the rural areas of Henan, and the one that can be least disputed: economic disobedience. Of 371 cooperative secretaries in Shangcheng county, 144 went along with or themselves engaged in cover-ups and the illicit sharing out of production in the course of 1957.[20]

This economic wrongdoing was first reflected in the neglect of collective labour and cropping plans.[21] Everywhere peasants were leaving their production teams to look for better-paid work. In the cotton-growing areas (where the autumn 1956 delays in grain deliveries had not been forgotten), the peasants demanded that priority be given to cereal crops and that poorer land be set aside for cotton. Despite the reprimands publicly addressed to the guilty counties, the province was ultimately able to sow only 800,000 ha of cotton, often in poor soils, instead of the 893,000 ha planned.

The most serious acts had to do with the unified purchase and supply system. The peasants wanted to receive as much grain as possible and deliver as little as possible.[22] Claiming exceptional conditions and feeling encouraged by the more indulgent attitude on the part of the authorities, cooperatives stepped up demands for food grains, justified or not. Thus five townships in Shangqiu special region demanded and obtained 20,000 metric tons of extra grain. In total, the state had to deliver more to the countryside (as well as to the cities where similar demands were being made) than in previous years and more than planned: 2.4 million metric tons between autumn 1956 and summer 1957, 48 percent more than the previous year and 250,000 metric tons more than planned.

At the same time, the state was finding that collecting grain was proving harder and taking longer than before.[23] To reduce the amount of grain delivered at a rate far below the prices on the free market, cooperatives made false declarations and concealed part of their output. Thus, in autumn 1956, Pingxing county declared the annual cereal harvest to be 723 metric tons as against the 875 metric tons actually in the granaries. After the summer 1957 harvest the authorities estimated that 10 percent of production had been concealed. In addition, after delivering their quota, cooperatives with a surplus resisted selling the regulation share of the increased production (60 percent and later 80 percent) at the official price.

Members of cooperatives usually shared out what was withheld from official requisitions;[24] 95 metric tons of grain was distributed in this way among 35 cooperatives in Huixian in summer 1957. Part was consumed and the rest sold in nearby local markets. At the beginning of September 1957, 150 metric tons of sweet potatoes were sold every day in the local markets of Neihuang county. Illicit sharing out of cotton was at least equally widespread, with peasants reselling it on the black market or spinning it at home. In Taikang county, 350 metric tons of cotton had been sold illegally by the end of 1956.

These share-outs were often carried on publicly within the cooperatives with the active agreement of the cadres. Numerous cooperatives in the suburbs of Zhengzhou, were transformed by astute leaders into real commercial enterprises that ignored the official contracts made with state companies and dealt directly, at very high prices, with small traders in the cities and even with the canteens of public enterprises. The national press highlighted the example of a cooperative in Runan county that had made contracts to deliver hemp and ropes to more than twenty Chinese cities, including Beijing, Tientsin, and Shenyang; by the beginning of summer 1957 this particularly enterprising cooperative had already made a profit of over 20,000 yuan.[25]

Because of this vast number of local acts of disobedience, state purchasing operations for the 1956 and 1957 harvests could not be completed on time.[26] By the end of November 1956 only 77.9 percent of the cereal purchasing plan for the whole province had been fulfilled. Even more time was needed to collect cotton and oilseed. By February 1957 Shangqiu special region had fulfilled only 35.2 percent of its 1956 cotton quota. The cotton purchasing plan was probably not fulfilled in 1957 either.

It would be interesting to be able to summarise the attitude of the Henan peasantry in the years 1956–1957 by portraying two peasants. The first would be one of those peasants hit by disaster in 1956 who just managed to get through the winter and only escaped hunger after the summer or autumn harvest of 1957. Details are not available for any particular such individual, although it is clear that there were many peasants in that situation. They did not have the right to speak out, let alone the means to do so. Their silence is the silence of poverty, a poverty that goes for nothing. It is possible, however, to sketch the picture of another type of peasant. This one is not rich either, but does have the means to escape poverty. Here then is Shen Xiaozhang, of Changge county. He is the head of an eleven-member family and received in all 3,500 kg of shared-out grain in 1956. In addition, pleading his family responsibilities, he managed to get extra rations from the cadres in his cooperative as "relief", which led the other peasants in the village to ask for some for themselves, too. To increase his income, Shen regularly sent two of his sons to sell grain and vegetables in the neighbouring market and he himself engaged in usury, lending soybeans for three months at 30 percent interest.[27] Then in February 1957 he refused to give his daughter-in-law 100 kg of grain and she denounced him to the authorities. An inquiry discovered a store of 3,710 kg of various cereals in Shen's house. But the local cadres, knowing that his case was not an isolated one, simply demanded reimbursement of the grants wrongly paid, and it was only in August that he was forced to put an end to his activities.[28] Shen Xiaozhang is typical of the peasants who made demands and knew how to fiddle on the side—typical of the peasants who had been so worrying the regime since summer 1956.

But such demands and manoeuvres remained chiefly economic, and except for localised incidents, never took a political turn. Therein lies a major enigma that runs through the history of the People's Republic of China: The peasantry, the regime's beast of burden, did not rise up against the wretched fate handed out to it, but simply endeavoured to survive, or at most, like Shen Xiaozhang, to make some temporary improvement.

Until summer 1957, the cities in Henan offered the same overall social appearance as the countryside. Although a minority agitated and made demands, the majority of the population simply extracted what advantage could be had from the new atmosphere. But there were two major peculiarities about the situation of city-dwellers. First, although they were equally marginal, the agitation in the cities was far more serious. More people engaged in it, and it was geographically more concentrated. Above all, it appeared more dangerous, since it was occurring in the very place where the new regime was based, sometimes only a few hundred metres from provincial offices. When a few cooperatives in a rural township refused to fulfil their quota of cereals to the state, it was a small affair, harmful only economically. When workers in a factory or students in a school became agitated, that very quickly became a political matter for obvious social reasons, but also for other reasons to do with the collective psychology of the CCP—the factory and the school were the favoured institutions of the new regime, where it put its most promising cadres and the children of its leaders. They represented the future.

Consequently—and this was the second peculiarity—the provincial press said much more about the situation of the cities than that in the countryside. The *Henan Daily* was in fact the newspaper of the province as seen from Zhengzhou, aimed first and foremost at Party cadres and militants, most of them actual or potential city-dwellers, and it spoke to them above all of what interested them most: their cities. This publicising of urban events, which was to contribute to the effectiveness of the Hundred Flowers campaign, makes the observer's task easier, enabling one to sketch a description of urban society in Henan in 1956–1957.

Life as Dreamed

A society is organised as much by its myths as its reality. In this particular case, myth and reality coincided: Living in cities was better. When asked about their career goals, pupils in the second year of the secondary school in Changge, a rural county in Xuchang special region, replied as follows: eighteen wanted to be cadres, seven officers, seven "experts", two pilots, two workers, two teachers, and only eight peasants. There was thus a marked preference for urban careers.[29] Everything confirms the pull of the cities on young people. If they sought to stay on at school or get themselves taken on, it was partly so as to find a way into or remain in the cities. Country girls, who could not hope for careers of their own, pursued cadres or workers to marry, running the risk of being unable to get used to the city and finally being rejected by a companion who found them too un-couth.[30] The city also attracted temporary workers who hoped to regularise their status and disaster-hit peasants who wormed their way in to engage in all manner of occupations. The available sources unfortunately do not enable an assessment of the scale of illegal immigration. It may be that the large towns in Henan, often still very much a part of their rural hinterland, were less attractive to the peasant-ry than the big cities in eastern and southern China.[31] But the repeated warnings of official propaganda and peasants' complaints about the inequality of condi-tions together with the facts mentioned above leave little doubt that the phenom-enon existed.

The myths were right. Life was undeniably better in the cities. First, city-dwell-ers enjoyed a higher and more stable income than peasants. According to a dep-uty director in the Statistical Bureau of the provincial government, the annual average wage of a worker was 498 yuan. Even taking into account the benefits in kind that a peasant enjoyed, this official calculated that the worker received 180 percent more in income than a member of a rural cooperative.[32] This compari-son is virtually meaningless. What was there in common between the ever-pre-carious and difficult life of a peasant and the regular cash income enjoyed by most city-dwellers? Even if all urban wages were not as high as those of workers, even if some categories of city-dwellers lived, as will be seen, a precarious exis-tence, for the vast majority, living in the city meant living in security. In addition, thanks to evening schools and the proximity of decisionmaking centres, one could rise up the ladder, and above all, get oneself into the Party. Living in the city enabled hope for the future.

A Dog's Life

But this life others envied, city-dwellers experienced as difficult. To begin with, although incomes were higher, so too were expenses. When peasants in Luoshan county complained that a young man from the village was earning 70 yuan a month as a worker, the man's response was to detail the expenses that he and his wife had to face each month, which left them only 14.4 yuan of savings. Doubtless these expenses were exaggerated, for another worker asserted, equally for the good of the cause, that with 47 yuan per month he could perfectly well support a family of five.[33] The complaints recorded by the press in spring 1957 suggest that city-dwellers were often experiencing great difficulties in making ends meet.

Two other major problems were omnipresent: supplies and housing. It was said that "the shortage of goods, queues at every corner, and the high cost of living are the distinguishing features of the markets of Zhengzhou".[34] Grain rations were often inadequate and had to be supplemented with expensive purchases on the black market. To receive their coupons or get their grain, people sometimes had to spend a whole day queuing. Furthermore, the street committee would watch out to ensure that people economised, and neighbours were often only too anxious to denounce any unusual sign of wealth. The most serious supply difficulties involved other food products such as meat and sugar, demand for which had been rising as the standard of living improved, most notably since the 1956 wage reform. Supply was not following demand. Complaints were particularly frequent about the supply of meat. After being increased by the cattle slaughtering of early 1956, arrivals of meat on the official market had been reduced by the poor condition of the remaining livestock and the development of the black market. Thus supplies reaching Zhengzhou fell by 21 percent between August and October 1956. The provincial government reacted by raising the price of pork and then beef in the official market and endeavouring (without much success) to eliminate the black market. Similarly, vegetables were hard to find in the official market, but plentiful in the free markets where prices fluctuated wildly. It was equally difficult to secure many manufactured items, such as clothes, despite repeated price increases that were themselves ill received by the population. However, it should be noted that these supply problems, especially serious in new cities like Hebi, Jiaozuo, Pingdinghshan, and Sanmen and the new areas of the big cities where commercial infrastructure was inadequate, were rarely mentioned by the sources for old country towns like Xuchang, Xinyang, or Nanyang.

The second problem of living in cities was housing.[35] The rapid growth of the urban population had stimulated demand in general, and the improvement in the standard of living led to demand for higher quality. Private renting was extremely expensive, up to 8 yuan per room per month in the centre of the big cities. High rents and the small amount of available housing forced many workers to pack themselves into slums. At the time of the main rains in July 1956 an official survey revealed that 58 of the 197 dwellings occupied by workers in the Zhengzhou insecticides factory were leaking. A universal concern was to get oneself allocated a dwelling in the new industrial zones, but waiting lists were long. At the beginning of September 1956, 1,000 basic-construction workers in Zhengzhou had no fixed accommodation. Of the 2,000 employees of the Luoyang tractor factory expecting accommodation in the spring, only half saw their requests granted. Normally, after operating for a few years, modern enterprises could accommodate only about half their employees, and apprentices and the unmarried had priority. It is not surprising that there were cases of subletting and even squatting.[36]

For the rest, although airier, cleaner, and more comfortable (even if they did not all have running water), modern dwellings were not wholly satisfactory. They were expensive to rent (at least one yuan per room) and involved heavy expenditure for water and electricity. Built according to Soviet plans, the new buildings proved to be unbearably hot in summer. Above all, the units were too small. The regulations allowed two-room apartments to be allocated only to families of more than six individuals. Unmarried people generally lived several to a room,[37] and if they married, had to wait several years for their own accommodation. In sum, despite undeniable advances, housing remained one of the sore points of urban living. In June 1957 an official survey covering 201 families in Zhengzhou revealed that the floor area occupied per person was no more than 4.39 square m; 72 families were living without electricity and 135 without running water.[38] Such conditions could not fail to produce harmful social consequences. Occasionally one glimpses leaders worrying about the spread of criminal behaviour amongst children in these bleak housing tracts. In Luoyang, the incidence of muggings, petty larceny, domestic disputes, and the like rose 31 percent between the first quarter of 1956 and the first quarter of 1957. The picture is classic, and it is equally true provincewide for the people of Henan. But one would like to have the information to spell it out in detail.[39]

A Caste Society

Life was not equally painful for everyone. There was a world of difference between a top leader like Pan Fusheng, who demanded a magnificent official residence and complained that "in Henan manners are uncouth" and that "Zhengzhou is so vermin-infested that one cannot receive foreign visitors there",[40] and temporary workers driven out of their village by a natural disaster. But there was an even more significant difference between, say, a station master who was illicitly occupying a two-room dwelling furnished with "loans" from the office[41] and a worker's family of ten people, including grandparents, crowded into a single room. The difference in conditions was easy to see in the street: There were the "aristocrats", those who moved about by bicycle (or more rarely by car), and the ordinary people, who walked.

The basic difference between the classes was not a matter of income. A "national capitalist" might very well earn more than 200 yuan a month and yet have difficulty in making ends meet, if only because of taxes. Cadres paid around 70 yuan a month might find themselves in a much better situation thanks to numerous official perks. In this society, both mobilised and dominated, it was not material advantages that counted most, but where each individual stood in relation to power. How much were the past prestige, the fine residences, and the concubines of some "democratic figures" worth in face of a government decision or even the bad temper of a petty cadre? With two rooms, the station master was scarcely better housed than the engineers, but the latter were dependent on him. In a society where everything had changed and threatened to change again, the essential difference was that between those who rectified people and those who were only the anonymous labour force of change and the target of rectifications.

Thus in 1956–1957 it is possible to distinguish three broad social categories in Henan urban society: the aristocrats, the cadres who controlled change and benefited most from it; the workers, and to a lesser extent students, who were in theory the beneficiaries of change and in fact its tool; and all the rest, who for one reason or another were excluded from power and at its mercy. The word *caste* for these divisions is provocative and perhaps false. Yet it has the merit of drawing attention to the rigidity of the social hierarchy, which was not the effect of any greater or lesser vitality of social groups, but rather the projection onto the body social of an absolute truth, the regime's ideology. If an individual or a social category was excluded, it was always on grounds of principle. It was for equally fundamental reasons that cadres enjoyed so many advantages—they represented the vanguard with correct ideas—and that workers were both well treated and dominated—they constituted the regime's natural social base.

The Aristocrats

The cadres occupied the top of the hierarchy. Their situation was envied. It was to become a cadre (*ganbu*) and then rise up through the hierarchy of power that people applied for admission to the Party and attended evening school. The regime saw cadres as leaders, but the population looked upon them first and foremost as individuals who did not work with their hands, or did not do so all the time—privileged persons who profited from the labour of others. In fact, the main attributes of a cadre were a desk and a pen. In bureaucratic parlance, a clear distinction was not always made between "cadres" and "unproductive personnel". Often, indeed, the best way of becoming a cadre was to enter management, which helps to explain the inflation of this category in industrial enterprises: 16.8 percent of the staff on average in all the factories in Zhengzhou, and according to a less reliable source, 30 percent in all the factories in Luoyang. The proportion of cadres was also necessarily high. For example, they made up 12 percent of the personnel of the Zhengzhou Number 3 cotton factory.[42]

Although envied, and in fact, highly privileged, the job of cadre was not without difficulties. It involved a heavy load of bureaucratic obligations. The proliferation of departments obliged cadres (especially the most senior ones and those most likely to be promoted) to hold several jobs at once. Thus, in autumn 1956, the head of the Kaifeng special region held fourteen different jobs. In general, basic-level leaders had at least two jobs, one in the Party and the other in the administration. They were permanently caught up in tasks of doubtful use, which were the life-blood of bureaucracy: endless paper, interminable meetings, "mass surveys", and the like.[43]

A second difficulty, which should not be underestimated, was to stay "in line" all the time so as not to lay oneself open to criticism and risk dismissal. When the line was clear it had to be applied unfailingly, giving rise to a sharp sense of authority that in some cases served to justify brutality and maltreatment.[44] But the "line" (*luxian*) was often not clear at all. In addition, it was almost constantly being modified. "Studying", that is, closely reading the newspapers and speeches by senior leaders, thus became not only a professional obligation but also a vital necessity. Fear of a false step meant that cadres participated in political debate only with the greatest caution. The frequent use of the expression "I approve in the essentials" is a typical example of such caution, signifying an overall agreement, but reserving the possibility of misunderstandings or disagreements that might be brought out later when the line changed. Clear-cut expressions were avoided and the conjunction *danshi* (but) was used with care; in Chinese political language it marks the point when something important is about to be said.[45]

Competition between cadres made such caution even more necessary—unpopularity with the masses was a lesser threat to a cadre's career than denunciation by a rival. Thus threatened, cadres who might otherwise be good and even dedicated people could be ferocious. Young "activists" (*jiji fenzi*) were officially encouraged to criticise their superiors. They did not hesitate to do so, for therein lay the sole route for them to make their way through the apparatus. Thus cadres were mistrustful of their juniors as well and endeavoured to hinder subordinates' careers. This explains the length of the probationary period for Party applicants and more generally the low level of recruitment in some enterprises and localities.[46]

A cadre also had to beware of colleagues. Information is unfortunately sparse on internal conflicts at lower levels of the bureaucracy, for the only incidents clearly described in the press involve the friction that often arose between local cadres and newly demobilised soldiers. Basic-level cadres were jealous of the great range of assistance that ex-soldiers received. At all levels, "committees to resettle demobilised soldiers" were responsible for finding them a job, housing, and even, if needed, a spouse.[47] For reasons of principle, but also because the authorities had confidence in the integrity and discipline that had been instilled in them during their service, demobilised soldiers were systematically favoured in hiring and promotion. Many were immediately recruited as cadres. In summer 1957, as many as 25,000 demobilised soldiers held leadership positions in cooperatives or townships. Of the 5,100 ex-soldiers and officers settled in five counties in Kaifeng special region in the first half of 1957, 3,000 at once became cadres. Similarly, in the cities, many site supervisors or factory managers were former officers of rural origin who had returned to civilian life at the time of the agrarian reform.

But the authoritarianism that cadres coming from a military background frequently displayed, notably during the first leap, left bitter memories in the population and raised hackles amongst other cadres. In many cases, despite official propaganda, local cadres and the population worked to hinder the recruitment of demobilised soldiers or force them to quit. Being the object of universal suspi-

cion and yet needing to make their way, the ex-soldiers had no hesitation in revealing petty local scandals and brutally imposing their authority.[48] Overall, however, it seems that the growing resistance they encountered meant that they did
not take over any but lower-ranking positions.

The difficulties of a cadre's life did not prevent, but rather officially justified,
the privileges enjoyed by anyone who had an iota of power—privileges that are
difficult to quantify but were much envied. First, cadres and Party members
in general were favoured in appointments, postings, promotions, and wage increases, as was clearly seen in the 1956 wage reform. The monthly income of the
head of the Financial(!) Department of Zhengzhou University rose from 50 to 110
yuan between the beginning of 1956 and the beginning of 1957. Various allowances were added to the basic wage.[49] If they ran short of money, cadres could
always ask for loans or assistance, which were granted to them much more liber-
ally than to the general public; and it often happened that the loans made to
cadres were never repaid.

In addition, every cadre was treated as a priority case in the allocation of new
accommodation and could arrange to occupy more space than otherwise entitled
to. Cadres often equipped their home with luxury items, such as a radio, that
belonged to their office. From always using the same official bicycle or being
driven in the same car, they ended up appropriating these vehicles for themselves.
Cadres could render considerable services to their kin. Obtaining a job as cadre
or employee for a spouse could improve the household's income.[50] Cadres could
secure places for their children in a school, a factory, or the administration and
give out precious "letters of introduction" that could be discreetly cashed in on
later.

These material advantages were perhaps less important than the prestige and
pleasure of dominating. Theatre performances were delayed until personalities
had taken their reserved seats. In factory canteens, cadres often had a special
room where unlike workers tied to a fixed schedule they could find a hot meal at
any time of the day or night. At the hairdresser's or the launderer's, in every shop,
cadres enjoyed priority. The arrival of a leader at a hospital was a disaster for the
staff, for such a person would demand to be examined at once, ask for the best
room and the prettiest nurse, and have no compunction about abusing and punishing doctors who did not effect a speedy cure. In Luoyang, the wife of a municipal official who came to the hospital for an abortion had the midwife sacked for
reserving the best bed for a woman in labour.[51]

Cadres ruled on how the laws were to be interpreted and implemented and if
they made a mistake they would benefit from attenuating circumstances unless
the mistake was of a political nature. In a factory in Luoyang, for the same trans-
gression (extramarital sexual relations), a worker was punished with two years'
imprisonment and a Party member with merely losing two grades. Of course, not
all leading cadres were like the head of the Party secretariat in Changge county,
who simply for his own pleasure, used to extend the performance of the local

theatre troupe to 3:30 in the morning.[52] But what is most striking in the picture of cadres painted in the sources—oppositionist as well as official—is the lack of shading. Except for a few petty cadres and some dedicated heroes, all the others are presented as belonging to a single narrow, pretentious, and authoritarian aristocracy.

Take for example this story told on 5 June 1957 by a tearful assistant secondary school head in Luoyang. One day when this teacher was chairing a teaching meeting, an official from the local municipal Party committee suddenly arrived. This official was at the same time chairman of the municipal trade union committee and thus an important figure in the city. He interrupted the meeting with these words: "I am a member of the municipal committee, my name is Wang!" And he announced that the funds originally allocated to the building of two classrooms and toilets for the school would in fact be used to pay for the completion of the trade union canteen. Seeing the teachers on the verge of protest, he added: "It is an order from the Education Bureau, do you accept it or not?" Finally he wheedled: "Comrades, these are simply contradictions within the people, we shall discuss them again later. If your school encounters problems, we shall help you to resolve them."[53]

The cadres' decisive advantage, which ultimately explains all the others and gave them the means to secure their domination and protect it, was their monopoly of useful information in a regime that was at once centralised and politicised: information from Beijing. Cadres were the only ones who knew the current interpretations of official ideology and their legal applications. Cadres at each level received specific documentation, which especially when it was of an economic nature, might not be divulged to ordinary mortals. In Zhengzhou in spring 1957 there was a library of 30,000 volumes specifically intended for cadres. Of course, a cadre would not know everything that Beijing wanted or did, far from it, for information was carefully measured depending on the grade of the recipient. According to a democrat from Luoyang, Mao Zedong's speech of 27 February 1957 on the "correct solution of contradictions among the people" (which was, it should be remembered, only published in June 1957 and then in a revised version) included 20,000 characters in its original form. The version designed for provincial-level cadres contained, 8–9,000 characters; that for cadres in Luoyang, 3–4,000; and for factory cadres, a few hundred sufficed.[54] Yet even factory cadres were much better informed than ordinary people in the street, who only had the press and official speeches, or quite unverifiable rumours.

After autumn 1956 a malaise settled over a section of cadres. Until then, they saw themselves getting stronger and stronger as the regime appeared to be fulfilling its targets and the country to be advancing towards socialism; but now the cadres' position weakened. On the one hand, the agricultural failure of 1956 had undermined their popularity. On the other, the central government itself was limiting their prerogatives, forcing cadres to listen to their flock, and in the event of conflict, no longer systematically backing them up. In the factories, cadres now had to convene often rowdy "workers' delegates' meetings".[55] They were mocked, sometimes insulted. During the rectification campaign, some of them would complain of no longer having the necessary authority. The spread of the black market and trafficking of all sorts cannot be understood without this weakening of control in the cities. As shown below, some cadres even took up oppositionist ideas. The press showed itself avid for details of a moral crisis, which in any event, lasted no time at all.

The "Creators of the New World"

The second favoured social category, situated just below the cadres, was industrial workers. They were, so to speak, the regime's legs, since according to the propoganda, it was their labour—under the correct leadership of the Communist Party—that was bringing about economic progress. Although well paid and respected, workers formed a much more heterogeneous category than cadres. They suffered from their subordination and in some sectors were even beginning to agitate for change.

The mythological as well as economic importance of the working class made it the central hub of urban society. The regime expected class behaviour—that is, political support and enthusiastic commitment to production—and in exchange granted a materially and politically favoured status. Workers in fact received monthly wages of 30–100 yuan and in Henan as in the rest of China enjoyed remarkable social benefits. Party membership was relatively open to them and their children were entitled to all sorts of special treatment. In a way, the worker was the only full citizen of the new regime.

But the reality was both less glittering and more complicated. First, workers did not feel themselves terribly privileged. Like other city-dwellers, they found it hard to accept the high cost of living and the housing problems. They felt their income to be insufficient and criticised the wage disparities between sectors and jobs, which the 1956 wage reform had aggravated.[56] Work was hard and even dangerous. The number of work accidents rose during the first leap, and then diminished again, but never disappeared, for machinery was old or unfamiliar and safety regulations were ignored.[57] A standing dispute pitted workers against their cadres over production norms, with workers refusing to improve both quantity and quality at the same time. They obliged their superiors, despite the exhortations of propaganda, to choose between those two imperatives. Quality targets, being less easy to include in statistics and progress reports, were usually the losers, unless special bonuses could be offered.[58]

Communist sources portray workers on the whole as careless and demanding. Genuine strikes seem to have been rare, but there are references to slowdowns, and more important, to poor morale in enterprises. The slightest symptom was an excuse to take sick leave.[59] Disciplinary regulations, usually rather severe, were rarely observed, especially in factories that had a high proportion of young workers or were particularly affected by the recession and ran only part-time. Playing games, fighting, even carousing appear to have been everyday occurrences. Official trade unions, sometimes made the target of mockery and abandoned, could not perform their disciplinary roles.[60]

The importance of the sectoral troubles that were exercising the "Henan working class" tends to suggest that this class should be seen as a composite of different milieux. The skilled workers transferred from eastern China, mostly employed in the Zhengzhou textile factories, formed a group apart. They were well paid, but complained about the poor welcome the people of Henan gave them, the differences of customs, and being separated from their family. Through strikes and the despatch of a delegation to Beijing, the director and workers in an Anyang factory successfully demanded the return of their enterprise to Shanghai.[61] The service sector was looked down on, since many women worked in it; in addition, wages remained low (15–40 yuan) and the work hard.[62] Basic-construction workers formed another distinct category, mostly temporary and 80 percent from rural areas. Poorly paid, brutalised by overseers, and looked down upon by the population at large, most of them yearned either to return to their village once their contract expired and the disasters ended or to regularise their status and become permanent, full-time workers.[63] Unfortunately there is little information about this subproletariat.

Cleavages could also be sharp between workers in the same enterprise. The press played up at least one such conflict, for it fitted well into what was said to be the situation: The gap that supposedly existed between the 30 percent of old workers who had grown up in the misery of the old society and were conscious of the benefits of the new one and the 70 percent of young workers for whom those benefits were just so many entitlements and who "spontaneously" introduced "nonproletarian" ideas into the enterprise. Such an analysis does not seem entirely accurate. It is true that on a number of occasions one sees old workers upset by the behaviour of their younger colleagues and by school-aged young people in general. But such annoyance had less to do with political differences than with disagreements over morals. What the old workers found hard to accept was the introduction by the regime, however cautiously, of new attitudes towards authority, the family, and child-bearing that broke with tradition. Available data do not show that old workers were more politicised or even proportionately more numerous in the Party than their juniors. No doubt had it been so, the press would have given plenty of details about it. Old workers may have been more disciplined at work, but that did not stop them from making demands just like their juniors. Alongside these differences of age and customs, authority relations introduced new cleavages. Supervisors, who were often ex-soldiers, were frequently loathed for their brutality, vulgarity, and incompetence.[64] Office staff, hardly distinct from cadres, were resented and unloved.

The most troubled sector among workers was young apprentices. Traditionally underpaid (less than 30 yuan a month) and humiliated by other workers, they normally received their confirmation at the end of very short periods of apprenticeship. But because of the recession, these were extended in early 1957. Feeling unfairly treated in a period when the trend was otherwise in the direction of relaxing constraints, and probably influenced by the school and university disturbances that were going on at the time, apprentices had no hesitation in using every form of protest up to and including strikes and sit-ins. Thus, in spring 1957, the 379 apprentices of the Luoyang tractor factory, who were being trained at the Zhengzhou textile machinery factory, set up a sit-in committee with the slogan "No to compromise, no to betrayal", although most of them gave in to authority.[65]

The "Green Shoots"

The apprentice problem was linked to the more general one of young people and education. Students—another privileged social stratum—posed a problem for the regime that was altogether new. Youth were obviously intended to benefit from the educational and vocational possibilities that the regime offered them as well as by the attention given to their intellectual and political training: They represented the future. But after summer 1956, various circumstances revealed the limits and even some drawbacks to the advances that had been achieved.

First, the failure of the first leap had many negative consequences for the schools. For many peasant families the burden of supporting their children's education was no longer bearable.[66] Poorly fed and clothed, secondary school pupils in Henan spent a difficult winter in 1956–1957 and often had health problems. In autumn 1956, half the pupils in one class in a Kaifeng secondary school had lost weight. Much more serious in the eyes of a population traditionally disposed to make sacrifices for the education of children, the slowdown in school-building, brought about by the recession, limited the number of secondary school places. At the beginning of the school year in autumn 1956 there were only 100,000 secondary school places in the whole province for 390,000 primary school leavers. The beginning of the school year in autumn 1957 did not look as if it would be much better, since only half the primary school leavers would be able to enter secondary school, and a third of the lower secondary school leavers, the higher secondary school. Provincewide only 3,000 of the 9,000 higher secondary school leavers would find places in the universities and specialist schools. A larger number of school leavers were thus arriving on the labour market just when industry's absorptive capacity was diminishing. Attempts were made to resolve the problem by encouraging the formation of "free secondary schools" and above all by sending or returning primary school leavers to the countryside, but initially without much success. Unemployment among the young in the cities exacerbated the crime problem.

The combination of material difficulties, enhanced competition in examinations, and uncertainty over job prospects explains the low morale in secondary schools.[67] School children protested against the poor state of their schools and the inadequacy of the food. After the failure of cooperatives and the events in Hungary, the agitation took an overtly political turn in at least some secondary schools. In Miyang, the cooperative movement was lampooned. In a secondary school in Lankao, the county boss had to intervene in person to bring about an end to the demands and prohibit pro-Hungary slogans. In sum, the social and political behaviour of Henan secondary school pupils seems to have been quite similar to that of their elders in higher education.

As will be seen, the older students were to play an important if not decisive role in the events of spring 1957. However, although available sources describe student activities at great length, there is almost no information about their material situation and their position in the social hierarchy. There are merely glimpses that students' favoured financial status (thanks to the scholarships that many of them enjoyed) did not eliminate all difficulties, especially for those who came from an ordinary family (food, buying books). It comes out even more clearly that in the eyes of the authorities the promise of a lucrative career as a technical or political cadre in the body social justified very strong ideological pressure and a political control that often interfered with school results. This ideological pressure justified the power of Party committees at all levels, power that inevitably clashed with the university hierarchy. Party control was exercised principally through the Youth League and secondarily through the system of class and year representatives for future cadres in apprenticeship. More even than the material difficulties, it was the ideological and political pressure suffered by students and the educational injustices that flowed from it that explain the violence of their protest in spring 1957 and the seriousness of the university malaise in the preceding months. In short, in the secondary schools as in the universities, the "young shoots" that the regime purported to be cossetting did not let themselves be strung along as docilely as planned.

The "Outs"

Beneath, or rather on the outer fringes of the privileged strata, several distinct social groups can be classified in a single category: the "outs". For however different their income and even their social status may have been, these groups basically found themselves in a similar situation: Not only did they have no share in power, but they depended on those in power for their survival.

The first circle comprised those who were outs on account of their profession. The degree of exclusion suffered by these minority professionals varied considerably. The medical profession, for example, represented an extreme case. The lack of equipment (despite the advances that had been made) and the length and strain of the work led to numerous complaints. Now under the direct authority of the state, medical personnel in general felt themselves unfairly treated. Although the regime devoted resources to public health, it was after all more concerned with society than with the individual—more, so to speak, with the soul than with the body. Those who cared for and transformed society—the cadres— occupied the high ground. In addition, personnel in every branch of medicine or on any medical staff had specific reasons for being dissatisfied. Practitioners of Chinese medicine felt disadvantaged compared to specialists in Western medicine. Those who had earned their qualifications before 1949, sometimes in Western universities, complained about the excessive influence the regime allowed Soviet medicine. In the hospitals there were protests against heavy workloads, low wages, and above all pressure by the Party. A surgeon declared: "By day, I have to operate, and at night, do my self-criticism"; and another: "Doctors have one foot in the hospital and the other in the courthouse". Nurses deplored their low wages, wretched housing, and above all the abuse they got from cadres and even from the cadres' drivers.[68]

But it must be observed that the income of doctors and nurses was almost the same as that of engineers and workers; they were a long way from the breadline. In addition, although under the authority of cadres, the profession as such was not threatened with disappearance. The discontent seems as much due to memories of the old regime and knowledge of the privileges won by doctors in the West as to exclusion from the new Chinese society. Finally, that this discontent is even recorded is because doctors and nurses had the intellectual and material means to express it; in that sense at least, they were favoured rather than excluded.

The case of artisans, although not extreme, appears more serious. They reacted badly to the brutal changes they suffered in 1955–1956. Forced into cooperatives that were often too large and poorly run, aware that collective constraints were being relaxed everywhere else, artisans ceased to put their heart into their work. Whenever possible they left the cooperatives.[69] A simple solution was even more widespread: to put in an appearance in the cooperative for form's sake but to organise what can only be described as underground workshops using illegal immigrant labour, often linked to one another and even supplying public enterprises. In the February Seventh district in Zhengzhou alone, in the autumn of 1957, 156 such "black enterprises" were counted.[70]

Artisans were looked down on and victimised in 1956–1957 for ideological and psychological, not economic, reasons, and after summer 1956 the importance of handicraft activities was once again acknowledged. Despite inevitable "petit bourgeois" tendencies, good artisans still had good chances of survival. That was no longer true of the small entrepreneurs—1,700 in Zhengzhou in summer 1957[71]—who worked rural fairs and kept the cities supplied in times of scarcity. Tolerated so long as the economic situation remained poor and the Party's prestige diminished, their occupational category was eventually condemned. Conscious of this threat as well as of the possibilities opening to them in the meantime, they took advantage of the last shreds of freedom left them by the regime.

Thus two traders in Huaxian accumulated a profit of 23,800 yuan in the first half of 1957 by going to Gansu to sell building materials.[72] Amongst the most commonly mentioned trafficking was the sale on the black market of vegetables grown in the suburbs, the resale of cereal or cotton coupons, and the repair of machines that some enterprises preferred to entrust to mechanics rather than official workshops. Reports suggest that in reality more or less everybody was simply trying to "get by". Consider two examples taken from opposite ends of the social hierarchy: A cadre sent on official business to Canton bought eight watches there for 80 yuan each and sold them on his return to Henan for 125 yuan each. An escapee from a labour reform camp set up a workshop for counterfeiting banknotes in Zhengzhou from which he made a profit of 580 yuan by pretending to be a "state cadre". The spread of all sorts of "business" was a major aspect of urban life in 1956–1957. But it should not be allowed to obscure the fact that all people living by their wits were in a very precarious situation; the regime could crush them at any time.

At least these economic crimes did not reach the highest level of seriousness. In contrast, the ethnic and religious minorities who peopled the second circle of outs were by definition suspected of the most terrible shortcomings. The national minorities represented only a tiny percentage of the population of Henan. The overseas Chinese, numbering a few thousand, and the 423,000 members of ethnic minorities in 1957 (including 402,000 Moslems) together made up less than 1 percent of the population of the province. Overseas Chinese were concentrated in the cities, where they sometimes held administrative or technical jobs. Moslems too mostly lived in urban areas or close to communication routes. Endeavouring to maintain their customs, they felt that they had many serious reasons for complaining. Their shops were abruptly nationalised or cooperativised in 1956; Moslem cadres trained by the regime were rarely assigned to counties where national minorities lived;[73] and in their own counties, there were fewer schools and less social infrastructure than elsewhere. Factories and government departments rarely recognised Moslem culinary and marriage customs. But at least they could invoke the law to defend themselves.

The situation was quite different for the few Christians, whose distress can be glimpsed in the rare bits of information available. In Nanyang special region Catholic and Protestant worship continued to be banned from the time of the agrarian reform. In Shangqiu special region, no building was assigned for Christian worship. The regime would not exert itself to implement its own policy, which in theory allowed priests and pastors who had broken with the West to practise. Thus a resolute minority, knowing its fate, opposed both the official church and the regime.[74]

The final circle, comprising the political outs (about 0.5 percent of the population[75]) must be looked on as the antechamber of death. By good behaviour some former capitalists associated with the Guomindang and Nationalist army officers had been allowed to remove their "hats". But the rest, whether or not they were watched, lived in poverty and sometimes died from abuse.[76] Such persons made up a good percentage of the "households in difficulties" that the 1956 disasters pushed into famine. In the cities, some tried to escape poverty by engaging in small businesses, but they lived under the constant threat of a repressive campaign or a false denunciation.

Generally, family members of such persons had been executed or sent to labour reform camps. Available sources unfortunately make only rare references to the camps in Henan. We know of the existence, within the provincial Public Security Bureau, of the Labour Reform Administration Bureau. At least one brick works at Pingdingshan and workers in the vast Minquan state farm came under this bureau. It may well be that the social agitation of the time did not spare the camps, for the press acknowledged two escapes and even some disturbances.[77]

The World In-between

Between the outs and the privileged there survived at this time a world in-between of those facing an uncertain fate. This included the "democratic" social groups the regime still intended to win over: the national bourgeoisie and intellectuals trained under the old regime. In this in-between world material conditions varied enormously. Some "democratic figures" still retained a grand life-style. The former owners of large and medium-sized factories enjoyed comfortable incomes, although they were not safe from tax demands and had no social security. Engineers and teachers enjoyed comfortable wages. But there also existed, especially in the large rural towns, a whole fringe of small businessowners ruined by taxes and retired teachers and petty clerks living on the brink of poverty. The example has been cited of the widow of a small businessowner who in order to survive had had to marry—horror!—a cook.[78] Such people complained of not being sufficiently defended by the democratic parties that in theory represented them. Overall, they wanted to change status and be absorbed into the working class so as to enjoy job security and social benefits.

The unity of this social stratum derived not only from the privileged past of its members but also from their uncertain present and future. Although surrounded by signs of respect and sometimes installed in positions of power, such persons were constantly watched and subjected to adverse decisions by the regime. Public opinion was not mistaken: Even when they held prestigious jobs (engineer, teacher), their reputation was not good. But after summer 1956, the regime reassessed their status and limited the power of cadres. Even before publicly asked to give their opinion in spring 1957, the democrats did not hide their aspirations: The optimists and the best-off were hoping for a strengthening of their social status and political role; the rest, habituated to fear of change, saw salvation only in absorption into the working class—a quite unrealistic goal. Certainly, all hoped for a clarification of their status. This was to happen abruptly in summer 1957 when this in-between world disappeared with all hands.

A Cold Society

One wishes to be able to describe everyday life in Zhengzhou, say, or Luoyang in 1956–1957 in detail, but the information available does not permit it. It is possible to get a reasonably clear overall impression: Barely emerged from the conformism and tragedies of the prewar period, the new society had given itself extremely hard masters. It was a cold society in which it was very difficult to maintain human relations other than family or professional ties.

Speakers in spring 1957 protested almost unanimously against the oppressiveness and pettiness of the Party's interventions in everyday life. People were afraid to organise even a small social get-together for fear of being denounced. After the Sufan, old friends no longer issued invitations to one another for fear of being accused of "factional ties" or "apolitical feelings" even if they exchanged only banalities. When they could not avoid each other, they talked about the weather. In the factory canteen, everyone ate in silence.[79] Furthermore, after destroying the traditional extended family, the new regime had partly rehabilitated a morality from the more distant past, which somewhat conflicted with its propaganda on women's emancipation. Children were firmly reminded to respect their parents. Unhappily married persons could secure a divorce only under exceptional circumstances, such as one's spouse being sent to a labour reform camp or having an affair with a couterrevolutionary.[80] In the factories, friendships between boys and girls aroused suspicion or provoked very pointed comments.[81] Moral conformism favoured the maintenance of certain traditional male privileges. In the big shops, male customers would sexually harass young saleswomen. Male cadres and even teachers would take advantage of their status to abuse their female subordinates or their pupils.[82]

But the picture was not all darkness. First, the regime did not seriously try to control family life. This vast area of social life remained largely beyond its reach, as is shown by its inability to persuade parents not to push their children towards higher education and the half-heartedness of the birth control campaign. In addition, the very heavy-handedness of the regime's ideological pressure produced countereffects. Popular ways of letting off steam were not always innocent. "Yellow books", that is, erotic novels, caused havoc in secondary schools.[83] There was brawling in the streets as well as in sports arenas and theatres[84]—whether from the traditional Henan love of the theatre or because disorderly conduct could take on a chauvinist or even oppositionist tinge. The provincial press frequently complained of the uproar set off by audiences and directed at groups from other cities, or other provinces, or even foreign countries.[85] At night, in the big cities the areas close to new areas were not always safe. In short, channelled or repressed in official life and during the day, violence took refuge in that part of social existence that the regime could not or would not control totally: sport, entertainment, night life—and the family. One would like to have more information on this uncontrolled part of social life so as to test in detail a hypothesis that is nevertheless worth stating: The political agitation of the Hundred Flowers movement was partly the effect of the severe moral and social repression suffered by urban society. The very excess of the "cold" may have been one cause of the flare-up of spring 1957.

*   *   *

To return to the initial question: Was it necessary—is it still necessary—to talk of a social crisis in Henan in 1956–1957? This concern does not, for once, derive from a lack of data. Even if the sources remain insufficient and uneven, they are more plentiful, more concrete, and more candid than before. Beginning in autumn 1956, the press published more "negative material" than before, and what was said in spring 1957 brought out realities that had previously been carefully hidden. The material dating from this time is amongst the richest there is on Chinese society after 1949.

The question is in fact a problem of definition. In everyday language, the word crisis indicates either a break compared to the norm or the considerable and rapid worsening of a malady. A social crisis affects a significant proportion of the population, which becomes aware that its material situation is deteriorating, blames the political rulers, and seeks to escape the law by protesting and breaking discipline in concrete ways; a social crisis takes the form of more or less violent demonstrations of discontent, disturbances. If the population does not give its discontent a direct political expression, aimed at replacing the political authorities, sooner or later social distress will nevertheless produce political consequences of one sort or another.

This definition of social crisis only partly fits the case of Henan society in 1956–1957. There was, it is true, a deterioration of the social climate. This deterioration was not limited to the strata that were victims of the reforms of 1949–1952 or 1955–1956; in fact, it even hardly concerned them, since landlords, rich peasants, and former capitalists had learned caution and were in any case too weakened to take action. Strictly speaking, the distress affected the "broad popular masses", whose relations with the authorities, hitherto confident, indifferent, or simply mistrustful, suddenly deteriorated. This was particularly visible in the countryside, as is shown by the spread of incidents, and more important, an almost universal economic rule-breaking. It was the peasantry as a whole that manifested its discontent, often collectively.

In the cities, the situation was less simple—or perhaps better known. Amongst workers the deterioration was less clear, because living conditions were already none too good, because situations varied a great deal from one occupational group to another, and because working conditions had not been ill affected by the events of 1955–1956 (workers had even received substantial wage increases). One may well see in the maintenance of a sort of grumblers' solidarity—not above making demands—between the CCP and the workers in modern enterprises one of the strengths of the regime. Yet the prestige of the regime fell in three ways in the cities. First, the cities had finally been affected by the economic crisis that aggravated the difficulties of everyday life, notably in supply, thus precipitating amongst what we may call consumers a discontent that was not, of course, politicised but was widespread in all sections of society and led to many disturbances and much trafficking. Second, some minorities—not all, for the political outs would remain remarkably silent—voiced an ever-rising discontent, whether they were affected by the economic crisis (temporary workers or apprentices), hit by the organisational changes of 1956 (notably artisans), or encouraged by the new political and social climate (Moslems, democratic figures). Finally, the agitation reached the fringes of the regime, amongst the youth in the schools and universities, and one can even detect hesitation in cadres about the Party line and resentment at its shifts and turns.

Is that enough to speak of a social crisis? It must be acknowledged that the deterioration of the social situation was not, especially in the countryside, on the same scale as the deterioration of the economic situation. The sufferings inflicted on the peasantry by a very marked fall in production and then by appalling natural disasters precipitated only numerous cases of disobedience, but no revolt, no violent, large-scale opposition movement. The masses endeavoured above all to limit the material consequences of the disasters by taking advantage of the freedoms that were temporarily restored to them. In the cities, a small minority agitated, but it had no economic or political weight. The majority was discontented but resigned. Furthermore, there was no direct cause-and-effect link between the social situation in China in summer 1956 and the launching of the rectification campaign in spring 1957, which was a political decision. The existence of a social crisis must have been only one of the motives (an important one, no doubt) impelling central leaders to launch that campaign, and more important, when it threatened to collapse, to call a halt to it. Similarly, the launching of the Great Leap Forward must be principally attributed to political causes. In short, everything suggests that in this period social phenomena played only a weak causal role in political evolution. In that sense, too, the term social crisis appears, at first sight, exaggerated.

To explain this state of affairs, one can invoke psychological factors: age-old habits of passivity and scepticism towards government, any government; the memory of the pre-1949 horrors; perhaps also, in some, a real hope in the ability of a still-young regime to correct itself; and finally, a characteristically Henanese sense of discipline. But it seems truer to seek an explanation in the very nature of the China-wide political regime founded in 1949. By definition, it is a dictatorial regime—a "dictatorship of the proletariat" exercised by its political expression, the Communist Party—and both arbitrary and imbued with the police ethic. It thus inevitably arouses feelings of resentment and hostility in the population. Yet, despite its imperfections, the Party's control of the population is for the most part powerful enough to inhibit open expression of opposition. A fortiori, large-scale popular agitation and an open social crisis, in the sense in which we understand it in the West, are physically impossible and even unimaginable in the People's Republic of China. Should the Party make a mistake or turn bloody, protest at the time would be extremely muted. It is the Party's rule over the population and the fact that politics rules the social that explain why in China errors that in any other regime would have precipitated a large-scale crisis had only slight social consequences and led to no major political change.

In fact, Chinese society is dominated to such an extent that any considerable social reaction to government policy can only come into being or develop with the permission of all or part of the central leadership. Society can only react in a perceptible way if it is allowed or called upon to do so. The permission may be more or less open and liberal; whence the difference between events like the crisis of 1956–1957, the Cultural Revolution, and even the April 1976 disturbances in Tiananmen Square or the challenge of 1978–1979. In the case of Henan society in 1956–1957, the popular reaction noted here could not have been expressed without the relaxation of social policy and the beginning of political liberalisation previously decided on in Beijing.

Yet the masses can never be completely manipulated, although moderating a tyranny is not only difficult but dangerous. It is difficult because a population still under the influence of previous fixed positions (and also equipped by experience with solid common sense) is slow to be convinced that the change is real and lasting. While awaiting decisive proof, the vast majority is satisfied to take advantage of any privileges it is granted. Danger arises from the possibility that the minority of those who have nothing to lose may take advantage of the opportunity to push aside the regulations and express a radical critique; setting no limits to its movements but incapable of giving them a positive aim, such a group can only engage in disorderly action. To the apathy of the masses corresponds the erratic agitation of minorities.

It is in this sense, and this sense only, that one can speak of a social crisis in Henan in 1956–1957. Given the dictatorial nature of the Chinese Communist regime, what Henan society demonstrated in these years represented *the maximum that the authorities would accept*. And one finds here all the main features common to all the other social crises in the PRC: the low level of incidents, their partial lack of spontaneity, and a sharp contrast between the apathy of the masses and the agitation of minorities. From this angle,[86] there are obvious analogies with the period of the "dark years" (1960–1962) and even with certain aspects of the Cultural Revolution.

These clarifications make it possible to pose more clearly the too rarely tackled problem of the relationship between the social crisis of 1956–1957 and the political crisis of spring 1957.[87] For even if the social crisis exercised no direct influence on the course of events, its indirect effects were of considerable importance.

The point is that the crisis helped to strengthen divisions within the Party. Maoist tyranny, it is true, walked on its head. Political authority had a thousand times more weight than the body social. Only the semifiction of the mass line guarantees the possibility of a two-way flow between the political and the social. In reality movement in one direction, from the political to the social, is much faster and more important than movement in the other. The regime is much readier to speak than to listen; that is why it hears so badly. On its side, the population can obviously not risk telling the truth, but it also cannot avoid saying something when its opinion is sought and thereby more or less clearly revealing its feelings. *The social crisis of 1956–1957 was the necessarily cautious expression of maximum discontent.* There was thus a sort of dialogue between the deaf (the central leaders) and the dumb (the people). By launching the rectification campaign of April 1957, that is, by taking for granted that the population accepted the goals of the Communist Party, Mao Zedong demonstrated a total lack of understanding of popular aspirations. His approach was dictated as much by deafness as by idealism.

But in this regime there are some who because of their situation and because it is, so to speak, their business are less deaf than others: the middle- and lower-level cadres who make up the vast majority of the Party apparatus. Between the two possibilities of spring 1957—giving the opposition movement time to define itself or abruptly shutting the door that had just been opened to it—these cadres' response was ready-made and almost automatic. Without having understood everything, they had read enough about the situation and knew enough to foresee that the challenge would threaten first their own power and then the regime itself. From this arose the lukewarm response, the more or less intentional blunders, and the deliberate obstruction that were to play a role in spring 1957. From this, too, came the divisions, at both provincial and central level, between the leaders most susceptible to the Maoist utopia (or the orders of the Central Committee) and those whose behaviour was primarily dictated by what might be called class interests.

Those in the second group were doubtless the more reasonable both from the standpoint of their own interests and from that of the stability of the regime. For the social crisis provided the challengers with explosive topics for public intervention and a public only too ready to approve them. As will be seen, the speakers in spring 1957 would often simply repeat out loud what was being whispered and report what they themselves had observed or experienced. In times of scarcity and discontent, such words could not but be grim. The debate could not remain academic. Behind the still-cautious statements by the liberals, a whole surge of popular discontent threatened to burst through, this time openly and violently. The social crisis was threatening to turn all those figureheads into revolutionaries. It offered them the formidable advantage of being able to be heard by the masses, and the regime being what it was, condemned them to an early death.

I will suggest a provisional and perhaps foolhardy conclusion: The tightness of the domination exercised by the Party over society explains why in Maoist China the scale of the social crisis is much smaller than what might be suggested by the seriousness of the ills that have precipitated it. It also explains why, far from directly influencing the authorities, the crisis depends on their relaxation to manifest itself; yet the development of the social crisis indirectly modifies the political debate by raising the stakes involved and fuelling disagreements within the Party.

PART TWO

The Political Crisis of Spring and Summer 1957

Strong dictatorial regimes can generally withstand a serious social crisis so long as it does not spread to the political sphere and has no effect on the apparatus of power. Although the Communist regime felt threatened in Henan in 1957, and to a degree indeed it was, this was not because of the economic and social crisis that followed the failure of the first leap. It was much more because a few months after that failure became clear a political crisis was superimposed on the social crisis and because there were grounds for fearing that the two crises would be mutually reinforcing.

The origin of this political crisis—the most serious that the new regime had so far experienced in Henan—is to be found in the launching by the central government on 27 April 1957 of the Communist Party's rectification campaign, often called the Hundred Flowers movement. This name is inaccurate, because as has been seen, the Hundred Flowers slogan was already being advanced at the beginning of 1956. By encouraging the expression of criticisms of the Communist Party, this rectification campaign brought to the surface a host of grievances and aggravated the division within the provincial committee. The crushing of the liberals in June removed all threat of subversion, but sharpened the internal divergences within the Henan leadership. Allowing the expression of contradictions among the people initially enabled a new and authentic voice to be heard, but then precipitated the emergence of a serious contradiction within the Party.

3

A Political Error: The Rectification Campaign in Henan (1 May–9 June 1957)

Whatever the real intentions of its promoters may have been, the launching of the rectification campaign by the centre must be regarded as a serious political error. Analysis of how the campaign unfolded in Henan shows that despite efforts to slow it down, the provincial authorities were beginning to lose control of the situation in some urban sectors by early June 1957. Although political protest was geographically and socially limited, the open airing of ills that were obvious to everyone revealed the true nature of the regime. After more than seven years of the CCP relentlessly extending its power over the population, the urban apparatus of the Party suddenly found itself on the defensive against criticisms from liberals. This attack came just as internal divisions deepened.

Overall, events unfolded in Henan much as in the rest of China. A period of latency was succeeded in late April by a phase of organisation followed by that of the great debates, which paved the way for the first disturbances. But the movement was slower in Zhengzhou than in Beijing, and in some smaller cities the delay was made up only by late May.

The First Months of 1957

According to available sources,[1] until April 1957, the political line overall remained what it had been in autumn 1956. Amidst continued criticism of the adventurism of the first leap, a more flexible rural policy was being pursued. Mao Zedong's speeches of 27 February to the Supreme State Conference, "On the Correct Handling of Contradictions Amongst the People", and 12 March before a national conference on propaganda work, which were later to justify extending liberalisation to the political sphere, were not published and produced no concrete follow-up.[2] Certainly rumours were rife about Mao's speeches,[3] but the periodic discussion meetings convened by local departments of the United Front continued to be largely academic. At a provincial conference on propaganda work convened in Henan in April the majority of provincial leaders condemned "neglect in political and ideological work", that is, the Party's inadequate political dynamism.[4] Others, on the contrary, accused some local committees of limiting or slowing down implementation of the new rural policy.[5] In short, in Henan as elsewhere, the first months of 1957 seem to have been a time of latency, debate, and hesitation.

Everything changed abruptly following the publication in Zhengzhou on 1 May of the Central Committee's directive dated 27 April 1957. This set off a rectification movement (*zhengfeng yundong*) of a new type. In the past the Party had always been the actor in rectification, but now it was also the object of rectification, required to welcome and even seek out views and criticisms from outside the Party in order to wipe out the three "isms" within itself: bureaucratism, sectarianism and subjectivism. The leaders were expected to set the example by truly mixing with the masses.[6]

Initial Planning

Until mid-May the leaders in Henan—including Pan Fusheng, who had suddenly returned—busied themselves without undue haste in organisational preparations. After meeting to draw up a "rectification plan" the provincial committee summoned a "working session on propaganda and education", during which the chief topics for discussion were set out.[7] Next, the committee disseminated the good word in two directions: in liberal circles in the province through the representatives who came together from 5 to 12 May for a meeting of the provincial committee of the Chinese People's Political Consultative Conference, and in Party committees in the cities and special regions.[8] At the same time provincial leaders went in great state to "engage in productive labour"—that is, physical work in factories or fields.[9]

Next, the various localities organised their jurisdictions on a similar pattern. Thus, in Luoyang the municipal committee met on 7 May to approve the provincial directives. The very next day its first secretary went to engage in production. The authorities took advantage of a meeting of the local Federation of Industry and Commerce to announce the good news to the liberals. The first organisational meetings of the movement in the city's three big pilot factories took place on 10 and 11 May. Yet it was not until 17 May that Li Li, the first secretary, publicly took a stand in favour of the rectification campaign, and not until 21 May that the municipal committee's rectification plan was distributed, envisaging that the movement would last until the end of September.[10]

The First Organised
Public Meetings

As it began to seem that the centre was sticking firmly with its new line and even Beijing was beginning to stir, provincial leaders had no choice but to move ahead. From 16 to 23 May the United Front Department of the provincial committee summoned the most senior figures in Henan and forty-four well-known democrats to a "discussion meeting". Meetings of the same type were organised in government departments and the leading sectors of activity in the cities. On 22 May, Wu Zhipu went to the University of Henan to encourage teachers and students to "bloom" and "contend".[11]

It was at this point that the rectification campaign got its first real boost. Intellectuals were called upon to express their "opinions". Opening the meeting called by the United Front Department, its leader exclaimed: "Say all that you know, keep quiet about nothing!" Before journalists of the *Henan Daily*, the head of the Propaganda Department of the provincial committee—(their real boss)—engaged in unheard-of self-criticism: He regretted having banned the play *Liu Hulan* in Henan. On 18 May, at the first discussion meeting called by the Zhengzhou Party municipal committee, a former businessowner said in substance: Hitherto I have expressed only 50 percent of what was on my mind, today I am going to say 90 percent. Wang Lizhi, the secretary of the municipal committee, immediately interrupted to call on him to express the remaining 10 percent, too. The press reflected this new orientation. On 15 May, it began to publish critical speeches and articles emanating from liberal circles. The Luoyang newspaper, which on 7 May had wondered "Bloom? Contend?", opened its columns on 18 May to a reader who challenged it ironically: "Set the example, you on the *Luoyang Daily!*"[12]

Resistance and Reservations

This second period also was marked by resistance on the part of the apparatus and reservations on the part of the democrats. From the beginning, Henan Party officials let it be understood that they were only agreeing to the rectification campaign decided upon in Beijing against their better judgement. On the occasion of the 1 May festivities in Luoyang, Li Li emphatically thanked the Soviet technicians present for their help, and Wang Tianduo, the local trade union chairman, cautioned that in discussions between Communists and others, everyone should "start from the will for unity".[13] The example came from the top: Wu Zhipu was later criticised for having deliberately omitted criticism of "sectarianism" in his speech at the working session on propaganda and education at the beginning of May.[14]

Although resistance among major leaders diminished by the middle of the month, amongst their subordinates it remained very much alive. On 13 May, in the middle of a meeting of the Luoyang Federation of Industry and Commerce a vice-chairman of the municipal Bureau for the Reform of Private Trading exclaimed to the former owners of mixed enterprises: "As for you, you are nothing but defrauders, thieves, oppositionists. After study sessions in Zhengzhou or here you are still more arrogant and disobedient". Newspapers liked to compare the rectification campaign to "a light breeze and fine rain"; but many basic-level cadres expressed the fear that it might be transformed into a "hurricane". Some simply banned all meetings. Others, more adroit, were content to copy the "rectification plans" adopted by higher echelons and transformed discussion meetings into sessions for the study of official documents.[15] When they authorised criticisms, they tightly controlled how far these might go. From provincial offices to basic levels, in each unit the first secretary of the Party committee was always the person in charge of the "leading rectification group". Each discussion was prepared and led by a Party leader. A meeting secretary recorded or noted all opinions expressed. Press accounts of the main speeches censored the names of leaders who were challenged, but not those of speakers, whose views were sometimes distorted.[16]

The "democratic figures" found themselves in a delicate situation. To fail to respond enthusiastically to the well-intentioned calls of the Party would be to show criminal indifference to the socialist cause. But on the other hand, how could they not be dubious about the regime's real intentions? "The thunder claps of the Zhenfan, Sanfan, and Sufan campaigns are still echoing in our ears. First they open the floodgates, then they round up, then they rectify", said a teacher from Luoyang. Wang Yizhai himself felt that, "Today, if one speaks one does not risk reprisals, but since the old cadres retain all power, they will be able to attack us when they want."[17] These fears were reinforced by a commonsense argument: If the old cadres really wanted to correct the regime's errors and abuses, would they compare the rectification campaign to a "light breeze and fine rain"? As for the small national capitalists, their hesitations were much simpler: They were not sure they knew how to express themselves in public and feared the wrath of the authorities.[18]

The result was that the democratic figures showed infinite caution. Everyone waited to be asked before expressing an opinion and made certain at the beginning of every meeting that the wind was still blowing in the same direction. All sought to get themselves represented by some well-thought-of figure such as Wang Yizhai. He at least would know what it was sensible to say, and anyway, he could be disavowed later. When the leaders of the small democratic parties could not plead illness (as Ji Wenfu did), they expressed themselves circumspectly. But their reservations with regard to the regime were generally known and they could not avoid mentioning them. Thus they had to at least partly tell the truth—while trying to remain sufficiently false. The only examples cited were ones everybody knew and the leaders admitted, and giving them any general significance was avoided. The speech thus became: In my unit, some cadres ill-treat me, which, thank God, is not the case elsewhere. When it became impossible to avoid pronouncing a judgement, one could still lose it in a welter of general assertions such as: Responsibility for the "chasm" or "wall" separating me from Party members lies with both sides; it certainly has something to do with the three "isms" with which the Party is afflicted, but it also has do with my social origins and my inadequate ideological level. Although speakers could not avoid raising certain basic problems, such as the monopolisation of power by the Communists and even the repression, most of the time they abstained from attacking senior leaders or challenging the regime itself.

Resistance and reservations were more and more open the farther one travelled from Zhengzhou. Information became scarcer. The local Party apparatus was less and less sensitive to the inputs coming from the centre and closer and closer to the rural areas, which were in principle exempt from rectification. Finally, liberal circles were more and more weak and isolated. Overall, the province lagged behind Beijing,[19] but Luoyang also lagged behind Zhengzhou. At the beginning of June, most administrative units in the special regions had not yet launched the movement. As for Nanyang, it had organised practically nothing.[20]

The Acceleration of Late May

Only a clear political decision by the provincial authorities could eliminate resistance and remove reservations. That decision was taken on the morning of 23 May by a session of the standing committee of the provincial committee of the Party. In a major speech, Pan Fusheng is said to have declared that, "China's entry into the period of building socialism means that social classes have disappeared", and then set out a list of "ten contradictions in Henan".[21] It was after this meeting that in response to a proposal by Pan Fusheng the decision was adopted in principle to step up the liberalisation of agrarian policy. But the real conclusions of this meeting had to do with the rectification campaign. The provincial committee officially acknowledged that it had not yet taken the necessary measures to convince all people to express themselves frankly. Implicitly disavowing its own United Front Department and most of the city committees, the provincial committee decided to convene discussion meetings itself in Zhengzhou and the major cities.[22]

That same afternoon, Pan Fusheng in person transmitted these decisions to the heads of the main departments of the provincial committee. To speed implementation, he summoned the fourth plenum of the provincial committee, enlarged for the occasion to include the leaders of the cities and special regions and a few counties. This meeting took place from 25 to 30 May. On the first day Pan Fusheng made a long speech in which he said in particular: "There are still ideological hesitations, people do not dare to bloom and contend. . . . Everyone must speak fully and clearly." Then Wu Zhipu presented a "self-criticism of the errors committed by the provincial committees in handling contradictions among the people". The plenum reaffirmed that the rural areas were to remain outside the rectification movement, but then reopened the question by introducing a quite extraordinary innovation, authorising criticisms of the provincial committee that emanated from within the Party itself, notably in the area of rural policy, including by way of wall posters.[23] It was thus no longer simply a matter of offering the abstract "Party" up for supposedly constructive criticism by non-Communists. Now it was a matter of handing over Wu Zhipu and his collaborators in the most concrete possible way to the potentially destructive attacks of their subordinates, as well indeed as the anger of the centre. In Henan Mao Zedong's great ideological design assumed the form of a bureaucratic manoeuvre.

The Return of the Mastermind

At this point, the petty details of history once again get tied up with the unfolding of great events. There is no doubt that the directives received from Beijing and the example set by other provinces backed Pan Fusheng. Henan was now so far behind in the rectification campaign that a sharp acceleration was the only real option. But the abruptness of its relaunching and the importance of its political consequences can only be explained in the light of the continuing conflict between Pan Fusheng and Wu Zhipu.

Pan Fusheng had been out of power since summer 1954. He waited until the very end of April before returning to Henan, that is, just when the centre's extension of liberalisation from the social to the political sphere offered him a serious chance of returning to favour and holding the position of procurator in Henan. Until 23 May he bided his time, positioning himself skilfully. Although he had recovered his hierarchical preeminence over Wu Zhipu, Pan left it to Wu to justify and organise a political movement of which Wu manifestly disapproved. For the first three weeks of May political authority in Henan was bicephalous.[24] Thus, in case the centre accentuated its liberal opening and Wu Zhipu, a prisoner of both his own statements and his supporters in the apparatus, failed to implement fully the directives emanating from Beijing, Pan would be able to compromise him decisively and regain complete power. Such was the manoeuvre that Pan felt able to embark upon on 23 May. It must be compared with those he had successively carried out in 1953 and suffered in 1954. Then, too, it had been a matter of taking advantage of a shift in the centre's policy to impose authority on the provincial apparatus. But this time, the two protagonists—already scorched by the experience of defeat—seem to have sought to get rid of each other once and for all. Such at least is what is suggested by Pan Fusheng's attempt to get not only non-Communists but also Party members to criticise both the general shortcomings of the Party and the political errors committed by his rival. This interpretation is confirmed by the counterattack Wu Zhipu launched in summer 1957 and concluded a year later.

The Big Meetings of Late May and Early June

It subsequently became apparent that by assigning an instrumental role to what ought to have been an end—criticism of the Party's mistakes—Pan Fusheng was demonstrating that he no more believed in the official objectives of the movement than did Wu Zhipu. After initially being reined in by the Henan party apparatus, the movement was really set in motion only to be diverted by its leader.

Pan's manoeuvre, petty though it was, had major effects. After the last week in May, the rectification campaign in the province made a new beginning. For its part, the provincial committee stopped holding back. With varying degrees of enthusiasm, committee members committed themselves to the movement. According to subsequent revelations, some of them did not mince their words. Wang Tingdong, the assistant head of the secretariat of the provincial committee, observed that "the masses say that Chairman Mao does not understand the situation, that the basic-level cadres are incompetent, and the middle cadres criminal toadies". Yang Jue, one of the secretaries of the provincial committee, admitted that "the Party cannot run science". Pan Fusheng himself expressed his agreement with Li Baifeng, the liberal poet from Kaifeng: The Sufan had been too violent; the *zhengfeng* must assume an ideological importance comparable to that of the 4 May 1919 movement. Pan is even said to have proposed (vainly) forbidding Party leaders from speaking at discussion meetings, so that they would not intimidate participants.[25]

In any event, even before the end of the enlarged session of the fourth plenum, the provincial committee convened in Zhengzhou the discussion meeting that Pan had announced. This went on from 27 May to 3 June. The twenty-four participants were no longer all content simply to make carefully balanced statements or individual recriminations. Now some interventions sounded loud and clear. Thus, on 2 June, Li Fudou, vice-chairman of the Yellow River Committee, and Li Baohe, vice-chairman of the provincial Irrigation Bureau set out a comprehensive critique of government policy in their area.[26]

The next day, Wang Yizhai made so bold as to ask what would be the practical follow-up of the movement. Had not the Party long known the criticisms that it was now hearing? At the close of the meeting, Wu Zhipu had to give assurances that the provincial committee would examine all the views expressed and, he promised, make the necessary reforms.[27]

The movement accelerated rapidly. In almost all the offices of the Henan government and some departments of the provincial committee,[28] members were called together to evaluate their activity. On the whole, the call from Pan Fusheng did not seem to be heard within the Party. A very small part of the criticism emanating from Communists reached the provincial committee. Non-Communist critics, however, became less and less intimidated and sometimes attacked leaders by name. The *Henan Daily* stopped censoring these criticisms and even encouraged them by revealing on 8 June the existence of a provincial circular dated 31 May on the rectification of work style in provincial offices and by criticising two senior officials in the province by name.[29]

In the special regions and large cities, the rectification campaign was given a real boost. The promised debates were held on 3–4 June in Xinxiang, 5 June in Luoyang, and 4–7 June in Kaifeng. They were run by delegates from the provincial committee, and except in Luoyang, were conducted in the absence of the municipal first secretaries. Before the 2,000 students and teachers of the Xinxiang Teacher Training School, Yang Jue made a resounding plea titled, "Let Us Sweep Aside Hesitations, Let Us Continue to Bloom and Contend". In Kaifeng, Zhao Wenfu had to listen to the complaints of the students. To the sound of jeers, he made a very liberal speech that the *Henan Daily* of 9 June had the charity not to publish in full.[30] During these meetings, numerous speakers questioned the Party monopoly and the repression.

Finally, starting in the last week in May, most Party committees in the special regions had meetings arranged by their United Front Department or the various democratic groups. In early June they committed themselves more explicitly by offering themselves to the criticism of those they administered, and in principle at least, their subordinates. Moreover, the continuing campaign was more and more commonly described in the meetings as a "criticism movement".[31]

Sweet-Smelling Flowers and Poisonous Weeds

Thanks to the boost given in May, the atmosphere began to shift sharply at the beginning of June. Speech became increasingly free, and at the same time, more radical and more dangerous. For their part, at the end of May the authorities abandoned the initial distinction between "scented flowers" and "poisonous weeds", which had worried a lot of liberals. In doing so they laid themselves open to having to inhale some very peculiar aromas.

Yet limits remained. Nothing could be more mistaken than to imagine these days as like the May days in France or even the Prague spring of 1968. Even as the other cities began to stir, in Zhengzhou itself suspicions were only slowly being effaced. Meetings, except at the university, remained restricted to the small elite of those who had a share, however small, of power and unfolded usually according to a ritual that stifled debate. All who attended expressed themselves in turn, then the Party official who was in the chair sent everyone home with some good words. Many interventions continued to be carefully balanced. The general tone shifted only slowly from complaint to recrimination and from recrimination to demand; rarely indeed did one hear anything like revolt. Whether from conviction or caution, some speakers demonstrated remarkable moderation. Jia Xinzhai, one of the non-Communist vice-governors, declared that only a few Party members had committed errors and moreover non-Communists were not entirely innocent. Others, even more skilful, embroidered on the theme that it was its very success that had led the CCP to make mistakes. Obscure cadres even thought the time had come for them to distinguish themselves by taking up the cudgels in defence of the Party. They argued that only some Party members had made mistakes, and that dogmatism must not be criticised with the help of revisionism, bureaucratism with the help of liberalism, and sectarianism with the help of a different sectarianism.[32]

It would also be a mistake to accept the accusations that some liberals in both Zhengzhou and Beijing had fomented an anti-Party plot. According to the official thesis,[33] two well-placed "rightists" in Beijing, Wang Yifan and Zhang Yunchuan, who formed a link in the centre with the "Zhang Bojun-Luo Longji clique", were supposed as early as April 1957 to have entrusted Zhang Zhonglu, head of the Transport Bureau of the provincial government and vice-chairman of the Henan committee of the Chinese People's Consultative Political Conference, with recruiting 100,000 new members in the province for the Peasants' and Workers' Party. Zhang Yunchuan was alleged then to have gone to Zhengzhou, from 8 to 12 June, to activate the operation. Meetings were alleged to have been held on the following days by Wang Yizhai, Zhang Zhonglu, Liu Jixue, and Luo Shengwu. On 16 June, a meeting was supposed to have resulted in two documents being drawn up along with a list of demands.

Such an obviously erroneous accusation is hardly worth refuting. I will simply note that an old liberal politician like Zhang Yunchuan had as a native of Henan and deputy for the province numerous personal and professional reasons for going to Zhengzhou and meeting former colleagues there. In April 1957 the idea of developing the small democratic parties was being mentioned in leadership circles and by Mao himself, and moreover, the Peasants' and Workers' Party being practically nonexistent in Henan, there was very little danger of it becoming a rival to the CCP. Finally, it might be noted that the alleged conspiracy was formed before the launching of the *zhengfeng* and put into effect after the halt to it was called on 9 June—surely a most bizarre way of proceeding. There is thus nothing to confirm the official thesis of a Henan plot. Contacts certainly existed between the various liberal figures the regime had consigned to the same ghetto. All doubtless aspired to live less dangerously. It seems that some of them began to hope for a genuine change in the regime. Some (Luo Shengwu or Wang Yizhai, for example) may have been thinking of cashing in on their popularity with intellectuals or students to gain favour with those in power. But none of them attempted or doubtless even contemplated the impossible. In fact, as often in a

Communist regime, the official thesis of a plot both concealed and reflected an extremely simple reality, but one that doctrine was powerless to explain: the spontaneous appearance in the early days of the movement of a political protest and the first real disturbances.

In fact, some speakers were no longer content simply to denounce political oppression, police repression, or the wretched lot of the people. They raised questions about the regime. Teachers demanded that the various parties take it in turns to run schools, which amounted concretely to rejecting the sacrosanct principle of the dictatorship of the proletariat. The power monopoly that the Communist Party enjoyed de facto became the target of a large number of attacks. Clear criticisms were made of Soviet aid and the Soviet model. Did not the alliance with Moscow explain, for example, U.S. aid to Taiwan and hence Beijing's inability to liberate that province? The supreme offence was committed by a certain Sun Defen, who edited the Zhengzhou University's journal. He said: "The Communist Party has oppressed me as much as the Guomindang. The United Nations ought to be concerned with people like us." Was the Chinese regime then just another dictatorship? "I feel", declared an engineer from Luoyang, "that China's liberation by the Communist Party was no more than a change of dynasty, we have simply changed masters."[34]

The First Sparks

More spectacular—and also more dangerous—were the disturbances that occurred in what might be called the superstructure: the press, artistic and literary circles, and the universities.

The agitation early on reached journalistic circles all over China, crystallising around a number of scandals such as the Zuo Ye affair.[35] Henan journalists had been quick to protest against the tyranny of the provincial committee ("It is just like being under military rule", said one of them) and against the poor quality of work that they were asked to carry out. In the course of stormy meetings, the editors of the *Henan Daily* demanded to be allowed to publish a number of censored articles and even to try out an independent newspaper. At meetings held on 4 and 6 June, the Communist Youth cells in the paper demanded that Pan Fusheng in person come to explain himself and adopted resolutions hostile to Party policy, which they immediately posted up around the newspaper building.[36]

The situation was more disturbed in artistic and literary circles. Actors, musicians, and writers criticised the officials placed over them. The protest was especially violent in Kaifeng and Luoyang. Artists and writers seem to have been more exasperated and bolder than many other liberals, since the most frequent criticisms of individuals by name came from their lips.[37] From late May the criticisms became more incisive.[38] "Look", railed one writer, "it is no longer so certain that Hu Feng is a counterrevolutionary." The historians also roused themselves: "If

Chen Duxiu had not committed rightist errors, Chiang Kai-shek would not have been able to turn on the Communists." Demands were made. The artists asked to form an independent provincial union that would publish a review and organise exhibitions. The writers were even more demanding and more active, perhaps because the regime had left them with more means to subsist and express themselves. The province's literary review, *Current*, which had been founded in January 1957 by Su Jinsan after the banning of *Garden of a Hundred Blades of Grass*, published impassioned issues, which quickly sold out. The July issue, set up before the centre's change of course, included a poem by Li Baifeng with the evocative title "Spring". The little intellectual world of Luoyang was scandalised by the arbitrary suppression in September 1956 of a literary monthly that sold out its 3,000 run in a few days. In Zhengzhou, the poet Ma Changfeng and the journalist Li Qing developed a proposal for a non-Communist literary review that would begin with a special issue on Ai Qing. And a political and literary newssheet published for a few weeks by a "democrat" in Anyang eclipsed the Party's own. In fact, no one lost sight of the political nature of literary problems, writers least of all. In Zhengzhou, to denounce the injustices committed at the time of the Sufan and call for reparations, they held meeting after meeting, such as what was effectively a mass meeting called on 30 May by Ma Changfeng and Li Qing where a collective petition was adopted.

But it was at the university that the most serious disturbances occurred. By the end of May the agitation had spread to all institutions of higher education. In Xinxiang, student assemblies met day after day. Kaifeng, an old university town, was plunged into tumult. Students and city-dwellers fought for *The Flame*, the bulletin published by Li Baifeng. In the Faculty of Medicine, the students, backed by their director, protested against the "lack of democracy and freedom". The Teacher Training School, where several famous scholars taught, was even more agitated. After the general meeting of 2 June, wall posters and the school newspaper revealed numerous excesses committed during the Sufan. The general meeting of 5 June, where some students called for a "living Marxism", debated the setting up of a "Hundred Flowers committee" to head the movement and threatened to send a delegation to demonstrate in Beijing if those locally responsible for the Sufan were not punished. Zhao Wenfu, sent by the provincial committee to give speeches, failed to calm student anger.[39]

The situation developed most dangerously in Zhengzhou. Curiously, the University of Henan was not at the eye of the movement, which is perhaps explained by bad memories of the Sufan. Yet, in late May wall posters there were already proclaiming: "We want true freedom and democracy! Let us put an end to spiritual oppression!" At the beginning of June, students and teachers unanimously denounced the poor equipment of the university, the authoritarianism of cadres, and the keeping of blacklists by the authorities.[40] In the Henan Institute of Agronomy a mimeographed newssheet published inflammatory materials on the Sufan. The official student union took up a position in the van of the movement. The committee elected with its support formed a "Sufan inquiry group", established links with other universities, and sent delegates to demonstrate in Beijing.[41]

The most serious incidents broke out in another institution of higher learning in Zhengzhou, the Specialised Teacher Training School. This school had encountered difficulties getting settled after its transfer from Kaifeng in autumn 1956. In addition, a recurring dispute pitted its director, Luo Shengwu, against CCP academic cadres. In spring 1957 true political disturbances commenced following material demands and protests against the Sufan. Luo Shengwu denounced the sabotage of the *zhengfeng* by Communist cadres and declared to anyone who cared to listen: "The Party committee at the university is oppressing democracy." As for the students, they were demonstrating to the cry of: "Support the school director!" On 4 June, Luo took a decision laden with consequences: on the excuse that it was pouring rain and the students must help get the wheat harvest in—but more likely far more concerned with not letting himself be overtaken by an uncontrollable strike—he temporarily suspended classes. From that point the situation worsened by the day. On 5 June students went off to demonstrate outside the provincial committee (in trucks provided by none other than the school management!).[42] Luo Shengwu hailed them in these words: "You have problems, I support you." On 6 June, Luo set up a "university reform group" under his chairmanship, including amongst its thirteen members only four representatives of what everyone then called the "right"—the Communist Party. On 7 June, Zhang Baiyuan hurried in to try and calm people down, but he only just managed to avoid being torn to pieces and had to leave the school under the protection of the last loyal batch of Communist youth with a crowd of students shouting at him: "Zhang, you are simply a bureaucrat, you cannot represent us!" The next day, Yang Jue, secretary to the provincial committee, and Wang Lizhi, Zhengzhou first secretary, had to come and explain themselves in person, before an assembly that was completely wild. In short, just when in Beijing the leading group of the CCP was deciding to call an abrupt halt to the movement, the Zhengzhou Specialised Teacher Training School found itself in a preinsurrectionary situation. Criticisms had been followed by concrete actions—holding general meetings, electing committees, organising public demonstrations—that were aimed at overthrowing the existing power-holders.

The scale of these disturbances was limited, but their seriousness was unprecedented. For they were occurring in a university, a place that by tradition and as a matter of policy was still highly respected. What if they spread? People were coming from all over to read the wall posters outside the school, attend meetings, and request tracts. The rural areas remained generally calm, but some suburbs and some county seats were beginning to be affected by the movement. Was there not a danger that once lit the first sparks might inflame the urban areas, and then if the movement lasted, the plain? To what extent does the scale of the threat coming from Henan help explain the sudden calling of a halt on 9 June?

When attempting to assess the threat represented in early June 1957 by those whom the press uniformly dubbed "rightists", it is difficult to avoid two exaggerations. The ease with which the regime wiped out the protest movement may create the false impression that the activities of May and June 1957 were nothing more than a confused intellectual agitation with no real social base. On the other hand, the scale of the crisis experienced by the Communist apparatus in both the centre and the provinces, plus the stubborn recurrence later of the themes developed by the rightists in 1957, may lead to excessive political and ideological importance being attributed to the protest of spring 1957. Let me say right away that a study of the Henan case has led me to a view that is closer to the second than the first argument. Despite its geographical, social, and political limits, and because of its predominantly intellectual and ideological character, the liberal protest movement had considerable effects, in both the long and the short term, on the solidity of the regime and its self-definition.

The protest movement's geographical and social limits are undeniable and well known. They have even been exaggerated. The rectification campaign was supposed to be restricted to apparatuses above the county level: provinces, special regions, municipalities. What happened in fact was that the boundary was not always so precise or so carefully observed. It was difficult to keep the often very densely populated suburbs of the cities out of things, and discussion meetings were organised in such places.[43] In addition, an exception to the rule seems to have been agreed upon for some traditionally commercial county seats. In the most remote counties, where the Zhengzhou newspapers were taken cadres and teachers closely followed events and there were some incidents around schools.[44]

But according to the provincial press, the rectification campaign remained an essentially urban affair. Despite their family origins, the rightists maintained hardly any contacts with the countryside. Among the eleven leading rightists denounced by the press in summer 1957, at least seven were of rural ancestry, but none worked in agriculture or even in a small town; all had lived in Zhengzhou or Kaifeng for many years. The liberals were even more urban based than the Communist Party.

It must be pointed out that in the cities the rectification movement spread to a number of productive sectors, notably the large stores and state factories. Study meetings were organised in such places to study the 27 April circular and became opportunities to express concrete criticisms of leaders. The "assemblies of workers' delegates" sometimes turned into criticism meetings not unlike those held in schools and universities.[45] There can in any event be little doubt that the agitation that prevailed outside the factories encouraged the wage demands and minority agitation mentioned above.

A Social, Political, and Intellectual Elite

In themselves, the rightists constituted a minority elite. Their total number was small. Officially, 200,000 individuals took part in the rectification campaign.[46]

From that total, numerous cadres and Party members must be subtracted as well as a host of democrats too cautious to breathe a word. But the official figure of 5,115 rightists denounced up to 30 October[47] seems too low, and certainly it does not include all those who managed to cover their tracks or were detained later. Taking into account the fact that Henan had 9,500 higher education students at the time and that there were many more secondary school students, there must have been several tens of thousands of active protesters. For a province with almost 50 million inhabitants, that is a very low figure.

This rightist minority was a social elite distinct from the world of production, as is shown by the case of specialist engineers and technicians. To call on them to express themselves was the reason that the rectification campaign was officially present in the factories. Yet they never spoke in the name of the workers as a whole, but only as members of an unfairly treated social category. The role of trade unions and the greater job security that workers enjoyed had made these specialists jealous.[48] Their criticisms of the Party's inability to manage factories usually ended in a plea for their own case.

Amongst the protesters were a fair number of members of formerly privileged classes. Of the eleven most criticised rightists, the seven whose social origin is known were all born to landlord families.[49] Many of them, especially the best educated, received comfortable allowances from the new regime. They had in effect been co-opted—more or less honourably, it is true; they were powerless, but integrated nonetheless into the privileged class of the new regime. Seven of the principal rightists were provincial leaders and the other four were academics placed well up the salary scale. Most of the rightists belonged to what might be called the public services. They included teachers, engineers, and technicians. Others were salaried leaders of small democratic parties or former businessowners' associations.[50] Both by origin and by profession, the rightists formed a materially privileged elite.

Above all, these persons formed an intellectual elite. The speeches made in May and June 1957 were couched in a language that was infinitely more varied and sparkling than that of official propaganda. These speeches often contain protests by intellectuals against the lack of culture and the uncouthness of cadres. They also testify to a high level of education: At least seven of the principal rightists in the province had completed university, two of them abroad. Many pursued intellectual professions. Wang Yizhai, the mastermind of the Henan plot according to propaganda, was an academic who had turned to politics. Born in 1895 into a ruined landlord family in Qixian, Wang went to study in Germany. After his return in 1929 he taught at the University of Henan and used his intellectual reputation to influence the course of events, advising the warlord Liu Zhenhua, mobilising students against Japanese aggression, and finally in 1948 joining and then leaving (because of disagreements) the pro-Communist university of the central plains. Despite his official position, he did not stop teaching after 1949.[51]

As members of defunct classes and defeated political groups holding intellectual jobs that the regime mistrusted, the rightists had already often suffered "criticism" from their new masters; this was the case for five of the eleven leading rightists and fourteen of the thirty-one other rightists. A considerable number of them had seen their family decimated during the regime's first repressive campaigns.[52] They were barely one remove from dangerous social circles and well aware of the cost of displeasing the Party of the proletariat. Being integrated into the regime's elite, they also knew what one false step might cost them, and from experience could have no illusions about the chances of a return to democracy. It was difficult for them not to speak out, but they had no interest in drawing attention to themselves by talking boldly or violently.

Those rightists who attacked the foundations of the regime thus did not do so out of self-interest or ambition. They knew they were socially and politically isolated and could not expect any great increase in power. Their criticism of the regime can only have been because of an inner sense of duty. They could do this and they should do it. This moral lucidity explains why instead of organising an uprising of the educated that would be doomed to fail, rightists in Henan were content to say what they were thinking. To the strength and cunning of power they opposed but a single weapon: truth. In that sense, the power of the protest movement derives from its very weakness.

It could in fact be said that the government was not threatened but felt itself hit. Speech had no sooner been set free than it struck home. It is not the agitation and disturbances of early June that best explain the ravages of the protest movement. It is rather that the protesters were speaking the truth and that their masters were partly ready to listen to them. Yet there can be no doubt that what was being expressed in spring 1957 included several different sorts of things. At least two must be distinguished: one specific, the other challenging the very nature of the regime.

Specific Demands

Specific demands were less dangerous. Since they called only for precise reforms, they could be stated cautiously. There came first the protest by national and social minorities. "The autonomous organs exist only on paper", one regretted. Numerous others denounced the ill treatment meted out to Moslems and overseas Chinese.[53] "National capitalists" protested against the harassment they had been subjected to.[54] Unlike most of their kind from other more traditionally industrialised provinces, those in Henan, who were mostly rather small-scale operators, did not seek extension of the (generally very low) interest rates that the state granted them, but rather their elimination. They wanted to get rid of their capitalist "hat" so as to enjoy the same advantages as workers.[55]

Teachers and artists deplored the contempt the new rulers had for culture. There were particularly sharp criticisms in Luoyang where investment in schools had been cancelled to pay for prestige expenditure. Artists asked that the ban on traditional works be lifted, and more generally, that they be trusted.[56] As for teachers, their demands frequently took a rather self-interested turn. A primary school teacher from Luoyang complained about the inadequacy of equipment, for example, the lack of a fence and the fact that there were too few toilets; another criticised the danger posed to children by the proximity of a busy road. The professional training of young teachers was deemed inadequate, promotion guidelines were unclear, the housing that went with the job often proved to be dirty and cramped, parents were not cooperating closely enough with teachers, and so forth.[57] But there were also demands about management. School heads appointed more for their political affiliations than for their professional ability came in for criticism for their authoritarianism. Teachers asked to be left to teach as they saw fit and to be consulted in school management.

Criticisms by engineers and specialists proved to be more telling when they touched on what the regime was most proud of: its development strategy. Numerous speakers made status-related demands. Engineers and technicians were conscious of their material privileges and demanded to enjoy them with more security. One engineer complained of having been reassigned nine times between 1952 and 1957, and it was reported that the post office at Boai had changed manager ten times in three years. A specialist told how he had been deprived of his room overnight.[58] The sharpest criticisms were of the Party's incompetence: "The problem is not so much that the Party wants to run everything, but that it is incapable of doing so." The mania for secrecy was the object of ironic comments: Had the Soviets actually told us about their latest discoveries? Were their automobiles superior to U.S. ones? The development strategy inspired by Moscow prompted direct criticisms of state factory managers. Why such big factories when there were still so many mediocre workshops? Why, asked a highway engineer, were there so many fine stone works when so many dirt roads remained?[59]

A last series of specific demands was by definition political: those emanating from the leaders of the small democratic parties. They deplored the fact that the Communist Party kept them systematically on the sidelines. Too many cadres put down "democratic figures" with the words: "You are only a landlord's son, your ideology is not pure, your past is complicated, you have never worked actively for us". United Front departments were criticised for holding only formal meetings made up of individuals chosen for their docility. These puppets experienced some nasty moments in May and June. Hou Lianying, an old democrat who chaired the Revolutionary Guomindang provincial committee, was taken to task: "What have you done to defend us?" Some democrats went further and criticised not only the situation in the past but also the recent signs of liberalisation. "We do not ask for mutual control but equality; we do not ask for equality between party and party but equality between person and person."[60]

Criticism of the Regime

In fact, the issue of the Party—that is, of the political regime—was in everyone's mind. The 27 April circular made it possible to raise the question since it called for criticism of the three maladies afflicting the CCP: bureaucratism, sectarianism, and subjectivism. This last notion raised few comments in Henan, perhaps because in an era of de-Stalinisation it referred to theoretical debates internal to the sacred texts of Marxism and the socialist camp, which seemed both complex and dangerous. Subjectivism was often replaced by the concept of "dogmatism", which was easier to understand and less delicate to handle. It was under that heading that interventions by the authorities in artistic and literary matters were criticised.[61] But whether because writers and artists were not numerous or because such proposals rapidly won general assent, the liberals preferred to direct their most serious reproaches elsewhere.

The concept of sectarianism made it possible to formulate more cutting criticisms by pointing at a fundamental political reality: the monopolisation of power by the CCP. One of the complaints most often expressed was of "having a function but no power". "To become a boss, one must first join the Party. The Party card is like a shield—it makes everything possible." One bold spirit concluded: "The dictatorship of the proletariat is the dictatorship of the few, it is the dictatorship of a party, it is tyranny." There was nothing surprising in Communists scorning regular institutions or elections being organised only in form: "Most of the deputies that we elect in fact come from the top."[62] Reminding the regime of the law by which it claimed to rule, the protesters denounced violations of the law. They showed that sectarianism was not simply an internal defect of the Party, but the hallmark of its action on society.

In Leninist-Maoist dogma, the concept of bureaucratism was less clear and open to varying interpretations. It normally referred to the red tape that was such a feature of the Communist hierarchy. The assistant manager of a hospital in Luoyang told how the recruitment of a doctor, suggested by the hospital in May 1956, was at first accepted by the municipal government and then delayed by its personnel section before being finally indefinitely postponed in February 1957 as the authorities had meanwhile changed their minds.[63] Cadres were also criticised for being remote from the masses. Secondary school teachers complained of never having seen their Party secretary. No leader from Luoyang, which administered it, had yet taken the trouble to go down the mine at Longmen. One day one of them stopped at the mine office for a glass of tea, and then went on, and telephoned from his office in Luoyang to ask for a full report from the officials that he had just left.[64]

The privileges that cadres enjoyed made their shortcomings more scandalous: "For some years, on the pretext of fighting egalitarianism, Communists have improved their own standard of living." The "personnel sections", which proposed appointments and decided on allowances in each unit, were the object of especial hostility. "They were", said one engineer, "effectively secret services."[65] The regime's propaganda about its own rectification campaigns fooled no one. It was known that for Communist cadres these were excellent opportunities to get rid of democrats, and for activists, to make their way in the apparatus. In short, although the arguments of the opposition intellectuals in Beijing like Lin Xiling seem not to have been widely disseminated in Henan, some bold spirits did not miss the chance to point out a parallel between principles and reality: "While claiming to make a tabula rasa of the past, the Party has made itself into a ruling class, a new aristocracy."[66]

Against Oppression and Poverty

Criticism extended to the social effects of Party rule. In the eyes of most rightists, the people were in a situation of oppression and poverty. There is nothing surprising about these critics aiming their most pointed darts at infringements of individual freedom; for they had themselves for some years been especially victimised in this regard. Several rightists, such as Li Qing, loudly demanded justice. Denunciation of the abuses committed during the Sufan was one of the most common themes. Cases of brutality and arbitrary arrest were quoted, such as that of a teacher locked up for a year before being freed without apologies or compensation. Some speakers did not hesitate to compare the Sufan to the ravages of the Emperor Qin Shi Huang Di, or to speak of "Beriaism" and even "Asiatic barbarism".[67] There was also criticism of the regime's other repressive campaigns, not simply disputing the sometimes mindless violence, but also the regime's very raison d'être: "Capitalists are human just like Communists and workers. How is it then that after seven years of so-called reform they are still no more than rotten eggs?" Even the instruments of repression, the army and the "labour reform camps", were attacked. Li Qing, who was always found amongst the boldest, concluded: "The Guomindang style is being reborn inside the Communist Party."[68]

It was less easy for the democrats to venture onto the strictly social ground. Some, prisoners of their origins and their privileges, visibly found it difficult to broaden their view to the masses. Others doubtless feared that they would later be criticised for having abandoned their professional area to get involved in political agitation. All this explains why although criticisms of a political and social nature were numerous, there were fewer that touched on the material situation of the people. These generally emanated from the most highly placed liberals in the hierarchy, who were better informed and more self-assured. They deplored the difficulties of urban living. Above all they painted a dire picture of the situation in the countryside. Liu Jixue, who had studied in Japan at the beginning of the century, taken part in the 1911 revolution, and then worked for the Guomindang in Henan before being made vice-chairman of the provincial committee of the Chinese People's Political Consultative Conference, had this to say: "In the old society, it can be said that the poor depended on the rich and the rich depended on heaven; now, with the unified purchase and supply system, wherever peasants go to find a pittance they return empty-handed."[69]

Rural poverty was unanimously attributed more to mistakes by the Party than to natural disasters. The Party's two great innovations were criticised: the unified purchase and supply system and the cooperatives, which, it was said, "were not socialist property but the property of the Party". The rural crisis was not overlooked. "In my village", said Zhang Yunchuan, "80 percent of peasants are discontented with the Communist Party."[70]

Why?

The rightists were not content to denounce the regime's mistakes. They also reflected about the causes, advancing two broad categories of explanations. The first was inspired by official propaganda: The line was right but the Party was not perfect. The early days of the regime, between 1949 and 1951, were recalled nostalgically as a time when Party members were modest and polite. Since then they had greatly changed. Excessively brutal mass campaigns and the monopolisation of power had spoiled the Party's relations with the population. Some adroitly quoted some recent saying of Mao Zedong's to suggest that the situation would improve once the CCP agreed to share a few shreds of power. According to this line of explanation, the Party's imperfections and mistakes were often attributed to some of its leaders. Late May saw the appearance of attacks on senior provincial cadres, especially in the area of propaganda and art. There were even criticisms of the central leaders. In case the references to Qin Shi Huang Di were not sufficiently clear, Mao Zedong was several times accused by name. Denouncing the cult of personality, a Luoyang Young Communist cadre declared: "If someone other than Mao had spoken of contradictions among the people, no one would have agreed." A technician in Pingdingshan blamed the chairman for the failure of the cooperativisation movement, and an agronomist added: "Chairman Mao's policy is not clever, it is dangerous." A cadre derided the growing cult of the chairman: "I think that if one shouts 'Long live Chairman Mao' one might just as well shout 'Long live Chiang Kai-shek.'" Other leaders were also lambasted by speakers.[71]

Not all liberals were satisfied with such limited explanations. Some proposed alternatives that involved more radical thinking. Questions were raised about the effects of the alliance with the Soviet Union. Should not the economic mistakes of the regime be attributed partly to Moscow's influence and excessive contempt for the West? In Henan as in the rest of China, many intellectuals felt barely disguised sympathy for the Hungarian uprising and hoped either that something similar might happen in China or that the Soviets would be forced to loosen their pressure on Beijing and the Maoist government to relax its pressure on the population. The Western camp was much more popular among rightists than the Soviet bloc. Several of them were accused of having listened to Voice of America broadcasts.[72]

But the USSR was on the whole little mentioned. Of the thirty-one second-rank rightists discussed earlier, only five were accused of anti-Sovietism. Whether from lack of information or as a matter of prudence, the liberals in Henan rarely referred to international events and even then did so almost exclusively only when China was involved (the war in Korea but not the war in Vietnam; the conflict over Taiwan but not the Suez crisis, despite the intense propaganda unleashed by the mass media in 1956; etc.). Even if they had no great affection for the USSR, the liberals in Henan were not much interested in the parallels between the Chinese regime and its Soviet model. They much preferred to compare the regime with its predecessors. For this was the most painful disappointment— that despite its ambition and despite its initial impulse, the Communist Party had not made a fundamental break with the past, but retained and reproduced some of the defects of the Guomindang regime, and more important, of the imperial regime, in that it was a tyrannical and unjust regime that functioned to the benefit of a parasitical social stratum. "I feel", said the engineer Chen Jishan, "that the liberation of China by the Communist Party was never anything more than a change of dynasty, the replacement of one ruling clique by another."[73]

A Nebulous Liberalism

In Henan, criticism of the foundations of the Communist regime was thus not initially inspired by nationalism and traditionalism, as was the case in some East European countries; rather, the regime was criticised precisely for not making a clearer break with the past. It is therefore not surprising that propaganda subsequently accused the rightists of having adopted "bourgeois" and "liberal" ideas from the West.

And it is indeed true that the one notion that appears to have united all protesters in spring 1957 was that of liberty in its most classic, even most "bourgeois", sense of individual freedom. Around this central reference point, other aims more or less explicitly articulated were also part of the classical panoply of liberalism: respect for the physical and moral integrity of the individual, participation of the majority in decisionmaking, access for all to information, and so forth. In that sense, the spring 1957 movement can be legitimately defined as a liberal and Westernising movement. The reference, common at the time, to the 4 May 1919 movement, is rich in meaning. Once again, the protesting Chinese elite was seeking the conceptual tools for a revolt in Western ideological models. The difference is that this time Marxism was no longer amongst the borrowings, but in its Sinicised form, the chief target of liberal attacks.

There, at one level, is what holds the 1957 protests together. Analyses that divide the protesters into two broad tendencies, one "democratic" and the other "radical", seem rash in the case of Beijing and false in the case of Henan.[74] Protest in Henan was never more radical than demanding freedom and democracy. The liberals were divided not on political or ideological lines but rather on their greater or lesser directness or vigour in expressing fundamentally similar aspirations. Once it is accepted that the boldest protesters were recruited from the universities, it is impossible to find systematic explanations for the greater or lesser vigour of this group or that group. Age, social background, and membership of one of the democratic parties appear not to be reliable indicators. Many young people, particularly students and apprentices, were very daring—but a large minority remained passive or faithful to the regime. Conversely, teachers like Li Baifeng, administrators like Luo Shengwu, senior officials like Li Baohe, and leaders of democratic parties like Liu Jixue, all over fifty, showed remarkable courage. Every professional milieu affected by the movement had its share of the bold and the time-servers. As will be seen, the movement struck a chord among the Communist youth and even within the Communist Party. Amongst non-Communists, it is impossible to determine with certainty the influence of political alignment, if indeed the expression is justified. I have been unable to distinguish notable differences in attitude between members of the various democratic parties. The most important ones, the Democratic League and the Guomindang Revolutionary Committee, are equally represented in the rightist samples.[75] In fact, each individual's attitude seems to have been determined less by any objective factor than by personal convictions and temperament.

There is a simple reason for this situation. The rectification campaign was launched late amidst disagreement and reservations, and it never completely eliminated protesters' uncertainty about the future or their consciousness of the risks they were running. If the movement had been launched earlier or more vigorously, and if it had gone on for some time, it would probably have become more structured and perhaps divided. But it did not have the time. Forty days have never in any place been enough to give an ideological and political structure to a revolutionary movement.

In the same way, the fragility and short life of the spring 1957 protest make any definition of the movement superficial and oversimplifying—a fortiori a liberal definition. Such a definition does not take into account the variety of the protests. Other references were made by the protesters, often contradictorily: the demand for social justice and the demand for respect for expertise; the call for human rights, and at the same time, for the most narrow corporatism. Often, too, no precise reference guided criticism inspired by simple common sense. Amongst most protesters, ideology was fluid and contradictory. The regime described it as "bourgeois and liberal" only the better to repress it, and in so doing attributed to all participants ideas that were clear only in a few and systematised by none. In fact, the numerous and active elements of liberalism present in the movement did not have the time to coalesce. The ideology of the protest remained somewhat hazy, ready for any shift and even its own disappearance. Its liberalism was defined less by "isms" than by aspirations too simple to be translated accurately into any ready-made format: a desire to catch one's breath, live less wretchedly, and the like.

The Ravages of Truth

This nebulous liberalism was to be dissipated before it had the chance to coalesce, and yet, over the span of a few weeks, its mere appearance precipitated ravages. To describe the medium-term effects of the failure of the Hundred Flowers falls outside my scope here. I will simply recall two commonsense hypotheses generally accepted for China as a whole that seem relevant to the case of Henan. The first is that the outcome of the rectification campaign marked the definitive separation between the CCP and the non-Communist elite that had been collaborating with the regime. The second is that since the spirit had on this occasion settled in the opposition, the permanent obsession of the Maoist regime became to muzzle it.

More interesting for my purposes are the two immediate consequences of the rectification campaign. First, the speeches by liberals, disseminated by the official press itself, sounded a chord among the people that cannot yet be measured precisely. The Maoist regime's need to dominate is not enough to explain why it was felt necessary, for many many months, not only to repress the rightists but also to refute their assertions point by point. One concludes that in wide swathes of the population people were saying: They are right.

The Party's obstinate efforts to convince also indicate that not everyone within it was convinced of the correctness of the official line. As often in the Chinese political system, a campaign of criticism and repression in fact masked uncertainties, divisions, and finally a purge within the Party. The Henan apparatus was divided over the protests by the liberals, and that was the principal short-term effect of the rectification campaign.

The fact is that although the majority of lower-level cadres were above all uneasy about the rectification campaign, as they also were about the relaxation of social policy, a sizeable fraction of them were whole-heartedly with the liberals. A small number of heads of Propaganda departments, whether from opportunism or conviction, supported the movement in ways later judged culpable.[76] Two other categories of cadres sympathised openly with the protesters. The first comprised rightists who were Party members. Engineers, journalists, and teachers, although members of the CCP, opted to take up the grievances of their colleagues against some of their comrades. A typical case is that of Luan Xing, since 1954 the head of the "group charged with setting up" the provincial Writers' Union. He had already come under fire for repeatedly defending Su Jinsan and the "ancients" against the "moderns", that is, the young amateur writers. As early as 18 May he flatly declared: "People should not be shut up!" Also in this category are relatives of leading democratic lights, such as Zhang Shumin, nephew of Zhang Yunchuan. Biographical analysis shows that these were liberals who joined the Party out of nationalism, but had stormy relations with their Communist comrades. Thus Luan Xing joined the CCP in 1938 and left twice before being readmitted in 1945. The engineer Deng Zhailin, who first joined in 1928, had come and gone three times by 1950. As for Zhang Shumin, he entered the Party in 1930, left in 1941, and was readmitted in 1949.[77]

Communist propaganda presented all these liberal Communists as "die-hard renegades", traitors to their class as well as traitors to the Party. But were they so isolated? It is interesting to note that a good number of non-Communist notables were also former Party members or fellow-travellers. Of the eleven most criticised rightists in the province, at least four had at one time or another between 1936 and 1949 worked closely with the CCP.[78] This makes it easier to understand why protesters were able to influence their former companions. Perhaps there even existed in Henan (and elsewhere?), on the fringes of the Communist Party and the small democratic parties, a small but active and sensitive community of more or less progressive liberals whom history and their own convictions had kept close to the Party without their ever feeling at ease there. This community broke with the regime in spring 1957 and was later to be one of those hardest hit by the repression.

A second category of cadres whole-heartedly supported the rightists on a single point only: rural policy. Their profile was different. In origins and careers they were not liberal intellectuals, but often cadres from rural areas who had risen from the bottom. Their prototype was Zhang Qingheng, who in 1956–1957, headed the state farms unit in the Rural Work Department of the provincial committee of the Party. Zhang was the son of peasants in Shanxi. He joined the CCP in 1943 and gained some secondary education before joining the guerilla movement in 1946–1948 in Wenxian county. Head of the secretariat and then assistant secretary of the Party committee in that county, he attracted attention by his marriage to the daughter of rich peasants and by his independence of character. After being transferred to the same post in the neighbouring county of Boai in 1951, he is said to have opposed the establishment of the unified purchase and supply system and the spread of cooperatives. Promoted to Zhengzhou, in spring 1957 he launched violent attacks on the Party's rural policy: "Every problem has come from the cooperatives. . . . The Communist Party favours the workers, it harms the peasants." The case of Zhang Qingheng is not unique. The criticisms that he expressed were widespread amongst the peasantry and were made by other cadres in the cities.[79] Persons like Zhang Qingheng were particularly dangerous because they had the capacity to form a link within the Party between the protests of the liberal intellectuals and the discontent of the rural population.

More generally, to an extent that is hard to measure, the whole Communist apparatus in Henan seems to have been contaminated by rightist ideas. There was not a demand or a complaint that was formulated solely by non-Communists. Some of the boldest protests came from low-level cadres. One can of course be virtually certain that the bold figures were a tiny minority. But what of those who hesitated and those who simply wanted to treat the people better? They seem to have been far more numerous. It seems as if the Communist apparatus was the target of a general but very uneven ideological impregnation.

It is true that the example came from the top. The provincial committee was split over both the rectification campaign and rural policy. Pan Fusheng, an advocate since 1953 of a cautious line in the countryside, was profoundly worried about the situation in the villages. He attributed responsibility for the incidents occurring there to the cooperatives' having "transformed people into beasts of burden". He advocated a relaxation of policy: "If peasants leave their cooperatives, that does not mean that they are abandoning the socialist path." At the end of May Pan took advantage of the relaxation of the general line and his political victory over Wu Zhipu to relax rural policy yet further. Although he did not succeed in getting the "seven ways of leaving a cooperative" made official policy, he intervened in a number of difficult cases, notably in Gaoxian and Linru, overruling local cadres who were preventing withdrawals.[80] It was on rural issues that Pan Fusheng and his supporters came closest to the protesters, both democrats and Communists.

Whatever its geographical, social, and political limits—all of which were evidenced by its brevity—the liberal protest in spring 1957 seriously affected the Communist regime in Henan and elsewhere. The loss of former fellow-travellers, a matter of great importance in the long term, could easily be made up for in the short term through a renewal of propaganda and repression. More dangerous was the aggravation of internal divisions within the Party. Even as the people in the streets were speaking of human rights, freedom, and democracy and the people at the top were preparing to shut everything down, a handful of officials in the corridors of the provincial committee were quarrelling over a few shreds of power.

4
Contradiction Within the Party (9 June–Late July 1957)

The halt called on 9 June 1957 and the launching of an antirightist campaign thus did not put an end to the political crisis. With all danger of subversion removed, the crisis simply moved inside the Party. In Henan, during June and July, the initially hesitant conduct of the antirightist struggle and the debates over rural policy evidence the intensification of disagreements among provincial leaders. After being struck in the heart, the Party was now being hit in the head.

In the political sphere, the provincial leadership had little room to manoeuvre. The furious editorials in the *People's Daily* left scant openings for interpretation, but provincial leaders seem to have done all they could, at least in the beginning, to halt the onset of a brutal campaign of repression.

Initial Moderation

In Henan the antirightist movement remained moderate until late June. Instead of the impetuous onslaught sought by the centre, there was a sort of steady fire that left the enemy time to retreat. Naturally, Zhengzhou did not miss chances to show Beijing its loyalty. After the issue of 8 June the leading editorials in the *People's Daily* were faithfully reprinted on the front page of the local press. In the main cities of Henan, as all over China, vast public meetings vented the great fury of proletarians against the rightists.[1] Since some guilty parties had to be produced, the names of a few highly placed democrats who had abused the trust placed in them by the regime and led their colleagues into temptation were revealed: Liu Jixue, Wang Yizhai, Li Qingzhi, and Guo Zhongwei. Like Christians to the lions, they were thrown to a group of long-fanged activists, who were mostly obscure cadres of the small democratic parties, not officially members of the CCP—people with every interest, one might think, in denouncing other guilty parties.[2] The threat was enough to send to ground the majority of those who had let slip some unfortunate phrase against the Party.

Yet, despite these bracing measures for public consumption, the antirightist campaign was as tightly controlled and bridled as the rectification movement had been when it began. Between 9 and 20 June, the *People's Daily* published three editorials, but the *Henan Daily* only one, and that a very moderate one, as the headline indicates: "Let us continue to bloom and contend, let us launch a debate". According to this editorial, the majority of views expressed in the course of the *zhengfeng* were right, but a small number of rightists had taken advantage of the campaign to denigrate and attack the CCP and socialism; the best way of countering them was to launch a great "open debate", as "the Hundred Flowers and hundred schools campaign adopted by the Party was an absolutely unchanging long-term policy".[3]

Of course, everybody knew that these assertions were a lie. It was perfectly well known that in Beijing there had been a decisive shift, and freedom of speech was dead and gone. Only a few illuminati, who in any case no longer had anything to lose, pretended to take such statements at face value. Their incongruous interventions provoked an uneasy silence and fuelled squalid settlings of scores.[4] However, the authorities showed obvious moderation. For a while longer, the provincial administration continued the moral campaign embarked on at the beginning of the month.[5] On 14 June a system of replying to letters and requests for action was officially instituted within the provincial government. The newspapers reported that Wu Zhipu and Zhao Wenfu regretted their bureaucratic behaviour in that area. A directive gave assurances that in future official bicycles would no longer be given to anyone below the thirteenth grade. Radios, furniture, and china improperly appropriated by cadres were restored to departments. At the Kaifeng Teacher Training School, it was announced towards the end of the month that teachers would in future be consulted over the assignment of graduates and even that an inquiry would be made into some of the abuses committed during the Sufan. Unable to debate the matter openly, the regime acted as if it could knock down the "wall" that separated it from the people by reforming itself concretely.

It could still be hoped that the inevitable repression would remain selective. Despite the newspaper headlines and the anger displayed by officials, political activity decreased and the police remained discreet. The discussion forums and protest rallies of early June gave way to a few big mass rallies with spectacular but well-worn ritual and the everyday business of committees. The get-togethers of the small democratic parties resounded to a new drum: Let us discuss, yes, let us discuss freely, but without attacking the Communist Party, and even better, so as to fight its enemies. It was a time for pacifying interventions by a few insignificant old progressives, such as the inevitable Hou Lianying.[6] To win clemency from the authorities the few named rightists hastily back-pedalled: Truly, they had not sought to criticise socialism, they had been misunderstood, please grant pardon.[7] Even the universities, where everybody now kept mum, were not yet visited by the police.

There is no denying that the antirightist campaign in Henan remained moderate until late June. The reason probably lies in the attitude of Pan Fusheng. He was surprised and upset by the central authorities' about-turn, of which he had quite clearly not been informed beforehand. He may well also have hoped that after risking their prestige in favour of liberalisation, the leaders in Beijing would prevent the antirightist campaign from going too far, and therefore held back the local movement as much as possible. "If the rightists have attacked us, it is because of our mistakes", he declared. Continuing to consider that most of them represented a "nonantagonistic contradiction", he tried to prevent their names being mentioned, their personal history published, or the methods of previous campaigns of repression being used against them.[8] Whereas before 9 June Pan Fusheng had been seen and heard everywhere, after that date he withdrew into a discontented silence.

The Attack on the Rightists

Pan soon had to admit his hopes had been misplaced. At the end of June the statements of the two central leaders who had initiated the Hundred Flowers policy, Mao Zedong and Zhou Enlai, dissipated any lingering illusions and heralded a full-scale hunting down of rightists. The publication on 19 June of the official, that is, completely revised, version of Mao's speech of the previous 27 February on contradictions among the people made the chairman's about-turn quite clear. There were still "antagonistic contradictions", and there was nothing even to prevent them from becoming, through a subtle shift in the arguments, the "principal aspect", since contrary to what some ill-intentioned individuals may have thought, the class struggle was not ended with China's entry into the era of socialism.[9] In short, as repression set in, it became impossible to hope to have recourse to the thought or even the clemency of the Great Leader. Moreover, the provincial committee set to work at once. On 22 June, a directive was issued to distribute the speech right down to the basic levels. On 25 June an editorial in the *Henan Daily* defended the "activists" against the calumnies directed at them. The editorial of 26 June marked an important new twist in the hostilities with the accusation against Liu Jixue of being opposed not only to the socialist revolution but also to democratic reforms. The rightists now constituted an antagonistic contradiction and had become class enemies. The publication by the *Henan Daily* on 27 June of the government report by Zhou Enlai to the National People's Congress spelled out the broad objectives of the campaign and detailed the arguments of the ideological counterattack. The repression was set squarely at the centre of the government's tasks. There remained no room for doubt. The Security departments were to be put to work. The *Henan Daily* of 29 June sounded the call: "Let us uncover and crush the rightist plot!"

From then on the guilty were pitilessly hunted down. Naturally, care was taken to ensure that everyone played the same tune. Propaganda recited the crimes of the rightists using well-worn themes and explained to the righteous the horrors threatening them. The implications and reasonings were drawn out with much fanfare. On 3 July an editorial in the *Henan Daily* asked: "Where are the intellectuals headed?" The issue of 14 July called for a "reasoned struggle".[10] Once launched, the repression was no different from earlier campaigns. The police raided the homes of suspects and seized their personal documents. Ma Changfeng's personal diary was put out for public entertainment. The press revealed the correspondence between Zhang Yunchuan and his relative Zhang Shumin. One may imagine how some denunciations, such as that of Guo Zhongwei by his own son, were obtained.[11] The violence of criticism meetings comes through in the press. Meetings would last all day and be repeated until satisfactory confessions were obtained. Li Qing and Ma Changfeng had to make at least four self-criticisms.

The method used by the prosecution was two-pronged. On the one hand, recordings and minutes of meetings in May and June were used to turn against the suspects everything they may have said at the time, abbreviating or altering quotations where necessary. In this way, in haphazard bits and pieces, the discussion meetings and disturbances of the spring were rerun. Moreover, private conversations did just as well. Second, each individual's past was gone over with a fine-toothed comb. The intention was to find something to show that the suspect was socially and psychologically destined to betray, and if possible, that this was not the first occasion. A torrent of denunciations fell on individuals hitherto held in respect. Sometimes well-known events were recalled. In 1948 had not Zhang Zhen, for example, used murderous operations to delay the advance of the Communist troops? Some revelations threw a new (but not necessarily accurate) light on little-known episodes of provincial history. Thus it was learned that in spring 1938 Guo Zhongwei, then administering northern Henan for the Guomindang, had bloodily put down an anti-Japanese guerilla unit led by a county head who was a member of the Communist Party; the Liehe incident (in Xiuwu) had led to the death of 110 partisans.

But the great mass of revelations were simply tidbits concerning minor faults. Was the behaviour of Luo Shengwu's wife in hurriedly selling her land just before the agrarian reform so outrageous? And did it take much away from her husband's merits? In a country where "talking like an Eighth Army trooper" is synonymous with talking crudely, who would feel that Liu Jixue had committed a crime by making fun of the military behaviour of a provincial committee secretary? Were not Wang Yizhai's good words for the homeless peasants of summer 1956 in accordance with the line as it then was? Were the authorities really unaware when they took one old democrat back into service that he had retained his five concubines after 1949?[12] The list of these dubious revelations could be longer; at the time they were enough to justify findings of guilt, ruin reputations, and destroy lives.

The accusations were not only minor or disputable but also often contradictory. Almost all ignored a prior and yet decisive question: How was it that a person now accused, whose past was well known and whose opinions were predictable, was not denounced before 1957? Had not Zhang Zhen and Guo Zhongwei already been pardoned for their massacres? Rather than openly admit—and also confess—its shifts and its cynicism, the regime preferred to distort history.

There was a serious reason for these contradictions. Like previous campaigns of repression, this one was not solely aimed at crushing its victims. It was also designed to teach a political lesson. The virulent outbursts published in the press served to pinpoint any interventions by people in each unit, who had to say something to escape falling under suspicion themselves. Every campaign of repression in China also serves a function of integration.

The same desire to teach a political lesson explains the multiplication of targets and the intensity of the propaganda that the regime disseminated about itself. After an initial period devoted to attacking the most dangerous rightists in the province, the small fry were targeted. During July, every unit had to dig up at least one rightist. In that way, the movement penetrated every sector of the administration and urban society. All were given the chance to demonstrate their loyalty to the regime and unmask this or that wrong-thinking colleague—and thus put themselves in the clear. In addition, from the beginning of the month, without losing its repressive function, the antirightist campaign was gradually transformed into a propaganda movement. The defeat and humiliation of the liberals was no longer a problem. Although some, such as Zhang Yunchuan, refused to say the most patent untruths, most had no choice but to give in, sometimes even to turn on each other publicly, like Li Qing and Ma Changfeng.[13] Henceforth, the principal target could be modified. It was no longer the rightists—who now were or would soon be under lock and key—but their influence, their ideas, that were to be extirpated. Propaganda trumpeted the regime's successes: economic construction, the Sufan, the purchase and supply system, the Sino-Soviet alliance, the political regime itself. After the central newspapers and then the *Henan Daily* had struck the first chord, the local papers took up the tune and published lists of figures and graphs designed to dazzle ordinary people.[14]

The net result of these frenetic accusations and resounding editorials is that the authorities returned to a very conventional discourse. This discourse rested on rocklike distinctions between socialism and capitalism, the principal and the secondary, successes and failures. It was articulated around a simple thesis: In the building of socialism in China, successes constituted the principal aspect and failures the secondary one. Only partisans of a return to capitalism could cast doubt on this truth, even in relation to problems previously defined as technical.

In short, there was a return to a lifeless language, foreshadowing a return to a lifeless politics.

The Rightward Shift of Rural Policy

What is interesting is that during the same weeks of summer 1957 the provincial committee's rural policy was moving in quite a different direction. The committee adopted new and very important liberalising measures. This development can be explained by three factors. First, in the centre itself, the launching of the anti-rightist campaign had not led to the adoption of a new general line. Aside from the judgement the regime was now making of rightists (and hence of itself), its attitude had not in principle varied on any of the great economic issues of the day. As Zhou Enlai's report to the National People's Congress clearly shows, the centre's rural policy continued to be moderate. The field was thus left open to Pan Fusheng who—and this is the second factor—had already adopted a very clear position in this area and made a number of promises. Pan Fusheng was a stubborn man, and feeling perhaps that Beijing would not run the risk of totally reversing itself, he speeded up the implementation of his rural policy.

Pan was encouraged—and this is the third and most important factor—by the situation in the countryside, which despite the beginnings of a recovery was not good. The drought had hindered the sowing and later the ripening of the wheat. By harvest time, 165,000 hectares had been affected by a locust invasion. A slackening of supervision, combined with the lack of discipline of many peasants, hindered the summer grain harvest, which totalled some 4.5 million metric tons instead of the 4.75 million called for in the annual plan. Wheat production in particular was no more than 3.75 million metric tons, a fall of 500,000 metric tons from the 1956 harvest and a return to the production level of 1954. The situation varied from one locality to another. In counties that had experienced major disasters in 1956, the harvest generally improved. Xinyang special region recorded a rise of 40 percent in wheat production, for example. But the situation was markedly worse elsewhere.[15]

One must not exaggerate, however. Taking into account the disasters of 1956, the low morale in the villages, and frequent deliberate underestimates, the summer harvest almost certainly represented a slight improvement, especially as the growth of the private sector, notably in livestock and secondary crops, brought the peasants extra cash income. Nevertheless, the stagnation in cereal production gave cause for concern and confirmed the opinion frequently expressed by the rightists that the problems of agriculture were not all due to natural disasters. If the bad run was continuing without any major climatic disasters, surely the problems had something to do with structural factors. Pan Fusheng himself did not absolve the cooperatives of all blame. People were also beginning to wonder whether food production could in future keep up with the rise in population. This concern, clearly expressed in Beijing during the rectification campaign, was touched on several times in the *Henan Daily*.[16]

In any case, the provincial government expected summer floods, and to avoid a repetition of what had happened the previous year, preparations were made. Announcing on 25 June 1957 the possibility that shortages could recur, the government outlined energetic measures. Cadres were to be ready to order fields resown, encourage secondary activities, lighten or postpone the collection of taxes, increase loans to cooperatives and households in difficulties, protect cattle, encourage all possible forms of saving, and finally, take the necessary relief measures to avoid peasants abandoning their villages.[17]

Above all, on the same day—which proves that the rural policy did indeed flow from one and the same concern—the provincial committee made public longer-range decisions with a much more political import (although in fact the document merely brought together and made official measures already implemented in some localities). "Important Points to Propagate to Encourage the Development of Agricultural Production and Secure an Excellent Autumn Harvest" promised a series of rewards, including exemption from taxes, to collectivities and individuals who notably increased production through improvements in infrastructure, land clearing, and increases in livestock. Cooperatives would in future only be required to observe the state plan for the main crops (wheat, cotton, oilseed, and tobacco). Private plots could now officially take up to 5 percent of the area and free markets would be set up everywhere. Cooperatives would be allowed to split, and in certain specified conditions, withdrawals from cooperatives would even be permitted. This vigorous and precise document set down solid bases for a rural policy based on both state planning and material incentives. A powerful propaganda campaign was commenced to disseminate the policy, and recalcitrant cadres were to be punished. A circular dated 6 July, followed by two meetings of county leaders, reacting to the silence of the local apparatus, insisted that the peasant masses be directly informed of the new measures and that all local newspapers publish them.

The floods of July 1957 initially caused panic among provincial leaders.[18] Fearing the worst, they made dramatic appeals for discipline and above all to the peasants' self-interest. For their part, the authorities set an example of behaviour that was more energetic and also closer to the masses than had been the case the previous year. A large number of leading officials at all levels personally led the campaign against the waters. In the end, the flooding affected only 1.8 million hectares in the Yellow River basin—hardly even a disaster. Nevertheless, the episode confirmed worrying weaknesses, including the inadequacy of many of the irrigation works built in 1956 and not subsequently maintained (notably on small water courses), the panic and lack of authority of some basic-level cadres, and finally the slowness and carelessness of rescue operations and the draining of the water. For provincial leaders of both stripes all this provided ample food for thought. Some readied themselves to argue that basic-level cadres and the peasantry needed to be taken in hand, but others saw in the failings a further reason to push on with their rural liberalisation policy.

The Political Contradiction

At the end of July 1957 Pan Fusheng found himself in a very uncomfortable situation. Forced to wage an antirightist struggle in the cities that was bound to undermine his prestige, he was also running into difficulties in imposing his rural liberalisation programme. These difficulties arose in large part from the ideological and political contradiction that was now out in the open. Socialism was reaffirmed in the cities but played down in the countryside. In one area the government was moving forwards, in the other back. How could the population be made to understand that private interest was sometimes a good thing and sometimes a bad one? The "general line" was too obviously a temporary amalgam of contradictions for the basic-level cadres to feel obliged to strict obedience. They had always been suspicious of measures being relaxed in the countryside, fearing reductions in their power. They could feel encouraged in their recalcitrance by the opposition of Wu Zhipu, temporarily put out of the game, but now beginning to look like a possible saviour.

The cadres' dislike and obstruction are confirmed in the provincial press.[19] At least one case of open opposition to Pan Fusheng on the part of a local apparatus is known. On 9 July, the Party committee of Yingyang, a county near Kaifeng, adopted a bold directive. Noting that the attacks by rightists had been sympathetically received among landlords, rich peasants, and even some cadres, the committee launched an ideological and political counterattack against the class enemies. The threat, for Pan Fusheng, was clear. Not only were the leaders of this rural county taking a stand firmly in favour of the antirightist movement, but more important, they were seeking to extend the movement to the countryside and thus resolve the contradiction that lay at the heart of the official line by a shift to the left in rural policy. The threat was all the more serious because the audacity of the leaders in Yingyang implied that they had powerful support. Pan Fusheng reacted ruthlessly. He caused the Yingyang committee's decision to be annulled by the authorities in Kaifeng special region. A directive from the provincial committee dated 13 July strictly banned extending the antirightist campaign to bodies below the county level, on the one hand because the key task now was to secure a good autumn harvest, and on the other because "the question of the support of the great mass of peasants for the socialist path was essentially settled".[20]

The difficulties encountered by Pan Fusheng in implementing his rural policy thus flowed from the contradiction between this policy and the antirightist campaign as well as from the existence of opposition at various levels of the provincial Party apparatus. The Party was emerging from the rectification campaign divided and hesitant. In seeking to suppress the break with the non-Communists, the Party had only succeeded in aggravating the contradictions amongst the people and then within itself. In the provincial apparatus there were two tendencies more sharply opposed than at any time since 1952. One faction, which in principle held power but in fact was already partly a minority, aimed to restore the rural economy by first reestablishing confidence through liberalising measures. The other faction, sidelined in spring but already partly rehabilitated as a result of the evolution of the central line, advocated relaunching the class struggle, that is, measures to mobilise people and restore discipline. The ongoing social crisis together with the urgency of the economic tasks to be done required prompt action to settle these disagreements.

PART THREE

The Emergence of
Henan Radicalism
(August 1957–September 1958)

So far, even during the first leap, Henan had never been a national model in either economic achievements or political activity. Furthermore, in mid-1957 the province fell deep into economic, social, and political crisis. Yet by the following December, the national press cited Henan as one of a small group of provinces in the forefront of the Great Leap Forward. And in summer 1958, Henan, with the earliest people's communes, was to be held up as a model to the whole country. During the whole period of the launching of the Great Leap Forward, the province's leaders spared no effort to do more and do it faster than elsewhere; it is in that sense that there are grounds for talking of Henan radicalism.

How explain the emergence of this provincial radicalism? Political factors—and more precisely the combination of central impetus and provincial ambitions—were decisive. In a first stage, the change in the political atmosphere in Beijing led to Pan Fusheng's being once again pushed aside and enabled his successor to carry through successfully an operation to reassert effective political and police control of the province (August–September 1957). In a second stage, the centre's definition of a new general line and an extraordinarily ambitious development strategy (October–December 1957) provided Wu Zhipu with the opportunity to risk both his career and the economy of his province in the adventure of the Great Leap Forward.

5

Reassertion of Control
(August–September 1957)

In the history of the People's Republic of China, what is the function of the little-understood months of August and September 1957? Was this, as is often spontaneously believed, a dynamic period of transition leading necessarily from the antirightist campaign to the launching of the Great Leap Forward? A study of events in Henan does not entirely bear out such an impression. The denouement of the provincial political crisis in favour of Wu Zhipu enabled the Party to reassert control of Henan and thus to launch a new mobilisation campaign, but it did not carry the seed of what was to be the policy of the Great Leap Forward.

Wu Zhipu's victory over Pan Fusheng made it possible to settle the political crisis in the province. The purge of Pan was effected in three stages. Politically defeated in August 1957, he was obliged to leave Henan in November 1957 and was officially deprived of all his posts in May–June 1958. With hindsight, the first of these three stages stands out as the most important one, and thus it was in August 1957 that Wu Zhipu secured the upper hand.

The Trap

Pan Fusheng was caught in the same trap he himself set a few months earlier, in May, for Wu Zhipu. Pan had bet his own future on the continuation of the centre's rightist policy and had to yield when that policy was abandoned at the end of the Qingdao central work conference.[1] This meeting was held towards the end of July 1957. It was probably intended to inform provincial leaders of the political compromise that the former advocates and opponents of the Hundred Flowers policy had just agreed on in Beijing. As is shown by a note from Mao Zedong distributed to those present, this compromise was favourable to the hard line. The chairman was not content to recognise only abstractly that the contradictions between "bourgeois rightists" and "the people" had become antagonistic and that the socialist transformation of the economy would have to be completed by a relaunching of the class struggle in the ideological and political spheres. He also approved the police repression, and more important, announced the launching of the Socialist Education Movement, principally aimed at the countryside.[2]

According to later reports, Pan Fusheng was surprised and unhappy with this U-turn by the apostle of the Hundred Flowers. Forced to protect himself, at Qingdao he did not make the triumphal report that he had prepared on his agrarian policy, but limited himself to a few noncommittal and ambivalent sentences. On his return to Henan he vented his anger in private: "Long live Mao! Queue up to eat stone bread". Then, before his peers, he endeavoured to water down the scope of the decisions reached at Qingdao, asserting in particular that the "points to propagate" were not called into question.[3] At a meeting of the secretaries of four counties designated to try out the Socialist Education Movement in the countryside, held from 31 July to 2 August, Pan accused his interlocutors of not implementing the clause about freedom to withdraw from cooperatives. It is true that he could no longer prevent the hardening of the general line. The conclusion reached at the meeting was "that it is highly necessary to launch a vast socialist education movement in the countryside and to carry out amongst county, district, and township cadres a movement to correct style and rectify the Party". But the communiqué still bore Pan's imprint in criticising rural cadres guilty of "commandism" who "confused contradictions amongst the people with antagonistic contradictions".[4]

Pan's enemies suddenly stepped up their activity, doubtless because they had been informed of the Qingdao decisions. Already at the end of July, while Pan was away, the provincial press had shown signs of change. First officials in Anyang special region, then in Xinyang special region trumpeted their decision to adjust their production targets for the autumn harvest upwards. Propaganda for the return of graduates to their villages had been somewhat stepped up. Above all, even before the official decision to extend the Socialist Education Movement to all counties was published, leaders in Yanshi, then in Xinyang special region started on their own.[5]

The official decision published by the Central Committee of the CCP on 8 August was followed the next day by a provincial directive ordering "the launching of a large-scale socialist movement aimed at criticising and punishing in the masses, but also in cadres, reactionary ideas and behaviour about the grain problem, cooperatives, and the rural standard of living".[6] At the same time, a string of angry news items hummed in the ears of ordinary people; the political situation in the countryside was decidedly very serious. On 16 August the communiqué of the fifth plenum of the provincial committee, which had met 4–14 August, drew the political lesson from developing events. Without concealing that the discussions had been heated, the communiqué marked a decisive swing to the left. It recalled the persistence of a struggle between the socialist path and the capitalist path. Criticising the "rightist ideology and feelings of many Party cadres" as well as the rightist errors committed by the provincial committee over grain, it indicated that in Henan the Socialist Education Movement would be not only what it was supposed to be in principle—a campaign to reassert control of the population—but also a pretext to purge the leaders who had overenthusiastically implemented the rural policy of previous months.[7]

The Return of Wu Zhipu

Reading between the lines, this communiqué revealed the defeat of Pan Fusheng. After vainly attempting to cut the meeting short, he had been criticised for his passive behaviour at Qingdao and his opposition to the new line. Attacked by Wu Zhipu, probably criticised by individuals like Zhao Wenfu whose chief loyalty was to the centre, more or less completely abandoned by Yang Jue and Wang Tingdong, Pan Fusheng was forced to make his self-criticism. Wu Zhipu, until then second in the hierarchical ranking, unofficially resumed leadership of the Henan Party apparatus, thus once again combining political and administrative leadership of the province in his own hands.

Yet Pan Fusheng's defeat was not complete. The communiqué of the fifth plenum was still moderate in tone; it did not specifically criticise the "points to propagate" and mentioned no names. Pan Fusheng remained titular first secretary. His two former colleagues in Pingyuan, Yang Jue and Wang Tingdong, remained at their posts.[8] Also, the centre had not yet explicitly abandoned the moderate economic policy adopted in summer 1956, although such an abandonment might now seem likely. So Pan Fusheng tried one last manoeuvre. Abandoning to Wu Zhipu the helm of the province as well as responsibility for any eventual mistakes, Pan set out to regain the favour of the centre. First he embarked on one of those grassroots surveys that Mao Zedong so delighted in and had commended to provincial leaders at Qingdao. This survey, which was published in the *Henan Daily* of 20 September and belatedly in the *People's Daily* of 18 October, is a strange document. In it, Pan analyses precisely, sometimes even brilliantly, the social and political situation in six cooperatives in Huixian and Xinxiang counties. Contrary to later accusations, a close reading does not reveal any basic differences between this text and the editorials of the time; differences lie rather in the greater rigour of the reasoning than in any alleged moderation. Justifying both his earlier pessimism and the new line, Pan Fusheng estimated that 15 percent of peasants were opposed to socialism and he analysed accurately the discontent of well-off middle peasants. He concluded forcefully in favour of the Socialist Education Movement. In fact, it seems that in publishing this general report, far from seeking to slow down or sidetrack the Socialist Education Movement in Henan, Pan Fusheng was seeking through an abrupt change of direction to seize its ideological and political leadership so as to win back Beijing's trust. To that end, he apparently also tried to turn to advantage a stopover by Mao Zedong in Zhengzhou in September 1957; he was later criticised for importuning the chairman by impudently pushing his survey report on him.[9]

It is not impossible that Mao, perhaps ill informed of the local situation, and more probably conscious of the obstacles still standing in the way of a leftwards shift in the general line, may have said a few kind words to such a persistent courtier and personally authorised publication of Pan's report in the *People's Daily*. But he did not give vigorous support to Pan Fusheng: The manoeuvre failed. Pan did not get back his power in the provincial committee. By mentioning his name less often than that of Wu Zhipu the provincial press clearly showed who was now the true boss of Henan.[10] The sixth plenum of the provincial people's Congress, held from 23 to 31 August, in the absence of Pan Fusheng, to follow up the meeting a few weeks earlier of the National People's Congress, gave Wu Zhipu an excellent opportunity to demonstrate his preeminence. Wu left to Zhao Wenfu the delicate task of making the "report on the work of the provincial government" (in which he himself had participated only half-heartedly since May), but took more important roles for himself. As messenger of the gods he "transmitted the spirit" of the National People's Congress plenum, and as high priest of dogma he summed up in his closing speech the line of the day with a vigour that seemed inspired from on high. On this occasion, he endeavoured also to appear as the apparatus's chosen one. The speeches by local leaders and reports by senior provincial officials were all so many ferocious counterattacks against the rightists and enthusiastic endorsements of socialist transformations, and amounted to a plebiscite in his favour.[11]

Moreover, it soon became apparent that the new boss of Henan was applying his own political approach to the problems of the hour. A working meeting was called from 2–6 September 1957 on the problem of combating natural disasters. Although adopting what were, all in all, conventional measures, it also threatened inefficient cadres and rejected the most rightist provisions advocated previously for disaster areas.[12] After the summer floods, an early drought foreshadowed a difficult autumn harvest, and efforts were made to mitigate its effects. In late September, a "meeting on financial and economic work" took a bold decision laden with consequences of all sorts: Economic construction must not suffer from an inadequate harvest; a propaganda effort would make it possible to "overcome" the people's food difficulties. The level of agricultural deliveries would, in any eventuality, have to be kept up, and to ensure this, the state monopoly on trade in the leading agricultural products would have to be strengthened, private markets controlled, and rationing in the cities made more effective.[13] In the Party's provincial apparatus, as in the centre, there was reason to believe that the change that had taken place at the helm of the provincial committee, far from harming its work, had rather enhanced its efficiency, since it represented a return to healthy principles and the real problems.

Yet, with hindsight, it appears that Wu Zhipu's return to power also brought two new sources of political imbalance. The first was that the elimination of Pan

Fusheng and the positions adopted by Yang Jue and Wang Tingdong abruptly deprived the provincial committee of its right wing. Unlike other provincial committees, which organised the antirightist campaign with the same cautious discipline that they showed during the rectification campaign, the Henan Party committee might be tempted to venture into an incautious "leftist" policy with no one to restrain it. The second was that Wu Zhipu's personality, combined with his political situation, might also push him towards adventure. He was ambitious, and his victory was still neither public nor complete. To impress the centre and to get his policy accepted by both his enemies and the mass of the undecided, he had to do more and better. The relative weakness of his position thus predisposed him to excesses. The centre's line would only have to move more sharply leftwards, and the Henan committee, in order to keep itself in the vanguard, would lurch into adventurism. These are the political and bureaucratic causes of Henan radicalism. There is no certainty that they were the least important.

It was, in any event, quickly understood that Wu Zhipu would not be content to impose his power and deal with the most pressing problems, but would also be restoring order in his bailiwick. To that end he would overhaul the Party apparatus, step up repression, and under cover of the Socialist Education Movement, combine a propaganda campaign with the authoritarian restoration of socialist discipline.

The Recovery of the Party

Wu Zhipu's prime concern, quite logically, had to be to rectify the Party, consolidate it, and restore it to its guiding place. There are several indicators that suggest that the Communist Party was threatened with a harsh rectification. Official documents stressed the need to criticise the "rightist ideology" inside the Party. Drawing the lessons of experience, the press developed an idea that was later to have a remarkable career: that the Party, even at its highest levels, can be contaminated by civil society, for sociological reasons, but also for strictly ideological reasons. It was discovered at the time that a large number of cadres came from the same social background as those who were thought to provide most agitators in the countryside: rich and well-off middle peasants. It was acknowledged that the rightist theses might be somewhat attractive to militants who entered the Communist Party at a time when the declared aim was not yet socialist revolution, but a "new democracy". The newspapers loudly denounced Party members and Young Communists who had allowed themselves to be influenced by the rightists. Zhang Qingheng was the one most violently criticised. This leader with bad social origins and a chequered political history became the archetype of all the cadres who had shown themselves as susceptible to the "irrational demands" and indulgent towards the "spontaneous tendencies" of the peasants.[14] An editorial in the *Henan Daily* issued a solemn warning on 15 September: "Party members are facing a serious examination."

What was the actual scope of the internal rectification of the Party? This is a rather difficult question to answer. Although forthcoming about the errors of many cadres, available sources mention only a few cases of punishment. It was only in summer 1958 that it was learned that a small number of cadres in the most disturbed counties such as Linru, Minquan, Yuxian, or Xiayi had been purged or demoted. According to available information, only a single leader at the county level was removed, the head of the General Bureau of the Yuxian Party committee. In the cities, only the Kaifeng and Jiaozuo committees were severely criticised.[15] It is tempting to think that in this particular case, the sources give an accurate picture and local purges were few in number and limited in scope. If the opposite had been the case the press would have had no reason to keep silent about it. Furthermore, the launching of a full-blown rectification movement in the Party in autumn 1957 does not seem consistent either with what is known about Wu Zhipu or with the political uncertainties of the time. Unlike Pan Fusheng, who had generally found himself in an outsider position, Wu had always endeavoured to maintain good relations with local apparatuses; the sharpness of his stands always contrasted with the cordiality of his relations with subordinates, even when they implemented his directives only very unevenly. But at the time, the need for a large-scale purge must not have seemed terribly obvious. The centre had decided to restore collective discipline and the primacy of the Party, but without adopting new nationalisation measures. It was still a question of "consolidating agricultural cooperativisation in three to five years".[16] Overall, this restoration programme was favourable to local cadres, and surely the majority of them implemented it all the more vigorously because it was in their interests.

It would be worth pursuing this discussion with the help of more—and more detailed—data from other provinces. For if it turned out to be the case that the purge of the provincial and local apparatus of the Party in autumn 1957 was very limited in most of China, as seems to have been the case in those provinces whose leaders were disgraced at the time,[17] it would be further evidence of the lack of preparation for the Great Leap Forward. The lack of any real prior rectification campaign would also explain why it was necessary constantly to step up the pressure on the local apparatus during the Great Leap. And finally it would help to account for the at once adventurist and passive manner in which that local apparatus implemented the centre's directives during the Leap.

Whatever the case, even if there was no purge, the Party now possessed a more coherent provincial leadership and a mission that was at last clear: to restore socialist order everywhere. This task was set to energetically, using as in the past a combination of police repression and ideological propaganda.

Police Repression

The impact of the Socialist Education Movement, which is widely acknowledged by observers, cannot be understood without the concomitant action of the Public Security departments, which is often overlooked or underestimated. Starting in August 1957, the police were no longer content simply to hunt down liberal intellectuals and members of the small democratic parties. They extended their activities to all sectors of society and incarcerated many peasants guilty of disobedience. In September and October 1957, 60,000 "harmful acts" were denounced in the campaign and 3,000 individuals tried; between August and December, 1,400 landlords, rich peasants, counterrevolutionaries, and bad elements surrendered themselves to justice.[18] At the same time, the police in the cities went after petty traffickers and unlicensed traders who had been growing in numbers for several months. They came down particularly hard on vagrants who had already been before the courts; in the city of Zhengzhou alone, ninety were arrested between the beginning of August and early September.[19] Full-scale roundups were even organised. Thus, on 14 September alone, Public Security in Zhengzhou arrested seventy "bad elements". These were generally what might be called juvenile delinquents, such as one youth who pretended to be a state cadre and importuned women in public toilets. But amongst them were a few who were accused of expressing unacceptable opinions, like the worker who, referring to recent strikes in Poland, threatened his bosses with a Chinese Poznan. At the same time, a few moribund sects and tiny illegal parties were suddenly discovered whose leaders were charged with conspiracy. That is how the identification of public order with socialist order was made manifest. And so that no one could be in any doubt about it, the sentences were not simply posted; they were carried out publicly. In Luoyang, on 24 September, before more than 5,000 people, a vagrant "formerly associated with the Guomindang" was tried and executed for having attacked PLA soldiers and Soviet experts and then murdered a demobilised soldier. In late December, it was announced that a secondary school student who had put up antiregime posters during the night had been arrested in Zhengzhou.

It is impossible to determine the total number of victims of the repression in the second half of 1957. Not only is the official figure for rightists (5,510) most likely underestimated, as has been seen, but there are no overall data on the repression of nonpolitical crimes. My subjective impression is that an overall figure of 15,000 sentenced to various penalties must be regarded as a minimum.[20] This figure excludes the mass of teachers humiliated and transferred, workers sacked, cadres demoted, and others who suffered in one way or another from the antirightist struggle and whose "errors" of 1957 were to condemn them to a subhuman existance for years to come. Although the number of direct victims of the repression seems to have been relatively small, indirect victims were more numerous, and for the rest of the population, the threat was clear. Quite possibly this is one of the explanations for the launching of the Great Leap Forward. That a reasonable and rather sceptical people allowed itself to be drawn into one of the wildest adventures seen in this century may be because it had no choice. Protest had been crushed; people were being shot in sports arenas; one had to keep one's head down.

The Socialist Education
Movement in the Countryside

Police repression alone could not restore a positive order. People had still to be told what was allowed and what forbidden, and this is where the Socialist Education Movement came in. The movement was organised between August and October in all social milieux, with widely varying intensity and effects.

The Socialist Education Movement in the Countryside assumed genuine political importance. After the rightists in the cities had been condemned, it was in the rural areas that the hardening of the regime first manifested itself at the end of July and it is there that it introduced the most significant changes. The primary aim was to combat the influence of "class enemies" by arousing the anger of the "peasant masses" and also by introducing reforms. In each county, the preparations went through three stages: the training of "pillars", who might constitute up to 5 percent of the population; testing in a few model townships; and finally, the despatch into the rest of the county of work teams who disseminated the example of these models. The movement then proceeded into two additional phases: the "great debate" and "rectification/reform". During the first phase, everyone, including the malcontents, was invited to "contend and bloom" and express "views". These were classified both by area and by degree of correctness or error. Then the local political leaders would reply to them, congratulating those who had spoken well but chiefly concerned with the rest. "Views" that were not considered to be antagonistic could merit an "explanation" of mistakes and the reasons for the policy pursued by the Party. Those whose criticisms were deemed to be unacceptable would become the object of a "struggle". They would answer for their "crimes" before tumultuous meetings and the most guilty would be handed over to the police. Then followed the phase of "rectification/reform". While "rectifying" false opinions and those who held them, the Party was supposed to admit some errors of detail and by making reforms deprive its enemies of any argument. For example, not only would a peasant who had wrongly taken grain belonging to the cooperative be punished, but so would any petty cadres who had closed their eyes, and a "reform" might be introduced such as strengthening the powers of the cooperative's supervisory bodies.[21]

The movement was supposed to arouse and channel the spontaneity of the masses. The press at the time stressed the "great debate" and the free expression of opinions very much as it had in spring 1957. In fact the propaganda referred to what ought to have happened at that time had it not been for interference and betrayals: a mass campaign combining democracy and centralism, free expression of opinions and criticism of class enemies. But the present movement was much more than that: It was also a disciplinary operation designed to restore the omnipotence of the Party apparatus in the countryside. The local apparatus of the CCP managed each stage of the movement, first obliging people to express themselves, then deciding who should be criticised. By the end of the movement, the Party had resumed control of all private activities, punishing those that were illegal and severely limiting the rest. "Individual peasants" were forced by a whole range of economic pressures to rejoin a cooperative.[22]

Finally, with the Socialist Education Movement in the countryside, the regime was pursuing another concrete objective, the consolidation of the unified purchase and supply system, which had taken quite a beating over the previous months. Provincial leaders frankly expressed their determination to avoid mediocre harvests and the resulting need to appeal for deliveries from the centre.[23] Deliveries would have to be maximised and consumption minimised. Of greatest concern was the grain harvest, justifying the introduction of a close checking of deliveries to the state. Most cooperatives had to undergo an audit. Many had to adjust their summer production figures upwards and increase their deliveries by 10 percent. Yuxian and Anyang counties had to make extra deliveries of 1,000 and 1,400 metric tons of grain, respectively. Vague or poorly enforced regulations, for example those relating to the share of the increase in production to be included in the calculation of obligatory deliveries (in principle 60 percent), or the exact quantity of grain set aside for cattle feed or aid to devastated counties, were spelled out and strictly enforced.[24] With things as they were, the best course (if only to avoid checks) appeared to be to promise spontaneously that the initial summer grain delivery plan would be exceeded—which is what the leaders of Xinyang special region did. At the same time, the illegal marketing of crops became more difficult with the publication and rigorous enforcement of a State Council directive dated 8 August. In the countryside as in the cities, the authorities now watched private markets closely, prohibiting excessive price fluctuations and verifying that the produce put on sale did not fall within the state monopoly.[25]

In sum, a distinction must be made between the disciplinary results of the Socialist Education Movement in the countryside and the strictly political results. The campaign silenced the opposition and largely restored the Party's authority over agricultural production, as was soon shown by the rise in state grain deliveries. The ending of the rural crisis that had appeared in summer 1956 must be dated from the Socialist Education Movement. The reassertion of the Party's authority was enough to put an end to the incidents that had been occurring for a year and to restore discipline in production. That was no small achievement. Not surprising, however, the peasants showed no enthusiasm for a political campaign that reduced their material benefits. There were also serious reservations among cadres, and as usual, more is known about them. Although basic-level cadres could agree to deliver more grain to the state, they were much less disposed to open "great debates" that would be hard to control. Some, compromised in previous accommodations, feared being criticised by activists. Others, judging higher directives to be still too liberal, led the movement high-handedly and settled a few personal scores as they went: "You insulted me, well, now I'm rectifying you." An even larger number quite simply disliked wasting their time on a political matter that they regarded as a secondary issue compared to the fight against disasters.[26]

All that explains why the movement developed very unevenly, although it was, for the Party, the top priority. At the beginning of September, just as the movement was ending in a few vanguard counties, the press felt that it was developing in only 25 percent of the cooperatives in the province, "soundly" in only 18.7 percent of them.[27] The Socialist Education Movement in the countryside gradually disappeared from the news during October without any overall figures being released. How many counties, although punishing the most serious excesses and imposing compliance with the grain regulations, had been content to summon a few symbolic meetings? The repression, the threats made by propaganda, the recovery of the Party apparatus, and the cautiousness of the peasants explain why "socialism" won out in the countryside, but usually without waging the ideological battle that the centre wanted. Thus, although the Socialist Education Movement made the restoration of the Party's powers and the main collective disciplines possible, it cannot be seen as an ideological prelude to, or political preparation for, later changes. That is yet another sign of the lack of preparation for the Great Leap Forward and a further explanation for the attitude of passive discipline that the peasantry was to adopt in 1958.

And in the City

The cities experienced a more radical change of atmosphere. It was there that the disorders of the spring had occurred, and there the unorthodox and the heretical were now hunted down. In addition, after the beginning of September, the regime undertook to tighten its control over the main sectors of activity, in each case mixing repression and reform.

The universities and schools suffered the harshest treatment. The *Henan Daily* editorial of 5 September 1957, which launched the Socialist Education Movement in those institutions, starkly reaffirmed the conventional principles regarding the leading place of politics in the school. The debate on teaching methods was settled in the most conservative possible way: The sense of community had to be stressed over individualism, and familiarity with Marxism-Leninism over intellectual independence. At the same time as it was unearthing the last rightists, the Party opened an ideological reeducation campaign. At least in the universities that had been most disrupted in the spring, such as the Specialised Teacher Training School in Zhengzhou and the Henan Institute of Agronomy, this took the form of compulsory political education courses taught and run by the very same Communist figures who had been most derided a few months earlier. More important, the Party decided on an unprecedented replacement of top administrative staff in universities and secondary schools. Not only were protesters criticised and arrested, and a few waverers removed and replaced by reliable functionaries, but the provincial committee organised a massive transfer of cadres from the productive sectors into schools and universities, over a thousand in the province as a whole, including twenty-eight high-level managers in Zhengzhou.[28] What a triumph for those cadres of rural origin, who had been derided a few months previously! Moreover, the time was approaching when teachers would have to volunteer to go and work in the countryside, thus leaving the authorities all the time in the world to complete their levelling work.[29] As for the students, they would be compelled to work on the work-sites of the Great Leap. In Henan as elsewhere, universities and secondary schools were entering an era of silence that would only be broken nine years later with the Cultural Revolution.

The repression was equally severe amongst craftsworkers and traders. Petty traders were hunted down. Craftsworkers who left their cooperative "to escape tax, the administration, and meetings", as one of them put it, only avoided fines, payment of tax arrears, and criticism meetings by rejoining. In the cooperatives that had not collapsed, the Socialist Education Movement boasted of the excellence of the socialist organisation of labour.[30]

In the factories, where the disorders of the spring had made few inroads, the Socialist Education Movement came later and was shorter and less repressive. Although already by late July it had overlain the antirightist campaign in a few big enterprises, its opening was only announced officially in about mid-August. It only really began on a large scale at the beginning of September,[31] and by early October was already winding down. Moreover, its intensity was never very great. In a few factories, organised discussions were the pretext for a severe dressing-down of workers and even more of apprentices who had demonstrated in the spring. It was made clear that disobedience, immorality, disputes, and absenteeism would in future be treated as antisocialist behaviour. A few trouble-makers were punished and the weakness of some leaders was censured. Yet in most cases there was no repression. In fact the newspapers of the time suggest that at the top the political consequences of the events of the spring had been learned. Although the liberal intellectuals were eliminated and the discontented peasantry disciplined, the working class—which as a whole had not demonstrated much—was to be rewarded; in theory as in fact, it was indeed a "pillar of socialism". Although discipline had to be consolidated, some of the workers' demands could be met. Since the government lacked the financial means for a new wage rise, rewards took the narrow path of psychological satisfaction and structural reforms. Promises were made to study demands about food and accommodation in a more liberal spirit, to clarify the rules governing promotion and the granting of social benefits, and even to consult workers when plans were being drafted. The incompetence, authoritarianism, and excessive benefits of some leaders were criticised. In each factory, a "reform group", headed by the Party secretary, encouraged workers to express their opinions and replied to them generally very positively. The group was even supposed to propose changes in the way the factory was managed and run.

Such an attitude could not last. Pointing to the leftwards shift of the general line, many leaders refused to feign moral reform. Thus the assistant passenger station master in Zhengzhou, who was criticised by his subordinates, refused to appear before their meeting, and following a tried and true method, summoned their representatives into his office. Moreover, the closer the end of the year came, the thicker came appeals to fulfil the plan. What a magnificent and classic pretext! A meeting organised in Zhengzhou from 17 to 23 September by the Industry Department of the provincial committee, called to discuss the Socialist Education Movement, was chiefly taken up with the production delays recorded in a third of industrial enterprises in the province, the disorganisation of transport, and the lack of job security in local enterprises. Towards the end of September, the convening of a provincial meeting on basic construction and the publication of an emergency directive ordering the completion of annual production plans confirmed that the Socialist Education Movement in the factories, hardly begun, was ending.[32] With few exceptions, the reforms envisaged ran into the sand. Late, short-lived, and finally ill-defined, this campaign does not seem to have had any lasting effects on the world of labour.

The City in Disgrace

Although the workers were spared qua workers, their fate was becoming more difficult as city-dwellers. City-dwellers had to suffer new privations.[33] As a poor cotton harvest was expected, beginning in about mid-August attempts were made to limit the consumption of textile products. On 27 July, a directive from the provincial committee called on each city-dweller to save 250–500 grams of grain each month. In future, requests for food relief made by poor families would be closely examined, especially for families that had come more or less legally from devastated rural areas. In short, people in the cities would have to tighten their belts.[34]

At about the same time, city-dwellers were faced with a new threat. Just when it was hardest to get food, it became harder to stay in the cities. A policy of sending secondary school graduates back to the township from which they came had begun several months previously, but it was only carried out forcefully after a meeting in late July of a provincial work conference on the topic. Despite many reservations, cadres had to set the example.[35] In total, of the 430,000 graduates of the lower and higher secondary schools who had failed to gain admission to a higher level, 360,000 were sent to the countryside. The economic motives for this measure—above all the economic slump that had been going on for almost a year—were not new, but the harshness with which the measure was applied was.

Similarly, there was a new impetus in the rectification campaign that for better or worse had been going on since spring in government departments. Cadres were no longer simply threatened with punishment for misappropriation, they now had to participate actively in production (or at least seriously pretend to do so). Even before the publication on 27 September of a circular from the Central Committee on this subject, all cadres at the provincial level were supposed to devote one day a week to productive work. By the beginning of October, 12,000 provincial- and municipal-level cadres were taking part every day in agricultural work around Zhengzhou. Furthermore, cadres were once again being sent to the basic level for lengthy stays, this time to lead the Socialist Education Movement and the fight against drought. By the beginning of September this was the case in Luoyang and Shangqiu special regions. The priority groups for being sent back to the basic level were surplus cadres, cadres disliked by their superiors, and cadres' relatives who had come to the city irregularly.[36]

Not only was urban life becoming more burdensome and insecure, but the official conception of the city was beginning to change. The major editorials of the period continued to view industrialisation, and hence urbanisation, as the very essence of socialism, but in actuality the regime, perhaps influenced by the criticisms made in the spring but more probably spurred by its new mistrust of city-dwellers, was in fact returning to a view of the city that was much closer to its economic possibilities. The provincial conference on basic construction that was held at the end of September 1957 criticised "uncontrolled urbanisation" and overambitious architectural projects.[37] At the same time, small rural industries that had suffered from the economic crisis began to be put back on their feet. Effort was focused on the creation of ninety-two small coal mines until a provincial work meeting proposed establishing small enterprises in other sectors.[38]

The reassertion of control in the cities thus proved to be more brutal, but also more significant than the reassertion of control of the countryside. The relaunching of local industries heralded and initiated a new development policy, more adapted to realities, which was to reach its peak during the Great Leap Forward, but without becoming an essential part of it (indeed it outlived it by two decades). Looking at the whole of Henan society, this seems a relatively unimportant innovation. The return to discipline and the change of provincial leadership clearly mark off the months of August–September 1957 from the weeks of crisis and hesitations that had gone before. But they did not herald the break of tempo in economics and politics that was to be the starting point of the Great Leap Forward: Any nonrightist policy remained possible.

6

Henan Radicalism:
The Great Days and
the Achievements
(October 1957–July 1958)

The Great Leap Forward and the Cultural Revolution are two high points of the history of the People's Republic of China. Yet, whereas the events of 1966–1969 have produced a dense and detailed literature, the story of the Great Leap Forward still largely remains to be written. The reason for this is obvious: The official sources are abundant but mendacious. After December 1957 provincial documents evidence the same shortcomings as the central press, unfortunately precluding their use in any detailed study of the development of the Great Leap line. But careful analysis of them can throw some light on two major, interrelated problems. The first has to do with the timing of the new policy in the province and the process leading up to its imposition. In particular, how much of the impetus came from central directives and how much from within the province? The second problem has to do with Henan radicalism proper—the nature of the provincial model that was to be celebrated throughout China after summer 1958 and hence the causes of political lying in a period of intense mobilisation.

The launch of the Great Leap Forward must be dated to the last quarter of 1957. Taking advantage of an unexpected improvement in the economic situation, the provincial leadership passed on the political decisions adopted by the centre with particular energy and embarked on a campaign of large projects, which given the shortage of equipment, could only be completed through exhausting physical labour performed under grueling conditions.

Economic Progress

After the worries of spring and the hesitations of summer, it suddenly seemed in autumn 1957 that the industrial crisis was lifting and the agricultural situation

improving. Overall, industry made some slight advances. Thanks to a resumption at the end of the year, due it seems to the impetus of certain investments, the
value of industrial production in 1957 rose to 1.2 billion yuan, against a little over
1.1 billion in 1956.[1] Most of the targets assigned to the province by the First Five-
Year Plan were attained or overfulfilled. Although the textile and food industries
suffered from the problems in agriculture, coal production rose to 6 million metric tons, as against 4 million in the previous year.[2] For the rest, a number of very
important projects, such as the Sanmen dam and Luoyang tractor and ball-bear-
ing plants, would soon be completed. New infrastructure works were planned,
including a second track for the railway between Anyang and Zhengzhou and the
building of a second bridge over the Yellow River. In short, 1957 would turn out
to be not as bad as had been feared in the previous winter, and it even opened up
some encouraging prospects for the future.

The available local data broadly confirm the impression of a slight improve-
Agriculture, even worse affected by the crisis, suddenly seemed to be recovering thanks to a combination of two different factors. First, the relaxation of rural
policy was at last bearing fruit. Despite an early drought, the autumn harvest was
fair, and certainly much better than expected. Both the area sown to rice and its
yield increased. Rice production increased accordingly to 1.22 million metric
tons, up from 0.76 million in 1953.[3] The raising of the official selling price for
sweet potatoes led to a 10 percent increase in production. With the autumn harvest, total cereal production for the year reached 12.3 million metric tons, an advance of some 3 percent over 1956.[4] Even per capita production (255.5 kg as
against 253.1) rose slightly.

The available local data broadly confirm the impression of a slight improvement. Xinyang special region, grievously affected by the disasters of 1956, made a
fine recovery. With 3.8 million metric tons, its cereal production was 53.4 percent
higher than in 1952. At the same time, because of the particularly severe drought
in the mountain areas, production stagnated in Luoyang special region.[5] Among
industrial crops, tobacco production continued to fall, but peanut production
rose, and more important, cotton recovered or surpassed its 1955 level.[6] Finally,
stock-raising made marked progress. In December 1957 the province had 6.30
million pigs (as against 2.85 million in the winter of 1956). Cattle improved in
quantity (6.2 million head as against 5 million in the autumn of 1956) and quality. In this area, the privatisation and decentralisation measures successively implemented since summer 1956 produced striking results.[7]

All these figures show that the crisis was being overcome and that Henan agriculture had resumed its forwards march, though at a rate slow enough to remain
worrying. In addition to the production figures discussed, there is of course another aspect that by definition does not appear in the statistics of the time: the
private gains resulting from the extension of family activities and the resumption
of rural trade. I am quite unable to put a figure on them, but available information, including above all the political concern over the issue, suggests that these

gains were considerable. Although short-lived, the liberalisation of rural policy in the end brought positive results.

In addition, the restoration of discipline made it possible for the regime to benefit from the rise in productivity of Henan agriculture. Since this rise was low, it would soon have been wiped out if urban consumption had continued to grow at the same rate as in 1956 and the state would have been unable to increase its revenues in proportion. But not only did the state deliver 19.4 percent less cereals than in 1956 to the deficit rural areas and cities of Henan, it also collected more and did so more quickly. Thanks to the Socialist Education Movement, the purchase of cereals and cotton was completed two months earlier than the previous year. The target for cereal collection was already overfulfilled by the end of November, with the result that a surplus of 175,000 metric tons was stored in granaries, although a shortfall of 250,000 metric tons had initially been forecast.[8] The regime also took a much harder line over rural loans. These were now granted only rarely, and repayment of those already due was demanded. Debts amounting to 60 million yuan, some of them outstanding for years, were collected in the last months of 1957.[9] In short, by increasing the amount it collected from the peasants, the government extracted maximum advantage from the slight increases in production and thus found itself in a better position to contemplate new investment at the end of 1957 than it had been a year earlier. The psychological effect of this economic improvement was possibly even more important, for did not the fact that the crisis had been overcome show the solidity of the regime and its leaders? The launch of the Great Leap Forward is hard to understand without this recovery of confidence.

The Decisive Turning-Point: October–December 1957

The change of atmosphere favoured the launch of the Great Leap Forward in Henan, but did not provoke it. From the beginning, the Leap had the character, which it was to retain to the end, of a deliberate policy drawn up and imposed by the centre. It would be mistaken to think that Henan anticipated the Great Leap or that its leaders were involved in planning it. Like every other province, it received directives from Beijing; Henan simply distinguished itself in implementing them.

The new general line was formulated by the centre and put into effect by provincial committees in the last quarter of 1957. The decisive event was the third plenum of the Central Committee of the Eighth Congress of the CCP between 21 September and 9 October. It adopted the first economic decentralisation measures. Above all, the upwards revision of the ambitious agricultural development programme that had been put on the back burner since autumn 1956 established the principles of a new economic development strategy focused on the country-side, based on local resources, and using the labour of the masses as the principal source of investment.[10] This was the strategy of the Great Leap.

The Henan leadership did not take long to fall into line. Wu Zhipu distributed the Central Committee documents during the sixth plenum of the provincial committee of the CCP, which met from 15 to 19 October and adopted a communiqué that justified launching the Great Leap: Henan being "in a period of socialist high tide politically and ideologically", "a high tide of agricultural and industrial production as well as economic construction" would inevitably break over the province.[11] Subjective factors suddenly came to the fore in the regime's ideological and political kaleidoscope; almost every day in October and November the provincial press headline read: "Determination is the master of things".

The Leap needed to be pointed in the right direction. This was the purpose of a series of meetings that were in principle devoted to irrigation problems. The first and most important, chaired by Wu Zhipu and attended by Tan Zhenlin, a national leader who had just been given responsibility for rural issues in the Central Committee, took place from 21 to 27 October in the presence of the main leaders of the province, special regions, and "key counties" intended to become models of the campaign in Henan. In a speech aimed in fact at the rest of the country, Tan Zhenlin set out the new policy: (1) priority of politics and the mass line (which meant that one must go forwards without allowing oneself to be stopped by practical obstacles), (2) priority of water storage and irrigation works over protection and drainage works, and (3) priority of small projects over medium- and large-scale projects. Tan justified this reversal of options by a critique of the inadequate results achieved since 1949 in irrigation and a violent attack on the passive economic policy pursued since July 1956. He set the first targets for 1958: raising the province's irrigated area from 2.8 to 4.2 million hectares and increasing agricultural production by 15 percent. Every unit, from cooperative to special region, would have to draw up its own irrigation programme. Already, some local leaders were being applauded for promising to overfulfil the prescribed norm without resorting to state grants. What was effectively a provincial irrigation congress was followed by meetings at all levels.[12] Once local plans had been drawn up, their coordination was encouraged. It was, once again, Tan Zhenlin who gave the impetus on about 10 November by calling together the leaders of the thirteen counties of northern Henan in the presence of Wu Zhipu. Tan exhorted his audience to draw up "global plans" applying for example to a whole basin.[13]

Yet it was never a matter only of irrigation. The "east wind"—the Communist wind as opposed to the capitalist wind from the west—was blowing everywhere, and it blew harder after each editorial in the central press. Decidedly a new era was opening. To spell out the new political guidelines and correct the now-obvious errors committed since summer 1956, each province summoned a second session of its CCP Congress. In Henan, this was held from 12 November to 2 December 1957, once again watched over by the ubiquitous Tan Zhenlin. As there was less concern to observe the Party rules than to propagate the "correct" line, this plenum preceded, often by several weeks or months, those that ought to have paved the way for it in the cities and counties,[14] and it unfolded both as a training session and as a rally. Wu Zhipu's introductory speech summarised the general line and was followed by three days of discussions in small groups. The provincial committee's long progress report, delivered by Zhao Wenfu, set out in detail the errors of the previous leadership without naming its leader and provided subject matter for the small group discussions that lasted until 26 November. The style and procedure of discussion was changed. It was no longer a matter, as it had been at the previous plenum, of delegates cautiously stating their concrete problems and even their political worries. Instead, one after another they expressed their enthusiastic support for the new line and endeavoured to show that they had concretely anticipated application of it. Those who had some error on their conscience were especially active. The delegates from Zhengzhou, where the rightist plague had flourished, promised in future to help the adjoining rural areas. The first secretary of the devastated county of Huaibin, who had been criticised a year before, promised a tripling of grain production in his area in 1958. In a climate of unanimity, provincial cadres swore true faith again and again and displayed wall poster after wall poster proclaiming their new convictions. Finally, the assembly heard from local star performers, including the illustrious Wu Zhipu.[15]

Political Centralisation

The principal aim of this pseudo-congress was in fact to convince senior cadres in the province that the change of political line was irreversible and fundamental. There would be no more hesitations and divisions. The Communist Party, fully united around its basic objectives, would take a decisive step forwards in the construction of socialism. Yet it is likely that the second plenum also adopted or laid the ground for more concrete measures. The most important ones strengthened administrative and political centralisation within the province. After winter 1957–1958, the trend towards breaking up administrative areas reversed. Indeed, it seems that the process that was to end in the foundation of people's communes began at about this time. That in any event is what emerges from some information on the number of cooperatives. According to a later account by Wu Zhipu, their number fell from 54,000 in spring 1957 to 30,000 in June 1958; according to the provincial press at the time, from 51,000 in November 1957 to 43,700 in April and 38,473 in June 1958.[16]

Other levels of administration were also caught up in this process of concentration. The number of townships (*xiang*) fell.[17] More important, Anyang special region was amalgamated with Xinxiang special region in winter 1957–1958 to recreate the old Pingyuan.[18] Henan now had only seven special regions compared to thirteen in 1949, nine in 1952, and eight in 1956. The process of administrative concentration that reached its peak in 1959[19] thus began at this time.

This observation is borne out by what is known about the strengthening of political centralisation that started in late 1957. Each level was now much more directly supervised and controlled by the next higher level. In the organisation of large irrigation works, production teams lost their autonomy to cooperatives. These appear to become merged into counties, and above all, districts. But now the biggest impetus was coming from the county (and not, as in 1955–1956, the township). As the *Miyang Daily* shows, county leaders were not content to draw up a mass of plans, they were constantly on the move to see the goals were fulfilled. The special regions sent work teams in an endeavour to exercise greater control over and coordinate action in the counties. They in turn received numerous delegations from the provincial committee, which attended important local meetings and convened provincial assemblies in the most suitable localities.[20] Political leaders at all levels seem to have become permanently incapable of staying in one place.

Not only did the leaders move about, but they got themselves established at the basic level. Starting late in 1957 the provincial committee effected a massive transfer of cadres to the rural areas. From then on, the despatch of cadres to the basic level meant something different and occurred on an altogether different scale. In the past, it had been chiefly designed to punish doubtful elements and save personnel. Now the main aim was to consolidate local Party committees, and far more people were moved. In May 1958, 5,000 of the 7,000 cadres in the city of Xinxiang were at the basic level. It is highly likely that the total number of cadres sent to the rural areas in the province—24,000 at the end of October 1957—was well over 100,000 by summer 1958.[21] Moreover, the quality of these missionaries changed. The Party and the administration now sought out good elements. In their new assignment, these cadres knew that the higher levels were watching them closely. The ambitious sought to make sure they were seen. Miao Huaming, previously assistant director of the provincial committee's Cultural Affairs and Education Department (a department that had much to be forgiven), was made second secretary of rural Dengfeng county and transformed his new unit into a model of the dissemination of education that was publicised all over the country. Zhao Guang, the head of the secretariat of the Party committee of Xinyang special region was assigned to Suiping county and made himself famous by setting up a proto–people's commune there, the famous "Sputnik farm".[22]

A final measure that ensured the obedience of local levels was the launching of a "work-style rectification campaign". In theory this was an extension to the county level of what had ended in the cities in an antirightist campaign. It also purported to allow everyone to have a say in separating "good" ideas from "bad" ones and carrying out the necessary "reforms". But the trap was now well known. The few cadres who let themselves be caught fell back on all those who had said some bad word, mostly people in education or the legal system. Thus the vice-chairman of the tribunal of Shangqiu special region, and in Miyang county a pro-fessor who talked too much, were criticised and arrested. The main effect of this repressive movement seems to have been to deter rural cadres unconvinced by the new line from any opposition activity—possibly thereby avoiding the need for several local purges.[23]

"War on Nature"

The strengthening of political controls within the provincial apparatus helps to explain the intensity of big projects. In this "war on nature", reported by the press in military terms, the first and most important battle involved irrigation. At the end of October 1957, 330,000 hectares were regarded as newly irrigated, but they were still concentrated in model zones in Xinyang and Xinxiang special regions or in vanguard counties such as Lushan and Jiyuan. Labour was mobilised prov-incewide for the first time in November, just as the ultimate target for newly irri-gated areas was raised from 1.3 to 1.6 million hectares. By 6 December, 70 percent of townships were engaged in the battle.[24]

After December 1957, the movement took off in every direction at once. It ceased to be a war and became a laughable game led by demented generals. Numbers poured out and by summer 1958, Henan became the first province of China to come under complete "hydrological control", that is, officially declared to be safe from foreseeable floods and droughts. At the same time, since the Great Leap Forward had to be "universal", and since therefore it had been decided to do "more, faster, better, and more economically" in every area at once, the press trumpeted victory after victory in the collection of manure, the reforestation of mountains, the elimination of harmful animals, literacy, and so on. The list would be long. The essential point is that it was claimed that every factor of pro-duction was being developed at once. Obviously, such an effort was bound to create contradictions, which today seem awesome. Thus, whereas logic suggests that the launching of the Great Leap Forward would produce an extraordinary need for labour, what happened was that the departments responsible for popu-lation control, which had previously laid low, suddenly awoke. They too had to "leap". The slogan of birth control was written into the "leap forward pro-grammes".[25] In addition, in December 1957 it was decided to evacuate 208,300 workers from the province: 65,000 were sent to Ningxia, and 143,000 (110,000 permanently) from twenty-five devastated counties went to farm the Jianghan plain in Hubei.[26] The confusion was total, because a policy that the Great Leap ought necessarily to rule out was actually being vigorously implemented as part of it.

So it is indeed to December 1957 that the launch of the Great Leap Forward must be dated. At that point, the news became all statistics. The nature of the press changed. Previously, it would still publish plausible—if not accurate—figures and acknowledge difficulties. Now, giant headlines leaped from the front pages, backed up by nothing but eulogies on the model units whose performances were compared in tables.[27] The Great Leap Forward in production looked like a Great Leap Forward in propaganda.[28] Certainly there was mobilisation of labour, but even more, there was mobilisation of the lie.

A "Sputnik" Province

A complete listing of the triumphs of Henan radicalism would be impossible. The key point is that starting in December 1957, Henan achieved a spectacular rise in the political hierarchy of Chinese provinces. From the beginning, by setting itself a target of 1.3 million hectares to be irrigated, the province had shown itself to be the most ambitious one in the country.[29] Subsequently, Henan maintained itself in first or second place in the irrigation movement, which a resounding editorial in the *People's Daily* of 7 June 1958 finally rewarded: "The people of Henan have provided a good model." Henan also won an excellent place in every other competition of the winter and spring: manure collection, "technical reform", literacy amongst others.

But it was in summer 1958 that the province experienced its hour of glory. Provincial leaders announced an extraordinary cereal harvest: 11.6 million metric tons, or almost as much as the whole of 1957. More important, it was in Henan that the first people's communes were set up, in particular the "Sputnik" commune, which was to be held up as a model for the whole country. The chairman himself bestowed blessings on the province. In an article titled "Presentation of a Cooperative" published in the first issue of *Red Flag*, the Central Committee's new journal on theory, he praised the way in which the Yingju cooperative in Fengqiu county was combating disasters. During his grand tour of the provinces in August 1958, the Great Helmsman stopped over in Xinxiang, Xiangcheng, Changge, and Shangqiu counties. His visit to the Qiliying people's commune in Xinxiang county was immortalised in a photograph in which one can see a gleaming, tanned face emerging from a field of cotton as well as the famous quotation: "*Renmin gongshe hao!*" ("The people's commune is good!")[30] Throughout the summer, Henan was described by propaganda as the place where people's communes emerged, the Holy Land of the people's communes movement.[31]

Economic Disaster

In fact, it is clear that the celebrated successes existed only on paper. Although "hydrologically controlled" according to propaganda, Henan suffered serious flooding in summer 1958. In June–July 1959 an invasion of locusts affected 61 counties and destroyed harvests on over 530,000 hectares.[32] Worse, the province suffered an appalling drought. This was caused by extremely poor rainfall in 1959, and was particularly deadly between July 1959 and March 1960. According to official sources it affected 6.5 million hectares in 90 counties. Drought conditions eased somewhat in March 1960 following a little rain, but a late frost and the spread of weeds aggravated the situation. Then the drought resumed in winter 1960–1961, so much so that in the following spring 1.3 million hectares had to be resown. The climate only gradually returned to normal in autumn 1961.[33]

During this period, delicately called the period of "difficulties" but more commonly known as the "dark years", the veil of words was torn. The irrigation works proved to be inadequate, sometimes even dangerous.[34] Silence descended upon the ambitions of 1958, and then it began to be gently put about that the figures already published were exaggerated. In any case, the production figures for 1973–1975 show up, sometimes comically, the exaggerations of 1958. How could anyone believe that Henan harvested 35 million metric tons of cereals in the earlier year when it produced only 18.7 million in 1974?[35]

Will it ever be known what the true harvest was in 1958? The impression that emerges from an examination of the few more or less reliable sources and interviews with refugees from Henan is that the harvest was perhaps slightly higher than that of 1957.[36] But there is no denying that production collapsed precipitously in 1959–1962. There are no figures available for this period. They must have been extremely low, since in 1965, that is, after three years of economic recovery, Henan harvested only 11.7 million metric tons of grain, thus recovering the level of 1954, and the 1957 production figure was only reached again in 1968–1969.[37] The excesses of the Great Leap Forward caused the waste of over ten years in Henan agriculture.

These overall estimates are confirmed by local data. In March 1960, only 20 percent of counties in the province had adequate grain stocks. In Xinyang special region, annual grain production for 1959–1961 turned out to be 40 percent less than in 1957–1958 and 33 percent of the 1953–1956 average, and shortages were acknowledged. Anyang special region also suffered a significant fall in grain and cotton production. In Nanyang special region, cattle were all but wiped out. Serious geographical journals noted that cereal production fell to its "lowest level in history" in Lankao and Yanshi counties. Emigrants report that Henan was hit by what were real famines, and all-too-rare documents refer to disturbances.[38] Without going into a tedious and pointless apportionment of responsibilities, I must, by way of conclusion, reassert what the Beijing regime admitted only far too late: In Henan as in the rest of China, the Great Leap Forward led only to a great fall leap backwards in production.

The Old Man Is Not Dead!

I now turn to another propaganda lie. At the time, it was claimed that the mass mobilisation for large projects was largely explained by a transformation of relations between leaders and led. Since the Great Leap line reflected the desires of the people, complete harmony was supposed suddenly to have appeared between the state and its citizens, which would account for so much hard work being done and such enormous progress being achieved.

But what little is known of the social reality of the time contradicts these propaganda assertions. Here are a few examples, consistent with the social situation of the preceding years, that show how popular behaviour towards the authorities continued to be what it always had been. In Xinxiang, in May 1958, the police had to be mobilised against people making forged cereal coupons and against children sent by their parents to cut still unripe wheat shoots in the collective fields. The first people's communes were not welcomed enthusiastically. In the "Let Us Overtake England" commune, which was to be one of the model communes in Henan, more than one family head in three took the risk of showing defiance at a time that propaganda expressly described as "crucial". The peasants took it very hard that production teams were deprived of their equipment, cattle, and money to benefit some infinitely larger unit with unknown and distant leaders, and that there was talk of suppressing all private activity. They would therefore sometimes take the initiative, and on the eve of "communisation", cut down their trees, slaughter their animals, and sell their grain reserves. In the people's communes at Pohu and Heshangqiao (Changge county), production teams sent some men to Zhengzhou by night to sell all the collective property. Of the 27 cooperatives that were to form the Dama commune in the same county, fifteen distributed the grain reserves to their members.[39]

Nothing suggests that, for their part, cadres had altered their behaviour. Some basic-level cadres, recalling the negative experience of the first leap, made known from the very beginning their reservations about overambitious production targets and advanced arguments that the regime summarised as "conditions theory"—that local geographical and economic conditions ruled out the rapid progress sought.[40] The opposition of some middle-level cadres, less discreet because less unacceptable to the regime, derived from more self-interested motives. Many county or township heads feared that once they had been sent to the new people's communes, they would lose their position as officials paid by the state.[41] Mentalities changed much less fast than the verbiage of propaganda. Many of the cadres sent to the basic level avoided mixing with the population and sought any excuse to return to the city.

Despite the new directions, the bureaucracy persevered in its ways. This is shown better than by any amount of statistics by what happened to Luo Yi, a young assistant mayor of the city of Xinxiang. The ambitious targets that this city had had to set itself implied a considerable increase in electricity use. The Ministry of Water Power and Electricity therefore allocated the city two generators, and in agreement with the provincial government, the municipality sent a mission to Shanghai in February 1958 to purchase the machines (which, moreover, could only be delivered in June and come on line in October). Immediately afterwards, the ministry changed its plans. Xinxiang would be supplied with electricity by a high-tension line from Zhengzhou and Jiaozuo and the two generators would go elsewhere. But it soon became apparent that the new line could not be completed before 1959. It was already April 1958 and the city Party congress had just raised production targets for the year by 70–114 percent! So the municipal committee sent Luo Yi to seek the advice of the provincial government. Officials there sent him, along with an assistant director of the provincial Industry Bureau, to Beijing where the responsible vice-governor was supposed already to be. But when the two men arrived by plane in Beijing, the vice-governor had just taken the train back to Zhengzhou. They therefore had to make their own way from office to office to secure eventually the despatch of the two generators and the promise that the high-tension line from Zhengzhou would be completed before October 1958.[42]

This story shows first that the traditional shortcomings of Chinese administration had not disappeared. Notwithstanding the new principles of decentralisation adopted in favour of the provinces, the provision of machinery for a modest city of 200,000 inhabitants was decided in Beijing, and the central administration was not terribly interested in local problems. To these old shortcomings were added others that had to do with the disorderly commencement of the Great Leap Forward. The arbitrary and continual raising of production targets forced central and local authorities to be constantly improvising; the whole Chinese administration was prey to a sort of Brownian movement. And then what on earth made Luo Yi run from ministry to ministry? The desire to do well and provide Xinxiang with electricity? Perhaps, though he had only recently been appointed to his position. Was it not far more likely he was concerned for his reputation and career?

What is striking in this story is not so much that Luo Yi had to resort to a universal practice—going from office to office—but that his success in getting the minister to honour the original promises made was portrayed as an achievement and inspired him not only to make a speech about it to the Xinxiang Party Congress but also to write an article in the journal *Economic Studies,* one of the country's most influential journals. The suspicion of arrivisme might also be extended to many another "vanguard leader" whose merits filled column after column in the press at the time, for example all those county secretaries who suddenly started digging away to leave their name on an "experimental field". Like earlier movements, the Great Leap Forward constituted an excellent opportunity for a host of careerist cadres to establish a reputation and secure appointments.

So the old man was not dead. According to the little hard information available, the Great Leap Forward did not significantly alter the attitudes of cadres or masses. Economic frenzy and political lying were the key components of radicalism. It remains to be seen why there had to be lying, and why in Henan lying had to reach such proportions.

There is an initial simple explanation for the lies of the Great Leap Forward in that the more unattainable the figures put about were, the more lying became the only possible behaviour for cadres. A doubling of cereal yields in a single year can only be achieved on paper. The highest officials in the CCP, who were old political pros, knew that perfectly well. That they risked themselves and their subordinates becoming known as the opposite of "frank and honest" is because they saw advantages, first and foremost the possibility of securing more enthusiastic and more total popular mobilisation.

Thus the first reason why lying became the rule at the time of the Great Leap Forward was because of infinitely more vigorous application than before of an established method of mobilisation. This method rests on two main principles: the centralisation of political incentives and the apparent decentralisation of economic operations. Like all earlier movements, the Great Leap Forward was both the consequence and the cause of a strengthening of political centralisation. As has been seen, this fact is obvious as regards the relations between the various administrative and political levels within the province—I have stressed how creation of the people's communes could be explained by the determination to make the Party's domination over the peasantry more effective. The strengthening of the centre's political control over the province is also glaring. That a leader from the centre like Tan Zhenlin ran or controlled the most important political meetings held in the province during the crucial months of late 1957 is obviously because he was responsible for Henan affairs. The sessions of the National People's Congress in February 1958 and then of the Eighth Congress of the CCP in May–June brought the whole Zhengzhou leadership to Beijing. More important still, no doubt, is the fact that from then on the central leadership, seized with a desperate urge for "surveys", was continuously on the move. Thus, although there is evidence that only three central leaders visited Henan in 1957, eleven inspections were made in the province in 1958: in the spring, Tan Zhenlin, Li Xiannian, Zhou Enlai, Peng Dehuai, and Chen Boda; in August, Mao himself and once again Zhou Enlai; in the autumn, Mao and Li Xinnian, again, as well as Liu Shaoqi and Kang Sheng.[43]

The second principle of any mobilisation campaign is the apparent decentralisation of operations. This means that once the broad targets have been set out and control by the central authorities assured, the localities retain freedom to arrange how to implement the directives sent them. This latitude only becomes freedom in the single sense that the localities retain the freedom to overfulfil the norms, if need be by inventing more "advanced" methods. This freedom is very organised; it is even tempting to say it is forced. For all the units are engaged in a vast competition for the title of "models" or "vanguard units". The principle of such competition involves considerable advantages for the authorities. To the extent that the process is engaged in, it enhances the chances of the plan being fulfilled. The existence of models also makes it possible to give a better explanation of the objectives of the movement and to publicise the principal "experiences" of it. Local leaders take part in it, in principle driven by their "level of awareness", but in fact by their concern to retain or increase their power. Such is the technique of mobilisation, already classic, that was used, on a scale previously unknown, during the Great Leap Forward.

The Henan Models

The question is what type of champions this competition produces. An answer can be extracted from the list of model counties in the irrigation campaign published in the *Henan Daily* of 16 January 1958 and completed by the same paper on 21 March (see Table 6.1). These counties were to remain in the place of honour until the following summer.

First, it will be observed that most of these localities are endowed with only mediocre natural conditions. In seven cases out of eight, the soils are not good. As elsewhere, rainfall is irregular. The irrigated area claimed for March 1958 is thus unlikely. This list does not include counties more favoured by nature such as those in the south of Xinyang special region (remarkably well watered, as will be remembered), despite the fact that most of them announced 100 percent irrigation in March 1958. The list is thus odd, both because it does not present the best results obtained and because those that it does include appear very dubious.

In my view the composition of the list is to be explained by motives of propaganda, concerned first with the agricultural economy. The majority of the listed counties experienced a bad cereal situation before and especially after 1956. As

TABLE 6.1   Model Counties in Henan (January–March 1958)

County	Special Region	Area Irrigated (%)	Soil	Annual rainfall (mm)	Agricultural Situation		Politics
					pre-1956	post-1956	
Changge	Xuchang	94	marshy	700	good	decline	rightism in 1956–1957
Dengfeng	Kaifeng	78	hilly	650	good	decline	early agrarian reform and despatch of a cadre
Jiyuan	Xinxiang	75	hilly	700	mediocre	improvement	irrigation model
Linru	Luoyang	73	hilly	800	poor	decline	rightism in 1956–1957
Linxian	Anyang	71	hilly	800	improvement	decline	guerilla area
Runan	Xinyang	73	?	900	mediocre	decline	?
Yuanyang	Xinxiang	96	marshy/salt	550	poor	decline	rightism in 1956–1957
Yuxian	Xuchang	83	hilly	700	mediocre	mediocre	rightism in 1956–1957

SOURCES: *Henan ribao* (Henan Daily), 16 January and 21 March 1958.

models for irrigation they thus highlight a break with the past—and the Great Leap was supposed to bring about a radical alteration in the face of the Chinese countryside. The question then becomes why were these counties chosen rather than others at least as backwards. The list includes no counties in Nanyang or Shangqiu special regions or the most mountainous areas of Luoyang special region. A preliminary response would doubtless refer to the need for the demonstration to have a minimum of credibility. Announcing records in areas that were too poorly endowed would have raised immediate doubts. This consideration also explains why the list includes only areas not too far from roads or urban centres. The second response is that politically there were particular reasons for highlighting at least six of these units: The leaders of Changge, Jiyuan, Linru, and Yuxian were seeking explicitly to atone for their rightism in 1957–1958; in Dengfeng, Linxian, and Yuxian there was a dynamic and ambitious political apparatus; and the same is probably also true of Jiyuan, which was chosen as provincial irrigation model.[44] Political factors also explain the predominance in the list of Xuchang and Xinxiang special regions, traditionally the best ordered politically and the most skilful at self-promotion; Nanyang and Shangqiu special regions, normally more passive, are not included.

To pursue the analysis in relation to areas that were the homes of the first people's communes in early summer 1958: Since the prize in the competition was purely political, one expects to find an even more marked predominance of Xuchang and Xinxiang special regions, along with the presence of other counties such as Yingyang and Yanshi that had already distinguished themselves by their hostility to Pan Fusheng and their activism in the Socialist Education Movement. But that is not the case. It is true that some counties in these special regions were in the vanguard. Lushan and Xiuwu, for example, each became a people's commune in summer 1958.[45] There are several model communes in Changge and Xinxiang (such as the famous Qiliying), and Yanshi won plaudits for its miraculous wheat harvest. But the most celebrated models of the communisation movement in Henan emerged from a special region previously known less for its political activism than for its agricultural problems: Xinyang.

The political rise of this special region poses an interesting question. It had attracted little attention before the serious flooding of the Huai in summer 1956, after which its leaders were criticised for their passivity. In 1957, it was more and more frequently mentioned in the press, first because of its agricultural recovery (its wheat harvest rose 46 percent compared to 1956), then for its achievements in the Socialist Education Movement, and finally for its large irrigation projects. By the beginning of December, 80 percent of the labour in the special region was already engaged in irrigation work. By January 1958, the special region had completed hydrological controls on 360,000 hectares out of the total of 1.56 million for the province and was promising a rise of 42.8 percent in its cereal production for the year.[46]

But it was in summer 1958 that Xinyang special region came into its political glory. At the beginning of August, the Chinese press announced to the world the great news that after setting up experimental people's communes in Suiping and Pingxing counties, Xinyang special region had by the end of July amalgamated its 5,376 cooperatives into 208 people's communes with an average of 6,200 households each. The "Sputnik" commune, the first one set up—which for a while embraced the whole of Suiping county—was to remain for two years the victorious emblem of the special region.[47]

This political rise is at first sight surprising. Except for the fact that Xinyang had been home to a Communist guerilla unit on its mountainous borders long before the closing years of the civil war, no known historical factor explains the political emergence of this special region. It may be that its leaders wished to redeem their "errors" of 1956; but unlike those of their peers in Xuchang and Xinxiang, their careers before and after 1958 are obscure.[48] Why then were their names on the front pages of the newspapers?

The Selection of the Henan Model

It seems that the selection of the Xinyang model is chiefly to be explained in the same way as that of the Henan model itself. Like their superiors in Zhengzhou, the leaders of Xinyang were chosen precisely because they had no past, no bureaucratic base, and no political autonomy; they could thus be easily manipulated.

The selection of Henan as a national model had nothing to do with economic considerations. True, with the province having been seriously hit by the 1956 disasters, its recovery could be held up as an example. In addition, its location between the Yellow River and the Huai gave it control of the flow of water towards Hebei, Shandong, and Anhui, and thus made it one of the keys to water development in North China. Finally, with its hundreds of streams prone to flooding because of beds raised above the level of the plain, the plain itself regularly threatened with drought although not truly waterless, and the great bare mountains cut by well-watered valleys, the province provided an excellent showplace for a high-prestige construction campaign designed more to achieve a large number of work-sites and rapid and spectacular improvements than a genuine and radical overhaul of the irrigation situation. Good and bad, these arguments may have come into play, if only to keep Henan among the provinces that merited the attention of the initiators of the Great Leap. But they are not enough. Other provinces had identical or superior advantages. Nor do these arguments explain the strictly political vanguardism of summer 1958.

In fact, at the end of 1957 the strengthening of political centralisation and the flood of ever more unrealistic production targets introduced a decisive factor into the competition between provinces: political selection by the centre. Once only false figures could be announced, the best province became the one that lied most, that is, the one that was most encouraged to do so by the centre: The best lie was the worst. Henan was chosen deliberately as a showcase for the Great Leap Forward. It is more than likely that the significance of Tan Zhenlin's long stay in the province (at least two months) at the end of 1957 was to encourage the provincial leaders to take the lead—and thus to lie more than was necessary—as well as to give them guarantees against any possible punishment. This would also partly explain why the province was visited by so many central dignitaries, including Mao Zedong himself twice.

It remains to ascertain for what political reasons Henan and its leaders were selected. Recent developments in the province were doubtless taken into consideration. Because Henan was one of the provinces most affected by the "right wind" in 1956–1957, it was not a bad idea, following a tried and true procedure, to make it a site for demonstrating the new line. But in my view, the principal argument was rather that its leaders, above all Wu Zhipu, could be disciplined and pliable tools. Wu Zhipu owed his return to power to the abandonment of the rightist line; he remained at the mercy of the centre, since Pan Fusheng had still not been criticised by name and retained more or less firm supporters in the provincial committee. Wu himself probably did not have highly placed protectors until late 1957.[49] The consolidation of his power, like his political rise, thus depended on the group in power in Beijing. When that group chose Henan as national model, it was in fact choosing an instrument that was at once convinced and servile: the first secretary of Henan.

All this is a hypothesis that is, of course, difficult to confirm. But it does throw light on a great deal. It becomes easier to understand the sudden familiarity with which Mao Zedong addressed Wu Zhipu when Mao visited Henan in early August. That date—like that in July 1958 when the removal of Pan Fusheng and his leading supporters, Yang Jue and Wang Tingdong, was officially announced—is not without significance. In April 1958, Mao was still telling the second plenum of the Eighth Congress of the CCP that Pan Fusheng had committed mistakes but had to be given the chance to correct himself.[50] The important event that occurred between April and July–August 1958 and that explains the chairman's sudden blessing is the miracle harvest in the Henan countryside, and above all, the establishment of the first people's communes. Wu Zhipu only received Mao's open backing after Wu had aligned himself totally with Mao.

The manipulation of which they appear to have been the object also throws light on the political fate of Wu Zhipu and the tribulations of the Henan model. After summer 1958 Wu figured amongst the best-known provincial leaders in the country. He spoke at central meetings, made statements to the New China News Agency, and wrote in the leading newspapers. A new star had appeared in the firmament of the Beijing regime, and it could even be foreseen that Wu Zhipu was destined to enter the Politburo of the CCP. This sudden rise was not to everyone's liking. Mao Zedong would say ironically "every time that the name of Wu Zhipu is mentioned, everybody becomes nervous".[51] And indeed, the first secretary of Henan stood out as one of the chairman's most fervent supporters, to the extent of supporting the Great Leap line at a time when no one else any longer believed in it.[52] And yet Mao became colder and colder towards him. In 1959 Mao was still backing Wu, this time lumping the unfortunate Pan Fusheng with the worst rightists, but he no longer totally endorsed Wu.[53] In high places the Henan model was less and less appreciated, despite its tiny blast furnaces and its large rural mess halls, its enormous agricultural production brigades and even the commune of Zhengzhou, covering the whole city. The fact is that with the chairman seeing failure looming, deciding on retreat, and donning the mantle of a realistic leader, faithful Henan ceased to be in favour. In 1961–1962, when the Henan catastrophe had become patently obvious and the political balance in the centre had shifted, Mao and his clan did not lift a finger to prevent Wu Zhipu's demotion to the rank of second provincial secretary and then his transfer to the Central-South bureau apparatus.[54] In 1964 the Great Helmsman had no compunction (when his position was decidedly stronger) about treating as a "leftist" a provincial cadre who had compromised his career for him, and then in 1967 letting him die in Canton amidst the insults of the Red Guards, even as his old rival Pan Fusheng was publishing triumphant articles in Chen Boda's *Red Flag*.[55] Since Mao had never seen Wu Zhipu and the Henan party apparatus in anything but instrumental terms, they lost all interest once their path, however "Maoist", became one that the chairman had abandoned.

If Henan radicalism was a radicalism based on a lie, it was in my view because it was the product of bureaucratic manipulation.

The Example of the First People's Communes

What is known about the formation of the first people's communes confirms my conclusion. With another look at what was being said officially, comparing it with what was actually happening, the falsification and manipulation become quite apparent.

The official story is remarkably simple. A typical example can be found in the article by Wu Zhipu published in *Red Flag* in August 1958: The large irrigation projects, and more generally, the launch of the Great Leap Forward in winter 1957–1958 led to the "development of productive forces"; from this "new situation" arose a "new necessity", transforming the relations of production by increasing the size of cooperatives and then broadening their aims and enlarging the range of their activities. After spring 1958, Wu argued, the masses, acting as spokespersons for history, spontaneously demanded the enlargement and transformation of their cooperatives, then themselves created certain collective institutions even before the foundation of people's communes under the auspices of the Party realised their aspirations.

To support this thesis, propaganda used a small number of concrete examples that are not without interest. In some counties, the fragmentation of cooperatives hampered irrigation projects. In one valley in Xixia 80 percent of small irrigation projects built by forty-eight different cooperatives were swept away by the floods of summer 1958. In Xinxiang, Suiping, and Lushan, cooperatives and even townships began spontaneously to join together in winter 1957–1958 to build big-enough dams and canals or to reforest the slopes. Soon, "new things" appeared: In April 1958, in Qiliying township, an old people's centre; in Malu township, mess halls, creches, kindergartens, old people's homes, and maternity hospitals; in Suiping, grazing areas and fish farms shared by several cooperatives.[56]

The first proto–people's communes appeared in March and April 1958. "Big cooperatives" (*dashe*) reappeared in some places, sometimes under different names ("agricultural farm" or "collective agricultural farm", a term hitherto used to describe Soviet sovkhozes). Their establishment was all the talk around Xinxiang. In Xinyang special region, "the masses" are said to have proposed one as early as March. The same month, in a township in Shangcheng county, fourteen cooperatives merged into four *dashe*. In April, the leaders of Xinyang special region agreed to start one *dashe* each in Pingxing and Suiping counties on a trial basis. The Sputnik farm was set up on 20 April 1958 in Suiping county. With 9,383 households and 44,328 inhabitants from twenty-seven cooperatives and four townships, it already had the dimensions of a people's commune and constituted the largest *dashe* in Henan. In May and June 1958 the number of *dashe* increased rapidly in Xinyang special region and they began to appear in other localities, notably in Xuchang special region.[57] But these *dashe* only introduced a change of size and were sometimes simply recovering their dimensions of spring 1956; they mainly made it possible to engage more labour and capital in large-scale works.

Starting in late June 1958, that is, after the summer harvest, the situation suddenly began to change much faster and much more radically. The number of *dashe* rose sharply.[58] Above all, the first true people's communes appeared, the largest *dashe* altering their name and their attributions. Thus, Qiliying contemplated calling itself "federated cooperative", "red flag federated commune", "federated farm", "Communist commune" and "building communism commune" before opting for the name "people's commune" (*renmin gongshe*). The Suiping Sputnik collective farm adopted the same name, subsequently approved by Mao at Qiliying. These new institutions extended their activities to areas previously untouched (industry, trade, education, militia) and assigned specialist brigades to them. In July 1958 the Sputnik commune was sending a daily average of 1,590 peasants to work in small industrial workshops and the mines. Everywhere, the number of mess halls, evening schools, kindergartens, and old people's homes was going up, at least on paper. The movement had even spread to Zhengzhou, where at the end of June, the textile machinery factory brought the families of its workers together in one people's commune that was developing subcontracting workshops, social services, and agricultural brigades. In August 1958 the most "advanced" people's communes attempted to establish a system for the free or almost-free supply of grains and clothes as well as a mode of pay by grades comparable to that of workers. In Suiping, Lushan, and Qiliying, nationalisation of land was discussed and sometimes even proclaimed, thus turning the people's communes into state agroindustrial enterprises. The first official appeals for caution came only after the publication of the Beidaihe resolution on people's communes in early September.

This account based on official sources calls for a number of comments. First, however attractive it may appear, the thesis that the development of productive forces necessarily leads to the transformation of relations of production is not proven. The organisation of irrigation projects on the territory of several cooperatives at once must have given cadres delicate administrative, financial, and labour problems, especially as "irrigation disputes" remained a lively tradition in Henan as elsewhere. The cadres may have been tempted to settle these problems by unilaterally reducing the autonomy of the various units, ready if need be to pass the measure off later as a "mass demand". But it remains to be seen whether such cases occurred as often as propaganda (which itself provides only a small number of concrete examples) asserted. One frequently gains the impression that the famous "big works" were only collections of small works. There is the further fact that the need to alter the size of cooperatives in order to carry out these works was only signalled by the press after the event, starting in summer 1958. There simply is no serious data to confirm or disconfirm the official line on this point.

Second, the alleged natural coincidence between mass spontaneity and the intentions of the Communist Party once again begs questions. How can the small number of the first people's communes and the absence of the sort of novel deviations and aberrant forms that any spontaneous movement inevitably spawns be explained? Furthermore, by a bizarre stroke of chance, all the first people's communes were situated in old model areas (Xuchang special region, Xinxiang county) or new ones (Xinyang special region). Were the masses in other parts of the country insensitive to the objective need to transform the relations of production? Again, the "new things" appeared in almost perfect order. Until June 1958 the *dashe* generally reverted to what they had been in the first leap. The first true people's communes date from the end of June and July. Hesitations over the name and hence the content of the new organ are interesting, but according to the information that is available, they seem to have been limited to the apparatus. Even after the beginning of August 1958, the avalanche of "good news" remained overall tightly controlled. The spread of people's communes was carried out in an openly authoritarian manner, with the press asserting ingenuously that "we must go from inside the Party to outside, from the cadres to the masses". Starting a people's commune became an extremely simple affair. The peasants in several

cooperatives (and generally in one township) were called together to approve enthusiastically the "proposal" made by one of their number, a proposal that the
Party had suggested and supported.

Not only was the creation of the first people's communes closely supervised,
but there is every reason to believe that where they were sited depended on precise political motives, though it is not clear what these were in detail. For example, the foundation of the Sputnik collective farm in Suiping, the work of Zhao
Guang, county vice-secretary, was supervised by regional, provincial, and central
officials. Chen Boda himself, according to a later source, was the direct inspira-
tion behind the excesses of summer 1958 in the Sputnik commune, to which his
journal did indeed devote a large amount of space.[59] The Maoist leadership
worked closely with the provincial and local authorities to create and cultivate
the model of the Sputnik commune.

The choice of other pilot communes seems to reflect similar motives. Cadres
in Xuchang special region were following a well-established tradition of vanguardism. Xinxiang special region, led by a dynamic and ambitious first secretary, had already attracted attention during the first leap. Precise political reasons
can explain the vanguardism of its model units.[60] As for the jewel of the special
region, Qiliying people's commune, where the first cooperative in the area was
established in 1955, it was founded "in the presence" and probably through the
good offices of a work team from the special region.[61]

The example of the first people's communes confirms and illustrates my conclusion about the launching of the Great Leap Forward in the province. Nothing
proves that they were the necessary product of historical development or the fruit
of a harmonious amalgam of mass spontaneity and the Party's political line. On
the contrary, everything suggests that they were a deliberate creation and even
the result of deliberate political manipulation.

Conclusion

A microstudy of Henan in the years 1956–1958 suggests two related categories of general comments, although in fact they remain no more than hypotheses. The first category has to do with the Chinese political regime, "seen from Henan"; the second is of a historical nature.

Central Power and Provincial Variations

First, the available sources throw some light on the workings of the various levels of power: centre, province, localities. The least uncertain conclusion is that in the Chinese political apparatus in the 1950s, provinces lacked a significant level of power. It is true that provincial organs played a considerable role in the economic and social sphere. They coordinated the drafting and implementation of the plan; distributed funds of their own; and helped, to an extent that is poorly understood, in the distribution of the infinitely larger amounts coming from the centre. They led the fight against disasters, helped regulate social life, and organised population movements. But this role was much less important than that of the central authorities and would have been wholly pointless without the action of basic-level authorities. Although the provincial officials coordinated the implementation of major decisions, those decisions came from the centre. What might vary somewhat was the degree of responsibility of the provincial authorities, not their decisionmaking power, which always remained virtually nil. The centre alone set the economic guidelines and made the basic decisions about how the budget would be allocated. As for cadres in the basic-level units, they saw to control of the population and ran the production apparatus under the more or less watchful supervision of the provincial authorities.

The weakness of provincial power was even more glaring in the political sphere. In this book, I have brought out the extreme centralisation of the Chinese regime. Of course, the centralisation was not absolute; that indeed would be at once unattainable and ineffective. Throughout China, economic and political importance, local traditions, and distance from Beijing doubtless meant that provinces varied in the extent to which they carried out directives from the centre. But Henan in 1956–1958 was surely among the provinces most directly tied to the centre. It was of no great economic importance, its leaders lacked a base in the bureaucracy, and the geographical and psychological distance from Beijing was small. Provincial officials carried out the often contradictory lines laid down by the centre with quite remarkable discipline. Politically, Zhengzhou was simply a suburb of Beijing.

The two cases in which the provincial leadership demonstrated even limited autonomy are themselves indicative of the predominance of the impetus from and control by the centre. The first case involves delaying tactics. Wu Zhipu restricted the relaxation decided on in summer 1956 to the economic sphere and contained the rectification movement in early May 1957.[1] Pan Fusheng used the same tactics when he endeavoured to attenuate the political U-turn in June and July of the same year. These various manoeuvres were aimed not at the heart of the central policy, but at some of its aspects. They were defensive and hypocritical, and therefore half-hearted; and that is why none of them succeeded in delaying implementation of a policy for more than a few weeks once that policy was clearly and vigorously commanded by the centre. In addition, each of these manoeuvres eventually earned its author a punishment. More important, what made them possible at all was divisions in the centre—divisions that were at once sufficiently serious and apparent for provincial leaders to dare to take political initiatives on their own (but keeping them more or less concealed), as Wu Zhipu did, from summer 1956 to mid-May 1957. When the reverse was the case, as it was after October 1955 or July 1957, and the central leadership was publicly united around a mobilising line, no stratagem big or small was of use. Political extinction threatened those who dragged their feet. That is when a second rather paradoxical form of political elasticity came into play. Provincial officials might no longer be in a position to delay or attenuate the movement, but they could implement it "impetuously", array it with new achievements, or in short, become a "model". There remained open to them the possibility of putting themselves in the vanguard of the movement, that is, of asking the centre for the favour of being put there. This second form of elasticity did not involve the actual content of the movement (since, as has been seen, models only exist on paper) but its symbolism, that is, its bureaucratic and factional effects. This form shows up even more than the other the supremacy of the impulses coming from the centre, since it was Beijing that as in winter 1957–1958 chose from among the candidate provinces (and their leaders) those to be held up as examples to be imitated.

The paradox is that this extreme centralisation did not prevent the existence between 1952 and 1958 of a very bitter conflict within the ruling apparatus in Henan. In its visible manifestations the conflict was primarily a personal competition for power between two leaders, Pan Fusheng and Wu Zhipu. Less visible but equally real was the factional aspect of the conflict. Each of the two protagonists had supporters within the provincial committee of the CCP. At least one of these two factions was backed by whole local apparatuses—Wu Zhipu had support in Xuchang and Xinyang special regions, as well as of some counties, such as Yanshi or Yingyang. The conflict had ramifications right down to basic levels, if one is to believe the revelations about various "affairs" and if my version of the story of the first people's communes is accepted. I have unfortunately not been able to determine the nature of the ties that held this faction together. One single comment is in order on this point: The great majority of these localities were the seat of early guerilla activity, were liberated early by the Red Army, or both. These ties were probably not initially political (at least in the sense of people sharing a common conviction). As has been seen, bureaucratic rivalries very largely explain the outbreak of the conflict in 1952–1953. In addition, the paradoxical positions that each of the two adversaries took up during the Cultural Revolution show that their political convictions counted for much less than factional affiliations and the accidents of bureaucracy.

But "politics" was not absent from their conflict. On the contrary, it must be noted that both were trained in the school of rural guerilla warfare, and Pan and Wu initially fell out over agrarian policy. Even more, far from calming down or remaining limited to one area, their conflict spread. In 1952, the disagreement was focused on rural policy; by 1957, it had become a conflict of political lines over the speed and methods of the transition to socialism, a conflict that bore also on a question originally of little concern to these two rural figures bred to a rather military-style communism, the problem of non-Communist intellectuals. Whatever may have been his innermost feelings, Pan Fusheng found himself identified with a moderate line according to which the transition to socialism must be a guided but cautious process, based not only on the determination to put principles into practice, but also on the acknowledgement of objective realities and the adherence of the popular masses—an evolutionary, unhurried process. Wu Zhipu, on the contrary, made himself the champion of the strategy of rapid transition that Mao Zedong set out and practised after 1955, a strategy proceeding by successive leaps, based in theory on mass "enthusiasm" and in fact on the constraint exercised by the people's conscious vanguard, the Party. It is as if Pan Fusheng and Wu Zhipu, at odds over personal, factional, and bureaucratic disputes, had been impelled to give their conflict a political content and then to identify themselves with the two rival lines that followed one another in central policy.

It must thus be concluded that the origin of the political purge suffered by the Henan apparatus in 1957–1958 lies not only in the change of policy by the centre and the need to find scapegoats, but also in a political conflict within the province that was both violent and persistent; the purge resolved a real local problem. But where lay the true origins of that local problem? In my view, in the centre itself. I am not here simply referring to the general argument (though it is one that contains more than a grain of truth) that political centralisation in dictatorships of the proletariat engenders uncertainty, intensifies factional struggles, and favours abrupt changes. What is at issue here is more precisely the increasing political swings and the growing bipolarisation of the Chinese regime in the 1950s. The shifts remained small in scale and the bipolarity veiled until 1955; after that year they became the key to the development of Chinese politics. They probably do not explain the birth of the personal conflict between Pan and Wu, but they do explain its politicisation, its persistence, and its very provisional resolution. Deep down, the Henan conflict was never more than the provincial expression or local projection of an internal ebb and flow and of a conflict affecting politics in the centre. So that if this case-study of Henan sets out a real provincial political history, limited, I agree, to the apparatus, but complex and capable of delaying or accelerating the implementation of whatever the central line was at any particular time, it gives no ground for seeing it as a counterweight or a limit to the omnipotence of the centre. Events in Henan on the contrary are the local products of a system that is at once both extraordinarily centralised and uncertain about itself.

The question is obviously to know whether the Henan case constitutes an isolated one or is simply the least poorly known of a series of intraprovincial conflicts. Of the three more or less complete provincial case-studies already written, two deny the existence of any major internal conflict, those dealing with Fujian and Xinjiang.[2] The third, Ezra Vogel's on Canton,[3] shows a different case. In Guangdong, sharp tensions engendered by the existence of a Communist guerilla base before 1949 and the colonisation by northerners of the provincial apparatus in the regime's early years culminated in a sweeping purge in 1957. These tensions were older than those in Henan and their geographical spread was at least as great, but they did not crystallise in a personalised and balanced conflict—the "locals" were always on the losing side. Furthermore, the Canton case exhibits a less direct link with swings in the central line. But the number of studies carried out so far is too small to make it possible to reach any conclusion on the representativeness of the Henan case.[4]

The Two Faces of
the Communist Apparatus

At least one might have thought that the way the Communist apparatus functioned would differ little from province to province in China proper. But there, too, the Henan documents reveal a greater diversity than expected. The Party apparatus, like the administrative one, showed two very different faces, depending on whether it was operating in a mobilisation phase or a consolidation phase.

A mobilisation campaign involved essentially the strengthening of the powers of the centre, and more generally, of all higher levels over lower ones. The amount of resources brought to bear to ensure a campaign's successful conclusion varied depending on the intensity of the campaign. Political resources, except naturally those that came directly under the Public Security departments, were mostly elicited through a vast competition for the status of model in which the risks and rewards might, depending on the case, involve only "face", or at the other extreme, the jobs of countless officials. The personnel resources specially assigned to a mobilisation campaign were the "work teams" that were sent down, selectively or en masse depending on the case, to the basic levels. These "teams" made sure on the spot that higher directives were carried out. Intermediate levels might also receive extra personnel, since their powers were enhanced by mobilisation campaigns. Each campaign in fact led to administrative concentrations at all levels and especially at one of them (the township in 1955–1956, the district or county, depending on the case, in 1957–1958). These concentrations worked to the detriment of lower levels and especially of the basic level; natural villages lost their autonomy de facto in 1955–1956 and cooperatives were merged into people's communes in 1958.

The purest examples of mobilisation campaigns affecting the working of the whole apparatus are the first leap and the Great Leap Forward. The various "leftwards" swings of the political pendulum, for example in 1952 and 1954, offer versions that are at once less pronounced, less complete, and less lasting. Mobilisation campaigns concentrated in a single sector of the apparatus have similar features that it would be interesting to study in more detail (for example, the reassertion of control limited to intellectual sectors in June–July 1957).

Consolidation phases show the opposite pattern. Whether they flowed from explicit political intentions or simply from an unavowed relaxation of controls, they always resulted in a return to greater autonomy of each level in relation to the next higher level. Extraordinary methods of control having been abandoned, government departments and Party committees would return to their routine and members of "work teams" to their original units. A process of administrative deconcentration would develop more or less rapidly, returning some powers to the basic units, whose number increased and size diminished. The absence or the discretion of political competition would enable each level to use particular local conditions to justify to its superiors toning down or attenuating the implementation of central directives without running too many risks, at least for the time being—and without, it is true, being able to look forwards to rapid promotion. During these consolidation phases local leaders would strengthen their power and young "activists" champ at the bit while they waited for the next mobilisation campaign when their "enthusiasm" could be expressed and their career take off. Local elites—professional and technical elites in the cities, "age" elites ("old peasants") in the countryside—would now be consulted more or less sincerely and completely, not of course about whether the policy being pursued was well founded or not, but about how it was to be implemented. In this a twofold process can be glimpsed, still timid and hesitant, of localisation and democratisation (on a property model of sorts), aimed at consolidating the links between the regime and the most "useful" section of the population.

Even the immediate aspirations of the masses would no longer be ignored.

Whereas in a mobilisation phase shortcomings in their conditions of existence would only be acknowledged in order to justify renewed efforts directed at a better tomorrow, now short-term demands would be considered, private interests would be taken into account, and even a blind eye turned to the more or less legal "spontaneous" activities in which the population indulged. The regime would no longer justify itself in terms of its dreams but in terms of its achievements. Whereas mobilisation derives ultimately from a conception of politics that is at once utopian and totalitarian, consolidation aims at reestablishing a system of power that is, of course, authoritarian, but is also more balanced and better attuned to the masses. These efforts were most vigorous between summer 1956 and summer 1957, but partial and temporary versions of them can be found at other points (for example in 1953 and early 1955).

One must not of course exaggerate the scale of the swings into moderation of the official line. Although hesitation persisted until 1955 over the precise nature of the regime's goals, and even more over the way in which it would implement them, from that date onwards, the ultimate goal of official policy was there for all to see. What the Party wanted was not only to develop the country but also to achieve socialism. There could no longer be more than respites on the road to transformation. The regime acknowledged the existence of a number of obstacles, but it also spoke increasingly of "leaps" that would make it possible to overcome them. China had entered the era of Maoist ambitions. The Party was even more united on methods of action than on goals, since methods were the province of the Party par excellence. Whether it was hardening or relaxing, at no time did it give up an iota of real power. In the countryside, when the regime was at the height of its liberalism, it would consult some, listen to others, and appear to ignore the rest—but it would never delegate its authority or recognise any objective and permanent limit to the enhancement of its power. In the cities, it took the insistence of the highest authorities in the centre for the apparatus to agree, for a few months, to regard as an issue the participation of non-Communists in public affairs. Even in a consolidation phase, the Party's fundamental modus operandi continued to be observed: absolute primacy of the Party over the administration, and of higher levels over lower ones, as well as refusal to grant true political status to the "spontaneous attitudes" of the population. Looked at from outside, the swings in the political practice of the Chinese regime seem slight: at worst, totalitarian tyranny; at best, a softened and hypocritical authoritarianism within the tried and true principles of the "dictatorship of the proletariat".

The Party-Masses Dialectic

If one looks at the regime from the inside and takes into account the concrete life of the Chinese, the recurrent swings between two lines and two styles of government must be given decisive importance. This oscillation is not simply an abstract mode of evolution of central and provincial policy. It also affects, often dramatically, the life of every man and woman in China. In a mobilisation phase, the peasant condition evolves towards a modern form of serfdom. Peasants are regimented on vast work-sites, sometimes in migrations of mammoth proportions; they have to work at night, private activities are banned, and their lot is exhaustion and deeper poverty. Workers seem more protected, for reasons both political and technical. But they, too, along with the mass of other city-dwellers, have to endure new meetings and further privations. Amongst cadres, many things change. Now suddenly the habits and petty privileges they secured for themselves during the consolidation phase are under threat. Their political virtue is being watched and failure to show sufficient moral rigour might be regarded as treason. At the same time as the apparatus is increasing its power overall (laying the ground for later, much less collective impositions), its members are taking a new "test" under the strict watch of their leaders. The swings in the regime's political line thus punctuate the life of every single individual, even those who are part of the apparatus, both concretely (after each mobilisation campaign, each unit resembles a valley devastated by flooding) and psychologically. For the abruptness and the root-and-branch nature of each swing is keenly felt, but so too is its contingent and temporary nature, for its political negation is already visible in the distance. Orthodoxy is both necessary and dangerous.

Historical studies of the People's Republic of China have sufficiently stressed the ideological or quasi biographical causes of these swings and the political divisions that explain them. A provincial case-study will hardly enrich the analysis. But to the extent that one opens up a more concrete historical space, one makes it possible to suggest a further explanation that has to do with the structural relationship between the Party and the popular masses. I feel that this relationship was formed in 1955–1956. Before then, it would seem to have been fluctuating— evolving from the honeymoon of the first few months towards a sort of balance of satisfactions and discontents—but overall not hampering or influencing the exercise of power. The authorities could conceive and implement new decisions without taking much account of predictable popular reactions. But after 1955 a period began marked by a gap between popular feelings and the Party's intentions. This gap was acknowledged by the two factions within the Party, but analysed by them differently. The Maoists saw it as the result of the bureaucratic and revisionist errors of the so-called moderates. But the latter were much closer to reality when they analysed it as the result of the excesses of the Maoist line. The fact is that relations between the Party (which supplied the vision and was the instrument of change) and the population at large began to deteriorate significantly and effectively in 1955–1956, becoming for two decades and more, mired in conflict. The decisive factor was both the passage to socialism and the economic crisis that it precipitated. Not only did the Party brutally give concrete form to a project that lacked the spontaneous assent of the people, but its tyranny was becoming less effective. The economic and social crisis that occurred in Henan (as indeed in the whole of China) between summer 1956 and summer 1957 inaugurated a cycle of relations in which the errors of one group and the mistrust of the other were mutually reinforcing. True, the Party retained vast power, sufficient not only to maintain sole rule but also to embark on a very ambitious process of mobilisation after a first and serious setback. It had not totally lost its original legitimacy either in the international sphere (despite the unpopularity of the Soviet alliance) or in economic and social policy—overall the gains as the First Five-Year Plan approached its end far outweighed the losses. Finally, although the internal divisions were already serious, they were not apparent, and until the Cultural Revolution, would not affect the organic unity of the central leadership. In 1956–1957 the CCP seemed—and to a large extent still was—more preoccupied with transforming the country than with tearing itself apart. Only a minority perceived its shortcomings as incurable ailments.

But two of these shortcomings were keenly felt by the broad masses: an excess of ambition and authority that did not adequately take into account popular feelings, and politically derived technical mistakes that compromised economic progress. The truth is that the novelty lay not so much in the appearance of these shortcomings as in the fact that they had become so widespread and were universally seen as such. The charm had been veiled; now it was broken. The failure of new enterprises, and for some categories of the population, the temporary return to their age-old misery deprived the regime of its aura. What was the point of tyranny if the results were so meagre?

At this point, I reach a difficult subject about which little is known; research to date has led to as yet fragile conclusions about popular protest. An initial conclusion is that the population as a whole was not content to suffer in silence the excesses and errors of which it was the victim. The people reacted, and their reaction took forms that were all harmful to the socialist order: economic disobedience, rural disturbances, low morale in factories, demands by certain minorities, and so forth. Furthermore, all this was understood for what it was. The regime set itself the task all through May 1957 of removing the "wall" and the "chasm" separating the Party from non-Communists. The broad outlines of this reaction, which was an essential feature of the crisis of 1956–1957, can be described and delimited; unfortunately, its various components and its precise effects remain very poorly known, especially in the countryside. The gaps in available information thus make it impossible to answer a key question: How, other than by the changes that had occurred within the Party in the meantime, can the crisis of confidence of 1956–1957 be distinguished from subsequent crises, especially the crisis of 1976 that was to bring down Maoism?

One thing is certain, and this is my second conclusion: At no time in 1956–1957 did the reinforced armour-plating of the Party allow a protest that was both united and political to see the light of day. Although popular reactions had a single origin, their manifestations, as has been seen, were extremely diverse. Most often they were silent actions: cutting down young trees, slaughtering cattle, hiding grain, slowing down the speed of the assembly line, and the like. Of course, these "antisocialist" acts carried a message, but one that was infinitely less dangerous for their perpetrators than a more narrowly political demonstration, which the regime would crush at once with the utmost violence. The only, or almost the only, ones to talk politics were those who had the knowledge and were granted the right to do so: the liberal intellectuals whom the regime in a moment of astounding carelessness encouraged for a while to speak out. The key feature of protest was that it was silent, cautious, and ready to dissolve at the first sign of anger from the centre. The regime was still too united externally and too strong for protest to be able to develop openly.

The upshot is that once it was seen that the Party could fail, it deserved hardly any better than the tyrannies that had preceded it: outward conformity, accompanied by a profound and active mistrust. The Party's perilous swings evoked a twofold reaction among the masses; the majority responded to the mobilisation campaigns with hypocritical discipline while a minority cautiously expressed its true feelings. This discipline was a poisoned gift for the Party, which could never fully realise its ambitions without a minimum of active support from the masses. The population's response to the triumphant war-game of propaganda was the time-honoured one of passivity and sabotage. That meant inevitable economic failure in which the most "realistic" faction that soon took up the reins would rightly see the result of a crisis of confidence. To restore confidence and revert to the lost middle ground it would loosen constraints. But the middle ground was now beyond reach, not only because of the internal faction fights but also because of popular attitudes. No sooner had the masses been granted the right to breathe than they wanted great gulps of air. They were no longer content with the petty freedoms allotted them; in a thousand acts of disobedience they called into question the foundations of socialism just when minorities were beginning to express themselves more freely. Soon the Party would feel itself threatened—or rather the "leftist" faction would gain the upper hand. The Party would then have to reimpose its authority, and to do so, repress and mobilise on a large scale—to the point where it all but stifled itself, which in the end would force it to relax its pressure, and so it would go around again.

The excesses and errors of 1955–1956 thus brought into being a vicious circle of relations between the Party and the masses. There is no doubt that the origin— the impetus of the first leap—was political and factional. Nor is there doubt that these factors subsequently continued to play a key role, if only to determine the length and nature of the various swings. But these also seem to have followed the equally quasi-pendular rhythm of relations between the Party and the masses at the base, a rhythm that did not depend solely on the whims of the Party, but partly on popular attitudes. The Chinese population, neither in revolt nor passive, had its own peculiar impact on political developments, an impact that was of course quite different from that of a revolt, but also more stubborn and perhaps in the long run more effective.

On the Origins of
the Great Leap Forward

In the same spirit, it can be said that the launching of the Great Leap Forward is to be explained above all by the Maoist impulse and the interplay of factions in the centre, but that it was not wholly without relation to reality, or such reality as could come through in the relationship between Party and masses. Its basic principle was intended as a rational response to the economic, social, and political crisis of summer 1957, and yet, it was inevitably to engender a frenzy.

I will summarise the sequence of events. At the origin of everything was the economic and social crisis that emerged in summer 1956. The failure of the first leap threatened not the existence of the regime but its future. The CCP's economic development project was threatened by the rural crisis and the industrial slump. Its programme for social transformation was more seriously compromised by the disappointment and apathy of the population at large.

The policy of economic and social relaxation gradually formulated starting in summer 1956 and completed in spring 1957 by a boldly conceived (but in practice hesitant and contradictory) attempt at political liberalisation constituted an initial response to this economic and social crisis. This response was in principle astute, since it sought to restore to the population the desire and the means to intervene positively in the process of production and to accept—even at the price of a few adjustments—the new collective structures. It was an attempt to get out of the crisis by appeasement. But this attempt failed, for two related reasons: The provincial apparatus as a whole did not implement the new policy sincerely, and more important, the population, especially the rural population, took advantage of the relaxation of constraints not to go along with them but to get away from them. Far from reestablishing confidence, the relaxation led to a deterioration in the social climate without producing any decisive advances in the economic sphere. Worse still, it led to the crisis spreading to the political sphere by introducing a double breach between the regime and the protesting section of the urban population and by intensifying factional struggles. The reality is that between May and July 1957, the Chinese Communist regime, at least in Henan, felt itself threatened (leaving aside the question of how real this threat actually was) in its definition as a people's regime by the social crisis and even more in its very existence (that is, in its dictatorship) by the political crisis.

A political regime unsure of itself and its power faces a dilemma: either it changes its character or it tightens the screws. After trying for a few weeks to change, the Beijing regime tightened the screws. For reasons that were less tactical than fundamental, deriving from ideology and history, the regime was deeply affected by the threat of the real world and responded to it by a radical reassertion of its own project: to rule, develop, and transform China. The launch of the Great Leap Forward must above all be understood as the brutal reaction of a young political organism that had just suffered its first serious wound, and suddenly, as if to prove to itself that it existed, returned to what, in its own eyes, was its very purpose for existing. People are balking? The Party will be able to bring them along by promising them progress, or failing that, by force. Agricultural difficulties threaten to compromise economic development? The main efforts will be focused on the countryside. Machines or fertilisers are lacking? Human labour will make up for them. It was with such brutal certainties and many more that the Chinese regime rediscovered itself in autumn 1957, just as it had made itself.

Let me reiterate—as I have stressed already—that this return to basics had many of the features of a return to reason (leaving aside of course any humanitarian considerations). Putting an end to social disorder, drastically reducing consumption expenditures, at least temporarily focusing on the countryside, resorting to the massive use of every available resource in human labour—all these methods in the service of carefully chosen and properly articulated targets could bring about economic progress. Note too that such a development strategy in theory applied quite well to the de facto situation in Henan in 1957 and rightly corrected a number of structural imbalances caused by the strategy of the First Five-Year Plan. It was, for example, reasonable to stress the rural areas that had long been neglected and recently been devastated; it was equally reasonable to turn to local resources of labour, money, and "inventiveness" after several years of excessive resort to government investment and advanced technology that was by definition scarce and costly. The principle behind the Great Leap Forward can be regarded as a rational attempt to overcome the crisis of 1956–1957 in Henan and the rest of the country.

But it is never enough to use only this sort of general, abstract argument. Not only did the Great Leap Forward produce a terrible catastrophe, but its political formulation and even more the nature of the Chinese Communist regime made the catastrophe inevitable. The Great Leap policy was reasonable only in the abstract. Formulated in the way it was by the Party as *it* was, the policy was bound to end in frenzy and catastrophe.

Analysis of the events of autumn 1957 in Henan clearly shows that there was not, as might have been supposed, a succession of the real (the crisis), the rational (the large projects), and the frenzied (the people's communes and the local blast furnaces), but an immediate move from the real to the frenzied in December 1957. The change in Chinese policy at that time was manifested in the change in the tone and even the nature of propaganda, the setting of targets that were from the outset overambitious, and the complete regimentation of the population in large projects and migrations on an immense scale.[5] The principal factor in the failure was already present in December 1957. The "general line", which was never formulated in a truly political way, was already drowned in emphasis and incoherence. The scale of the ambitions was already in stark contrast with the muddiness of the formulation. Action programmes combined general promises and piles of figures, but never set out priority targets realistically or the means to achieve them. Ambiguities and contradictions were legion. Was not the principle of the new line "overall development", that is, precisely the refusal to make choices? Here was one of the most authoritarian regimes on earth lapsing into the most complete anarchy over its programme. It wanted everything, it promised everything, immediately. Since the real world had not ceased to exist, instead of formulating a coherent and articulated policy in a number of stages, it launched a series of "campaigns" that one after the other combined all ambitions and mobilised all efforts: the large projects of the winter and spring, the summer harvest and the people's communes, the local blast furnaces. In short, from general principles that were in themselves quite unobjectionable, there emerged what was in effect a political frenzy evolving in successive avalanches.

This degeneration was inevitable for two series of reasons. First, the ideological infatuations of the Maoist faction found disciplined and (in the case of Henan) even servile instruments in provincial and local apparatuses. But it may also be thought that the same reason that had made the Party aware of the failure of the first leap, the deterioration of its relations with the masses, largely explains the follies of the Great Leap. It was from wishing through an act of will to seize back a lost legitimacy that the Party even more dramatically than in 1955–1956 compromised its social image. Far from abolishing the vicious circle of its relations with the population, which had come into being in 1955–1956, it followed and consolidated the cycle by repeating even more violently and more stubbornly the errors of the first leap. Thus, because the warning of 1956 had not been heard, a tale of catastrophes opened that would only be ended, perhaps, with the death of Mao Zedong. After 1958 the Chinese Communist regime developed at the tempo not of its achievements but of its failures and crises.

Notes

The following abbreviations are used in the notes:

DGB   *Dagongbao* (Impartial)
GMRB   *Guangming ribao* (Clarity Daily)
HNRB   *Henan ribao* (Henan Daily)
HQ   *Hongqi* (Red Flag)
JJYJ   *Jingji Yanjiu* (Economic Studies)
JPRS   Joint Publications Research Service
LYRB   *Luoyang ribao* (Luoyang Daily)
MYRB   *Miyang ribao* (Miyang Daily)
PI   *Pékin Information*
RMRB   *Renmin ribao* (People's Daily)
XHBYK   *Xinhua banyuekan* (Xinhua Fortnightly)
XHYB   *Xinhua yuebao* (Xinhua Monthly)
XXRB   *Xinxiang ribao* (Xinxiang Daily)
ZGNB   *Zhongguo nongbao* (Journal of Chinese Agriculture)
ZZRB   *Zhengzhou ribao* (Zhengzhou Daily)

Preface

1. See especially Gil Delannoi, *Les années utopiques,* Paris, La Découverte, 1990.

2. For an introduction to the climate of French research on China in the early 1970s, much can be gained from a reading of Claude Aubert, Lucien Bianco, Claude Cadart, and Jean-Luc Domenach, *Regards froids sur la Chine,* Paris, Le Seuil 1976.

3. Gilbert Padoul, "Comment connaissons-nous la Chine?", *Le Débat,* February 1981, pp. 96–105.

4. Jean-Luc Domenach, *Chine, l'archipel oublié,* Paris, Fayard, 1992. This book is currently being translated for the Free Press.

5. Frederick C. Teiwes, *Politics at Mao's Court: Gao Gang and Party Factionalism in the Early 1950's,* Armonk, N.Y., and London, M. E. Sharpe, 1990; David Bachman, *Bureaucracy, Economy and Leadership in China: The Institutional Origins of the Great Leap Forward,* Cambridge, U.K., Cambridge University Press, 1991.

Introduction

1. On this vital question see the works of Lucien Bianco, notably chapter 6 of his *Origines de la révolution chinoise*, Paris, Gallimard, 1967, and his contribution "Les paysans dans la révolution" in Claude Aubert, Lucien Bianco, Claude Cadart, and Jean-Luc Domenach, *Regard froids sur la Chine*, Paris, Le Seuil, 1976.

2. The title of the book by Claude Cadart and Cheng Ying-hsiang, Paris, Le Seuil, 1977.

3. One of the first and best U.S. case-studies on the working of the Chinese political apparatus is the work by A. Doak Barnett, *Cadres, Bureaucracy and Political Power*, New York, Columbia University Press, 1967.

4. Gilbert Padoul, "Comment connaissons-nous la Chine?", *Le Débat*, February 1981, pp. 96–105.

5. The best of these works (but falling short of Merle Fainsod's masterpiece *Smolensk Under Soviet Rule*, Cambridge, Mass., Harvard University Press, 1958) is the work by Ezra Vogel, *Canton Under Communism: Programs and Politics in a Provincial Capital*, Cambridge, Mass., Harvard University Press, 1969. See also Victor C. Falkenheim, *Provincial Administration in Fukien*, New York, Columbia University Press, 1972; Kenneth Guy Lieberthal, "Reconstruction and Revolution in a Chinese City: The Case of Tientsin, 1949–1953", Ph.D. thesis, Columbia University, New York, 1972. Among the provincial case-studies published since in the United States special mention should be made of Keith Forster, *Rebellion and Factionalism in a Chinese Province: Zhejiang, 1966–1976*, Armonk, N.Y., M. E. Sharpe, 1990. Ezra Vogel has also produced a follow-up to his case-study of Guangdong: *One Step Ahead in China: Guangdong Under Reform*, Cambridge, Mass., Harvard University Press, 1989.

6. The collections include several local newspapers and numerous booklets published by Henan People's Publishing House.

7. Parris H. Chang, *Patterns and Processes of Policy Making in Communist China, 1955–1962: Three Case Studies*, New York, Columbia University Press, 1969.

8. See in particular Wang Tianjiang, *Taiping jun zai Henan* (The Taiping army in Henan), Zhengzhou, Henan People's Publishing House, 1974.

9. This guerilla unit was quite active up to 1932. See the memoirs of its principal leader, Chang Kuo-t'ao, *The Rise of the Chinese Communist Party*, vol. 2, Lawrence, University of Kansas Press, 1972, pp. 171–294; and an article by Robert W. MacColl, "The Oyüwan Soviet Area", *Journal of Asian Studies*, November 1967, pp. 41–60.

10. Nine of the twenty-five counties in northern Henan were at least partially amalgamated with the Shanxi-Chahar-Hebei and Hebei-Shandong-Henan border regions in 1947. See *Yijiusiqi nian shangbannian lai qu dangwei guanyu tugai yundong de zhongyao wenjian* (Important documents on the agrarian reform movement from the CCP border area committee since early 1947), n.p., n.d., available on microfilm at the Toyobunko in Tokyo.

11. Among the six known leaders of Henan and Pingyuan between 1949 and 1952, four spent most of their career in the big bases in North China and only two were natives of Henan: Wu Zhipu and Ji Wenfu. But Wang Guohua, the sole important cadre known for certain to have served in Henan in the 1930s (see his memoirs in *RMRB*, 1 September, 28 November 1961, 24 January 1962), held only second-rank positions (vice-governor and then provincial secretary 1956–1961).

12. See particularly Zhengzhou shifan xueyuan dilixi (Department of Geography of

the Zhengzhou Teacher Training School), *Henan dili* (Geography of Henan), Beijing, Shangwu yinshuguan (Commercial Publishing House), 1959; Sun Jingzhi, *Huabei jingji dili* (Economic geography of North China), Beijing, Kexue chubanshe (Scientific Publishing House), 1957; *Nongye jingji quhua ziliao* (Materials for an economic definition of agricultural regions), Beijing, Nongye chubanshe (Agricultural Publishing House), 1958.

13. *Henan dili*, p. 86; *HNRB*, 5 September, 24 August 1957.

14. See in particular George B. Cressey, *Land of the 500 Millions*, New York, Toronto, and London, McGraw-Hill, 1955, pp. 245–284; Theodore Shabad, *China's Changing Map*, London, Methuen, 1972, pp. 118–123; Thomas R. Tregear, *A Geography of China*, Chicago, Aldine, 1965, pp. 215–227.

15. The worst floods were in 1931, 1933, and 1938 (when to delay the invader, Chiang Kai-shek had the idea of diverting the Yellow River, and the water flooded 450,000 square km, leaving 3.1 million homeless in the province), not to mention the damage caused in 1946–1947 by the return of the river to its bed.

16. The drought of 1920 affected 57 counties (Marie-Claire Bergère, "Une crise de subsistance en Chine, 1920–1922", *Annales, ESC*, November-December 1973, p. 1374); that of 1928–1930, 118 counties and 15.5 million people in Henan (François Godement, "Accident climatique et guerre civile en Chine: la crise alimentaire de 1928–1931", Third-cycle thesis, Ecole des hautes études en sciences sociales, Paris, 1978, pp. 73–74); that of 1942, surely the worst, left three million dead (*XHBYK*, 8, 1960, pp. 44–45; *RMRB*, 17 October 1959), half the total deaths caused by natural calamities between 1937 and 1945 (*Henan dili*, pp. 58–59).

17. *Huabei jingji dili*, pp. 158–159; *Henan dili*, p. 88; *ZGNB*, 12, 1957, p. 17. This average masks numerous irregularities: Thus, in 1950 the Nanyang region harvested only 0.37 metric tons of grains and less than 0.1 metric tons of cotton per hectare (*HNRB*, 10 September 1957).

18. In Henan there was quite a large minority of rich and middle peasants (37 percent of rural households possessed more than 0.66 hectare) in 1925–1927, according to Roman Slavinski, "Les piques rouges et la Révolution chinoise de 1925–1927", in Jean Chesneaux, Feiling Davis, and Nguyen Nguyet Ho (eds.), *Mouvements populaires et sociétés secrètes en Chine aux XIXe et XXe siècles*, Paris, Maspero, 1970, p. 395 (Eng. tr. *Popular Movements and Secret Societies in China, 1840–1950*, Stanford, Stanford University Press, 1972). According to a slightly later survey on two counties, the properties of rich peasants were hardly smaller than those of landlords; see Xingzhengyuan nongcun fuxing weiyuanhui (Committee of the State Council for Uplifting the Countryside), *Henan sheng nongcun diaocha* (Survey of the countryside of the province of Henan), Shanghai, Shangwu yinshuguan (Commercial Publishing House), pp. 6–14.

19. These estimates are extremely fragile, especially the one for the population of Henan in c.1900, which Communist sources may underestimate. The figure that seems the least fragile is the one for 1923, obtained by extending to the whole province the percentage increases between then and 1957 in thirty six counties, a third of the total. The 1949 figure is a probability (the first serious census gave the figure of 43 million for 1952).

20. *ZGNB*, 8 August; *HNRB*, 27 November, 31 December 1957; *Huabei jingji dili*, p. 158; *Henan dili*, p. 88.

21. It is most likely only in 1974 that the theoretical per capita production regained this level. For a probable population of 64 million, cereal production was 18.72 million metric tons that year (*PI*, 11 August 1975), or 292.5 kg per capita.

22. On the significance and meaning of the role of these cities, there is much to learn from Marie-Claire Bergère's article "Shanghaï ou 'l'autre Chine', 1919–1949", *Annales, ESC,* September-October 1979, pp. 1039–1068.

Prologue

1. Zhengzhou shifan xueyuan dilixi (Department of Geography of the Zhengzhou Teacher Training School), *Henan dili* (Geography of Henan), Beijing, Shangwu yinshuguan (Commercial Publishing House), 1959, p. 104. In July 1951, of the twenty-six publicly managed enterprises in Henan, fifteen had been confiscated and eleven were newly built (William Brugger, *Democracy and Organisation in the Chinese Industrial Enterprise, 1948–1953,* Cambridge, U.K., Cambridge University Press, 1976, p. 109).

2. On the industrialisation strategy of the First Plan in Henan, see in particular Sun Jingzhi, *Huabei jingji dili* (Economic geography of North China), Beijing, Kexue chubanshe (Scientific Publishing House), 1957, p. 178; *Henan dili,* pp. 107–108; *RMRB,* 31 March 1957.

3. *RMRB,* 28 November 1954.

4. On the notorious People's Victory Canal, see *RMRB,* 3 June 1956, and two works devoted to the programme to control the Yellow River: Zhongua renmin gongheguo shuilibu bangongting xuanchuanchu (Propaganda section of the general bureau of the Ministry of Water Conservancy of the PRC), *Genzhi huanghe shuihai, kaifa huanghe shuili* (Completely control the nuisances of the Yellow River, develop its irrigation resources), Beijing, Caizheng jingji chubanshe (Financial and Economic Publishing House), 1955, pp. 72–73; Wang Weiqun and Hu Yingmai, *Weidade Huanghe* (The great Yellow River), Shanghai, Xin zhishi chubanshe (New Knowledge Publishing House), 1956, pp. 60–65.

5. The best sources for the construction of the Sanmen dam are the two works cited in the previous note, along with two articles in the journal *Xinjianshe* (New construction), 9, 1955, pp. 1–7, and 11, 1955, pp. 29–33. It was not until 20 December 1974 that the *RMRB* revealed that the reservoir rapidly silted up and ended up irrigating only the adjoining countryside.

6. *HNRB,* 29 September, 1 October 1957. It reached 5.6 million metric tons in 1957.

7. *Huabei jingji dili,* pp. 172–173.

8. On the urban population of Henan, see *HNRB,* 13 June, 15 and 20 August, 4 September 1957; *Henan dili,* pp. 76, 81, and 131–138.

9. A yearbook published in 1990 gives a higher estimate but a comparable advance in the population of cities and towns: from 2.65 to 4.45 million inhabitants; see Guojia tongji ju zonghe si (State Statistical Bureau General Company), *Quanguo gesheng, zizhiqu, zhihaishi lishi tongji ziliao huibian (1949–1989)* (Collection of historical statistical materials in all the provinces, autonomous regions, and directly administered cities), Beijing, Zhongguo tongji chubanshe (China Statistical Publishing House), p. 523.

10. *RMRB,* 10 March; *HNRB,* 29 September 1957.

11. *HNRB,* 24 August, 4 and 5 September 1957; *Renmin jiaoyu* (Popular education), 4, 1958, p. 12.

12. On these schooling problems, see *HNRB,* 16 September; *ZZRB,* 17 July 1957; *Renmin jiaoyu* (Popular education), 4, 1958, p. 12. Zhengzhou had fifteen of the twenty-eight specialised schools in the province.

13. *HNRB*, 16 July, 21 October, 16 November 1956, 15 August, 12 and 25 September 1957. In November 1957, 36,000 national, provincial, and local newspaper copies were distributed daily in the city of Xinxiang; see *XXRB*, 10 May 1958.

14. *HNRB*, 27 November 1956.

15. On the excessive cost and the absurdities of the new construction, see especially the protests by two engineers in the *LYRB*, 25 and 28 May 1957. In Zhengzhou, 733 hectares of agricultural land were taken up by new buildings in 1951. See *Zai xin renwu mianqian* (Facing new tasks), Hankou, Zhongnan renmin wenxue yishu chubanshe (Central-South Literary and Artistic Publishing House), 1953, p. 33.

16. *RMRB*, 16 August 1955. Until the first meeting of a provincial congress of the Party in 1956, the assemblies of delegates of the CCP were the supreme political body in the province: This one was the eighth.

17. *RMRB*, 16 January 1955.

18. *HNRB*, 29 November 1956, 25 August 1957.

19. This is because, as will be seen, the priority for industry was reduced in 1957.

20. *RMRB*, 14 January 1955.

21. *Henan dili*, p. 88. This work rests on serious documentation but is influenced by the political line of the time; it may well have played down the gains of the First Five-Year Plan period.

22. According to sources of the time (*PI*, 9 October 1972, 11 August 1975; *GMRB*, 18 April 1973; *RMRB*, 15 December 1973), cereal production in Henan between 1969 and 1974 rose from 13.5 million metric tons to 18.7 metric tons, an increase of 38.7 percent in five years.

23. Henan supplied other provinces with 155,000 metric tons of grain in 1953, 370,000 metric tons in 1954, and 470,000 metric tons in 1955 (*HNRB*, 12 July 1957). In 1974 it exported just 3,200 metric tons (*PI*, 11 August 1975).

24. This is according to a comparative table presented by Frederick C. Teiwes in "Provincial Politics in China", in John Lindbeck (ed.), *China: Management of a Revolutionary Society*, Seattle: University of Washington Press, 1971, pp. 186–187.

25. *HNRB*, 22 September 1956, 4 July 1957.

26. *HNRB*, 23 November 1956.

27. *RMRB*, 24 February 1956.

28. The irrigated area reached almost 1 million hectares in 1955 (*RMRB*, 10 November 1955). The cultivated area under rice rose from 410,000 hectares in 1952 (*HNRB*, 4 June 1958) to 458,000 hectares in 1955 (*HNRB*, 12 August 1956).

29. A significant run of the *Henan Daily* is available only for 1956 onwards, requiring reliance on publications in the centre. But later revelations, confirmed by Beijing newspapers, leave no doubt that the case was as I have stated.

30. *Quanguo gesheng*, p. 524. On the Henan working class, see in particular *RMRB*, 17 October 1954, in which an article describes the low morale that had prevailed since the end of the year throughout the new Zhengzhou Number 2 cotton factory: between January and June accidents, fights, and acts of disobedience prevented any increase in productivity.

31. *XHYB*, 8, 1950, pp. 834–844. For a similar example in Zhengzhou, see *XHYB*, 5, 1950, pp. 77–78.

32. The first buses in Zhengzhou went into service only in mid-1954 (*HNRB*, 11 September 1954).

33. *Zai xin renwu mianqian*, p. 46; *RMRB*, 11 September 1954.

34. For an example of an affair involving corruption, see *XHYB*, 8, 1950, pp. 844–845.
35. *RMRB*, 16 January, 24 June, 5 October 1955.
36. *RMRB*, 21 March 1955.
37. *RMRB*, 17 April 1955.
38. See the examples contained in Zhongyang nongyebu jihuaju (Planning Bureau of the Ministry of Agriculture of the Central government), *Liangnian lai de zhongguo nongcun jingji diaocha huibian* (Collection of surveys on the economic situation of the Chinese countryside in the last two years), Shanghai, Zhonghua shuju (China Publishing House), 1952, especially pp. 152 and 163.
39. Detailed examples will be found in *Liangnian lai* (especially pp. 155 and 164–165, where it is noted that in four villages in Qingfeng county, 5 percent of families engaged in usury) and in *Zenyang banhao huzhuzu* (How to establish mutual help teams successfully), Kaifeng, Henan renmin chubanshe (Henan People's Publishing House), 1954, p. 7.
40. The sources are less inadequate than in the economic sphere and especially the social sphere, principally thanks to the revelations later published by the provincial press.
41. On the administrative system within Henan, see the handbook successively published in Beijing by the Law Publishing House in 1957 and the Cartographic Publishing House in 1962, 1965, and 1977: *Zhonghua renmin gongheguo xingzheng quhua jiance* (Summary of administrative divisions of the PRC).
42. The eight special regions of Henan from December 1954 to the end of 1957 were Kaifeng, Luoyang, Nanyang, Shangqiu, Xinyang, Xuchang, and in the former Pingyuan, Anyang and Xinxiang. Although there were repeated changes to the boundaries and the regions they came under, the number of counties in Henan remained stable (around 110) between 1920 and 1980, except during the short interlude of the Great Leap Forward when 18 of them were abolished.
43. *HNRB*, 23 September 1956, 26 May, 3 September 1957; *RMRB*, 11 October 1958.
44. Political leadership and administrative leadership were separated in 1956–1958 in two of the four cities whose leaders are known, Luoyang and Kaifeng, in two of the three special regions, and in seventeen of the eighteen counties.
45. On Zhang Zhonglu, see in particular *HNRB*, 26 and 28 August, 11 September 1957.
46. On the origins and practice of the United Front in the PRC, see Lyman Van Slyke, *Enemies and Friends*, Stanford, Stanford University Press, 1967. On the democratic parties and groups represented in Henan (the League for the Advancement of Democracy and the Workers' and Peasants' Party had no branches in Henan), see in particular *HNRB*, 30 November 1956, 19 May 1957; *RMRB*, 12 February 1957.
47. On Ji Wenfu, see *XHYB*, 10, 1954, p. 28; *HNRB*, 23 and 24 August, 7 September, 20 and 21 October 1956, 22 and 26 June 1957; *RMRB*, 17 October 1958. On Jia Xinzhai, see *XHYB*, 4, p. 143; *RMRB*, 6 February 1955; *HNRB*, 24 October, 2 November 1956, 17 and 19 May, 2 and 5 June, 4 September, 20 October 1957; *XHBYK*, 11, 1960, p. 112; *RMRB*, 25 April 1964.
48. In 1954, Su Jinsan sought to block publication of a novel by Li Zhun, one of the leading figures among these "young writers", titled *We Must Not Take This Path*, which developed the themes of the new orthodoxy (*HNRB*, 9 August 1957). On the conflict between Wang Yizhai and Ji Wenfu, see Wang's self-criticism in the *Changjiang ribao* (Yangtze Daily), 14 July 1952.
49. *RMRB*, 7 July; *HNRB*, 15 and 27 August 1957.
50. On the building of the Communist Party in Henan between 1949 and 1957, see *HNRB*, 22 September, 6 and 17 November 1956, 25 July, 22 August, 23 September, 29 De-

cember 1957. Membership of the Youth League rose from 824,000 in 1953 to 1.8 million in 1957. By 1956 there were one party school at the provincial level, thirteen city or special region schools, thirty-one schools of administration, and a training class in each county (*HNRB*, 23 September 1956).

51. Figures for other provinces are: Hebei (3.18 percent), Shanxi (2.92 percent) and Shandong (2.14 percent). See Teiwes, "Provincial Politics", p. 165. These provinces have a longer established Communist presence.

52. Of the population in Yancheng county, 0.51 percent belonged to the CCP (*HNRB*, 15 May 1956) but 1 percent of that of the whole of Xinyang special region; see Xinyang diwei bangongshi (General Bureau of the CCP committee of the Xinyang special region), *Wei gonggu fazhan renmin gongshe er douzheng* (Struggle to consolidate and develop people's communes), n.p., 1958, mimeographed document for internal circulation, p. 21.

53. For example, in September 1956, the new city of Sanmen still had only 201 Party members for a population of 30,000 and at the beginning of the same year, only 1.3 percent of the population of Xinxiang were members of the Party (*HNRB*, 26 May, 23 October 1956). On the CCP in Luoyang, see *LYRB*, 15 May 1957. On the Party's establishment among miners, see *HNRB*, 22 November 1956, 20 August 1957; *RMRB*, 15 February 1959.

54. *RMRB*, 6 December 1956.

55. *RMRB*, 13 December 1955.

56. Thus, a township in Yuanyang county was systematically ripped off for three years by what was in effect a gang of cadres (*HNRB*, 18 August 1956).

57. On the agrarian policy pursued in Henan up to 1955, see in particular *Zai xin renwu mianqian*, p. 39; Liu Shaoqi et al., *Tugai zhengdang dianxing jingyan* (Model experiences of agrarian reform and Party rectification), Hong Kong, Daqun shudian (Masses Bookshop), 1949, pp. 34–36; *XHYB*, 2, 1950, pp. 959–960, 4, pp. 1472–1474, 5, pp. 83–84, 7, pp. 561–562; *Tudi gaige tiaolie* (Rules of the agrarian reform), Canton, Zhongnan Xinhua shudian (New China Bookshop of the Central-South), 1950, 15 pp.; *Tugai hou de nongcun xin qixiang* (The new atmosphere in the countryside after the agrarian reform), Beijing, Renmin chubanshe (People's Publishing House), 1951, pp. 71–85.

58. One such figure was Wang Yizhai, the head of the secretariat of the University of Henan, in 1952 (*Changjiang ribao* [Yangtze Daily], 14 July 1952).

59. *XHYB*, 3, 1950, pp. 1430–1433. This affair was highlighted for the explicit reason that it was not isolated.

60. Resistance was still continuing a year later in what was otherwise a model county like Yingyang county (*RMRB*, 17 November 1954). In fact, the complaints did not dry up until 1957.

61. See, for example, *XHYB*, 8, 1952, pp. 35–37.

62. For example, Song Zhihe, mayor of Zhengzhou, between 1948 and 1956 (*ZZRB*, 17 July 1957).

63. These speeches are reproduced in *Yijiusiqi nian shangbannian lai qu dangwei guanyu tugai yundong de zhongyao wenjian* (Important documents on the agrarian reform movement from the CCP border area committee since early 1947), n.p., n.d., available on microfilm at the Toyobunko in Tokyo. A violent rectification of the Party followed this speech, which Yang Jue apparently carried out particularly vigorously in Anyang special region (*HNRB*, 25 and 29 July 1958).

64. Examples of this moderation will be found in *Liangnian lai*, passim and p. 156. Pan's action in Pingyuan was violently criticised in *HNRB*, 4 and 29 July 1958.

65. *XHBYK*, 15, 1958, pp. 76–78.

66. On Wu De and Chao Zhefu, see *Who's Who in Communist China*, Hong Kong, Union Research Institute, 1969, pp. 25 and 730–731. Wu Zhipu's personal antagonism towards Pan Fusheng, which comes through clearly in the 1957–1958 crisis (*XHBYK*, 15, 1958, pp. 76–78), probably arose in part from the fact that he felt himself superior in the political hierarchy. His reputation at the national level was not inconsiderable, as witness, inter alia, his contribution to a compilation in which the illustrious names of Liu Shaoqi and Zhu De figure, *Sixiang zhinan* (Ideological guide), Hong Kong, Beifang chubanshe (North Publishing House), 1949.

67. These political twists and turns are very well analysed at the central level by Thomas P. Bernstein, "Keeping the Revolution Going: Problems of Village Leadership After Land Reform", in John W. Lewis (ed.), *Party Leadership and Revolutionary Power in China*, Cambridge, U.K., Cambridge University Press, 1970, pp. 239–267. The policy pursued by Pan Fusheng in the countryside in 1952–1954, and its consequences, are fully described in *HNRB*, 4, 23, 25, and 29 July 1958; and *XHBYK*, 15, 1958, pp. 76–78.

68. On this affair, there is an interesting source, a compilation published in Wuhan which I translated and annotated with Ch'en Ho-chia in *Une ténébreuse affaire: le faux rapport de Lushan*, Paris, Publications orientalistes de France, 1978.

69. On Zhao Tianxi, see *XHYB*, 11, 1954, pp. 64–65; *HNRB*, 23 July 1957; *RMRB*, 15 May 1958. On Ma Jinming, see *HNRB*, 9 September 1956, 2 February 1958; *RMRB*, 1 November 1960. On Wang Yantai, see *HNRB*, 3 March 1958; *RMRB*, 21 August 1974, 27 December 1975. On Qi Wenjian, see *Who's Who in Communist China*, p. 129; *HNRB*, 4 September 1957; *RMRB*, 20 September 1961. Ji Dengkui, who reappears in Luoyang in 1957, is only mentioned in existing biographies after 1959, when he took over leadership of Luoyang special region.

70. *Zai xin renwu mianqian*, p. 34; *XHYB*, 7, 1950, pp. 562–563.

71. *XHBYK*, 15, 1958, pp. 82–85.

72. An article in the journal *Xin Zhongguo funü* (Women of the new China), 6, 1954, describes Ji Dengkui showering fatherly advice on Wen Xianglan and getting a loan of 200,000 yuan made to her cooperative.

73. It is told in detail in *RMRB*, 11 September 1954.

74. *HNRB*, 4 July 1958.

75. See, for example, *RMRB*, 26 January, 6 February 1955.

76. *RMRB*, 26 January, 6 and 11 February 1955.

77. *RMRB*, 24 November 1954.

78. *RMRB*, 28 May, 16 November 1955; *XHYB*, 6, 1955, p. 123. The press commonly began to use the term "leap", which was to have a great career a few years later.

Chapter 1

1. All the chairmen of local writers' unions were "rectified" during this campaign (*ZZRB*, 21 May 1957).

2. There were 200–300 arrests for Zhengzhou itself. On the Sufan repression in Henan see in particular *HNRB*, 5 October 1956, 12 June, 19 July, 10 September 1957; *XHBYK*, 16, 1957, pp. 115–116 (where vice-governor Jia Xinzhai estimates the weapons seized at the time as 16 machine guns, 1,129 guns, and 80,000 cartridges, which seems very little for a prov-

ince with over 47 million inhabitants that had only emerged from civil war a few years earlier).

3. *HNRB*, 7 April, 12 May 1956.

4. *HNRB*, 4 September 1957. A "rich peasant" guilty of several murders, who had remained hidden in a cave for a year, surrendered to the authorities in Xiayi county at the instance of his family and was treated "indulgently" (*HNRB*, 30 May 1956). My subsequent work leads me to think that these figures are lower than the true ones, though my analysis here essentially stands: The novelty of this campaign of repression lies in its qualitative targeting of social strata that had come over to the regime. See Jean-Luc Domenach, *Chine, l'archipel oublié*, Paris, Fayard, 1992, pp. 118–121.

5. See *HNRB*, 30 November 1956, for the example of Changge, Yexian, and Yuxian counties; and 4 September 1957. Note that in Guangdong, according to Ezra Vogel (*Canton Under Communism: Programs and Politics in a Provincial Capital*, Cambridge, Mass., Harvard University Press, 1969, p. 136), only 3,670 "counterrevolutionaries" were uncovered during the Sufan.

6. *HNRB*, 11 June, 10 July 1957. Note that 6,000 cadres were specially assigned to collecting "materials" to back up the accusations.

7. For the examples cited below, the sources are *ZZRB*, 22 May, 5 and 11 September 1957; *HNRB*, 27 July 1957; *HNRB*, 10 July, 9 August 1957; *ZZRB*, 11 September 1957; *HNRB*, 30 July, 15 August 1957.

8. There is a balance-sheet of the "high tide of socialism" in the industrial sector in *HNRB*, 30 November, 13 December 1956.

9. On the development of the cooperative movement in Henan, see *RMRB*, 10 October 1955; *HNRB*, 19 October 1955, 29 September 1956; *HQ*, 8, 1958, pp. 6–7 (article by Wu Zhipu). The performances of other provinces are reported by Frederick C. Teiwes, "Provincial Politics in China", in John Lindbeck (ed.), *China: Management of a Revolutionary Society*, Seattle: University of Washington Press, 1971, p. 168.

10. *HQ*, 8, 1958, pp. 6–7.

11. For *dashe* in the first category, see *JJYJ*, 11, 1958, pp. 16–23; *HNRB*, 16 June, 7 November 1956; *RMRB*, 1 February 1956. For those in the second category, see *RMRB*, 8 February; *HNRB*, 8 November 1956; *XHBYK*, 10, 1960, pp. 101–102. Note that Xinxiang special region had just welcomed a new leader, Geng Qichang, and the largest cooperative in Lushan was headed by Su Dianxuan, a famous model of labour.

12. This is essentially because of the lack of frankness in the available sources.

13. On the general problem, see Thomas P. Bernstein, "Leadership and Mass Mobilisation in the Soviet and Chinese Collectivisation Campaigns of 1929–1930 and 1955–1956: A Comparison", *China Quarterly*, July-September 1967, pp. 1–47. On the organisation of the movement in Henan, see *RMRB*, 19 October, 19 November 1954; *HNRB*, 10 April, 23 September 1956; *Xuexi* (Studies), 4, 1956, pp. 3–6; *HNRB*, 7 July 1956. In the whole of China, the number of townships fell from 210,000 to 100,000 (see Roy Hofhcinz, "Rural Administration in Communist China", *China Quarterly*, July-September 1962, p. 146).

14. This was the case of Zhang Qingheng, one of the leading cadres in the Rural Work Department of the provincial committee, who was to be violently attacked in summer 1957.

15. See for example *HNRB*, 26 May 1956. Around 3,500 head of cattle were slaughtered by peasants in Anyang special region in February 1956 (*HNRB*, 9 May 1956).

16. Bernstein "Leadership and Mass Mobilisation".

17. MacFarquhar's is an excellent work, the best available on the period 1955–1957 and full of intelligent and often accurate insights; see *The Origins of the Cultural Revolution, 1. Contradictions Among the People 1956–1957*, Oxford, U.K., Oxford University Press, 1974, pp. 26 et seq.

18. The provincial budget devoted to "economic construction" rose from 78 to 153.6 million yuan, and the value of "basic construction" completed in 1956 exceeded by 105 percent that of 1955 (*HNRB*, 23 November 1956).

19. *Henan renmin* (People of Henan), 9, 1956, pp. 4–18.

20. *HNRB*, 16 November 1956, 27 June, 8 February 1956.

21. See, for example, in *RMRB*, 2 April 1957, a report that defends this state-of-the-art technique, and in *HNRB*, 20 July 1957, another that criticises it. In *HNRB*, 19 November 1957, the secretary of the Qiliying cooperative described the opposition aroused by the new technique; a work published recently on Qiliying acknowledges that the cooperative's cotton yield fell by two-thirds in 1957 (Chen Li and Tien Chieh-yun, *Inside a People's Commune*, Beijing, Foreign Languages Press, 1974, pp. 70–71).

22. *HNRB*, 7 August, 15 November 1956; *HNRB*, 29 September 1956. It was not uncommon for people to work at night by the light of an electric lamp (*HNRB*, 9 August 1956).

23. *ZGNB*, 8 August 1957, p. 13; *HNRB*, 4 January, 24 August 1957. Guojia tongji ju zonghe si (State Statistical Bureau General Company), *Quanguo gesheng, zizhiqu, zhihaishi lishi tongji ziliao huibian (1949–1989)* (Collection of historical statistical materials in all the provinces, autonomous regions, and directly administered cities), Beijing, Zongguo tongji chubanshe (China Statistical Publishing House), 1990, p. 534, estimates cereal production for 1956 at 12.1 million metric tons, but it is said to have already reached 12.5 million metric tons in 1955. The value of agricultural production apparently fell from 3.47 billion yuan to 3.30 billion yuan and the index (1952 = 100) from 119 to 113 (pp. 532–533).

24. *ZGNB*, 8 August 1957, p. 13; *HNRB*, 21 December 1957. The 1990 *Quanguo gesheng*, pp. 534–535, provides comparable figures for cotton production (from 167,000 to 140,000 metric tons) and cattle (from 6 million to 5.6 million head) in 1955–1956, but not for pigs (from 3.8 to 3.7 million between 1954 and 1965).

25. *HNRB*, 12 August, 29 November 1956.

26. Cereal production in Nanyang special region rose by 3.7 percent (*HNRB*, 1 September 1957); in Luoyang special region, the wheat yield rose from 0.9 metric tons per hectare to 1.11 metric tons per hectare (*HNRB*, 13 July 1956). Amongst the counties in low-lying areas where cereal increases were recorded were Boai, Changge, Changyuan, Luoshan, and Shangcheng.

27. *HNRB*, 22 September 1956.

28. *HNRB*, 18 September 1957; *RMRB*, 21 July 1956; *HNRB*, 12 January 1957; *HNRB*, 27 November 1956, 24 August 1957. In addition, at the end of 1956, 30 percent of the cattle were in a very bad state (*HNRB*, 9 July 1957).

29. *HNRB*, 8 November 1956.

30. *HNRB*, 13 June 1956. In July 20–30 percent of wheat harvested in the province was rotten or infested with insects (*HNRB*, 14 July 1956).

31. *RMRB*, 6 August 1956.

32. *XHBYK*, 15, 1957, pp. 19–20. On the 1956 floods, see issues of *HNRB* for July, August, and September, from which the details mentioned below are drawn.

33. *HNRB*, 20 August 1956, 25 August 1957; *XHBYK*, 10, 1959, p. 115. The "record flow" at Huayuankou, the highest since 1933 according to this latter source and "for a hundred

years" according to *RMRB*, 28 May 1971, was recorded in July 1958 as 22,300 cubic metres per second.

34. See, for example, in *HNRB*, 4 June 1957, the criticisms by two irrigation experts, Li Fudou and Li Baohe.

35. In a cooperative in Shangshui county, 80 households out of 476 included at least one sick person; in one village in Yuanyang, there were 84 sick people for 315 inhabitants (*HNRB*, 2 and 8 September 1956). At the beginning of 1957, a flu epidemic was only controlled with difficulty in Luoyang and a meningitis epidemic hit Zhengzhou (*LYRB*, 27 May; *ZZRB*, 24 June 1957). On this topic, see further *HNRB*, 7 July, 4 and 5 September, 27 October 1956.

36. *HNRB*, 10 November; *RMRB*, 29 August 1956.

37. See *HNRB*, 9 August, 3 September, 23 October 1956, 4 January 1957. In May 1957 the protesting students at the University of Wuhan carried out a survey on the situation along the Jinghan railway (*HNRB*, 16 August 1957).

38. On organised emigration and its problems, see *HNRB*, 14 July, 8 September, 14 October, 2 November 1956, 5 June 1957.

39. *HNRB*, 20 September 1956.

40. They seem to have been rare, although fifty-six townships in Huaibin benefited from them (*HNRB*, 8 August 1956).

41. *RMRB*, 10 March 1957.

42. On delays caused by cadres, see for example *RMRB*, 11 June 1956; *HNRB*, 27 July, 7 September, 11 November 1956. On misappropriation, the most important sources are *HNRB*, 11 and 28 November 1956; see also 11 and 14 July, 12 September, 6 and 24 November 1956. The amounts cited are often small. Such practices must have persisted and even spread, as shown by the purge of the provincial apparatus decided on in autumn 1978 because credits intended for the victims of the 1975 flood had in part been misappropriated (*RMRB*, 8 September, 13 November 1978).

43. Amongst them was Hao Zhongshi, who was to become vice-minister of . . . agriculture. It was revealed that 550 peasants in Guangxi had died of hunger and 14,600 had fled their village (*RMRB*, 18 June 1957). Amongst the discreet allusions in the sources, I note a peasant found dead on the roadside near Luoyang (*LYRB*, 7 June 1957), four suicides in a production team, and five deaths amongst people fleeing along the Jinghan railway (*HNRB*, 16 August 1957).

44. See examples of missions of inquiry in *HNRB*, 7 August, 2, 3, and 5 September, 7 and 16 November 1956, and 10 January 1957. For examples of missions of condolence, see *HNRB*, 7 and 27 August, 11 September 1956. On the despatch of cadres, see *RMRB*, 25 April 1957; *HNRB*, 24 December 1956, 4 January 1957.

45. *HNRB*, 4 January, *RMRB*, 10 March 1957.

46. *HNRB*, 9, 10, 16, 22, and 30 May 1956.

47. There are useful analyses of the political debates in the centre during this period in Parris H. Chang, *Patterns and Processes of Policy Making in Communist China, 1955–1962: Three Case Studies,* New York, Columbia University Press, 1969, pp. 40–66; and MacFarquhar, *Origins of the Cultural Revolution,* pp. 99–165.

48. On the provincial congress of the Party, see *HNRB*, 11, 14, and 18 July; *ZZRB*, 21 July; *RMRB*, 25 July 1956.

49. *XHBYK*, 21, 1956, pp. 216–218.

50. *HNRB*, 21 October, 8 November 1956.

51. *HNRB,* 29 November 1956.

52. On these minor events, the sources are *HNRB,* 17 July, 23 and 24 August, 28 August, 12, 19, and 29 August, 9 September, 11, 15, 21, and 30 November, 25 December, 15, 17, and 23 August, 10 September, 25 October, 17 November, 29 August, 8 October, 6 November 1956.

53. Editorial in *HNRB,* 1 October 1956.

54. On the first of these two local cases, see *HNRB,* 30 November 1956. On the second case, see *HNRB,* 6 November 1956; *RMRB,* 26 March 1957; *HNRB,* 14 August, 27 November, 25 December 1957.

55. *HNRB,* 11 August, 18 September, 26 November 1956; *LYRB,* 17 May 1956. On the wage reform, see also *HNRB,* 13 July, 11 and 17 August, 1 September, 25 November 1956.

56. On the price reductions, see *HNRB,* 20 July, 16 August; *ZZRB,* 7 and 15 September, 31 October, 24 and 26 November 1956. On housing, see *ZZRB,* 4 July, *HNRB,* 14 July, *ZZRB,* 18 July, *HNRB,* 4 September 1956. On educational problems, see *HNRB,* 13, 16, and 27 October, 12 December 1956.

57. On the improvement in working conditions, see, inter alia, *HNRB,* 15 May, 15 June, 18 July, 16 August 1956. On the "one-boss system", see *ZZRB,* 24 November; *HNRB,* 20 December 1956, 4 January 1957. For a criticism of abuses of power committed by cadres, see *HNRB,* 17 August, 14 September; *ZZRB,* 24 November 1956.

58. The first of these two affairs is reported in *HNRB,* 27 June 1956; the second in *ZZRB,* 4 and 12 September, and *HNRB,* 16 October 1956.

59. On this whole process, see above all the after-the-event account published in *HNRB,* 17 November 1957; *HNRB,* 23, 24, and 26 August 1956.

60. On these various measures, see *HNRB,* 19 October, 16 and 19 December 1956.

61. MacFarquhar, *Origins of the Cultural Revolution,* pp. 177–199.

62. *HNRB,* 10, 12, and 23 January 1957.

63. *RMRB,* 26 March; *HNRB,* 17 November 1957.

64. The main 1958 source is a vengeful article written in the summer by Wu Zhipu, according to which the shift was completed by spring 1957. However, many local examples point in the opposite direction. Shangqiu special region, for example, which already had 4,000 cooperatives in September 1956, still had 4,559 in August 1957 (*HNRB,* 13 October 1956; 20 August 1957).

65. *HNRB,* 27 November 1957; *HQ,* 8, 1958, pp. 6–7 (article by Wu Zhipu). The shift was most radical in Xinxiang special region where the number of cooperatives rose from 1,539 at the beginning of 1956 (with 506 households in each) to 5,439 in August 1957 (154 families per cooperative); see also *HNRB,* 31 October 1956, 27 December 1957.

66. *HNRB,* 13 August 1957; *JJYJ,* 11, 1958, pp. 16–23.

67. They rose from 17,000 to 26,000 and 23,500 to 45,300, respectively (*HNRB,* 17 May, 31 August 1957). Note that for this period of retreat there is little information about another special region, Xuchang, ever quick to put itself forwards in times of mobilisation.

68. The counties were Changge (*HNRB,* 29 September 1957) and Jiaxian (*HNRB,* 14 August 1957).

69. *HNRB,* 20 September, 13 October 1956.

70. *HNRB,* 28 July, 14 September, 12 December 1956; *RMRB,* 26 January 1957; *HNRB,* 11 and 12 September, 6, 8, and 9 November 1956. The unhappy situation of the handicrafts sector was deplored at length at a meeting to which old practitioners of twenty-seven traditional specialities, thirteen of which had disappeared, were summoned in October 1956 (*RMRB,* 24 October 1956).

71. *HNRB*, 11 July, 17 September, 23 October 1956; *RMRB*, 16 January 1957.

72. *HNRB*, 17 July, 11, 14, 21, and 25 August, 4, 6, 8, and 15 September; *ZZRB*, 21 September, 23 November 1956. The "discussion" was summarised in *RMRB*, 2 November 1956.

73. *HNRB*, 4 July 1958. The distribution of plots of land led to disputes in the villages, as is shown by a report in *RMRB*, 9 July 1957: All the peasants asked for nearby plots and all in one block. The plots were supposed not to exceed 5 percent of the cultivated area, but in four cooperatives in Wenxian they accounted for 50 percent of the area sown to cereals (*HNRB*, 2 June 1957).

74. The permitted margin in Huaxian at the beginning of September was 10 percent for wheat and 5 percent for soybeans (*HNRB*, 5 September 1956).

75. *ZZRB*, 21 November 1956; *RMRB*, 24 December 1956, 26 January 1957; *HNRB*, 6 October 1956.

76. *HNRB*, 28 November 1956, 24 August, 13 September 1957.

77. But only 50 percent of available medicines were used (*DGB*, 26 April 1957).

78. See, for example, *HNRB*, 11 December 1956, 11 August 1957.

79. The Henan provincial budget can be reconstructed from the data in *HNRB*, 29 November 1956, 25 August 1957.

80. *HNRB*, 22, 27, and 30 November 1956.

81. *DGB*, 15 March; *HNRB*, 20 March 1957.

Chapter 2

1. A slightly modified version of this chapter was published in *Annales, ESC*, October-December 1979, pp. 1069–1093, as "Une crise sociale en Chine, la société henanaise de l'été 1956 à l'été 1957".

2. *HNRB*, 4 July 1958.

3. Miyang is a remote county in Nanyang special region. I was able to consult this local newssheet (hereafter *MYRB*) for the period October 1957–May 1958.

4. In *HNRB*, 10 November 1956, there is the precise example of Xiuwu county.

5. In August 1957, out of 811 households in a Linxian cooperative, only 121 had the means to face the famine by themselves (*HNRB*, 14 August 1957). See also *HNRB*, 7 and 24 July 1957. On the food problems experienced by Henan, the sources are *HNRB*, 17 May; *RMRB*, 31 May; *HNRB*, 11 June, 26 June, 14 August 1957. On clothing problems, see *RMRB*, 28 November; *HNRB*, 25 December 1956, 24 May 1957.

6. *DGB*, 8 August 1957; *HNRB*, 10 January; *RMRB*, 26 March; *LYRB*, 23 and 28 May 1957.

7. On the various procedures adopted, see in particular *HNRB*, 22 June 1957, 18 and 25 July 1958.

8. On withdrawals from cooperatives, see in particular *HNRB*, 22 June, 14 July, 3, 13, and 18 August 1957; *RMRB*, 20 March 1957; *HNRB*, 20 January, 4, 17, 18, 20, 25, and 29 July, 4, 7, 8, 11, and 18 August 1958.

9. Ezra Vogel also provides the rather low figure of 130,000 temporary withdrawals and 20,000 permanent ones in Guangdong (*Canton Under Communism: Programs and Politics in a Provincial Capital,* Cambridge, Mass., Harvard University Press, 1969, p. 204).

10. For the examples cited below, the sources are *HNRB*, 9, 10, and 15 August, 3 September; *ZZRB*, 4 September 1957.

11. On these incidents, see _DGB_, 5 and 8 August; _HNRB_, 2, 3, 10, 11, 15, 18, 28, and 29 August, 8, 15, 20, 25, and 29 September, 4 and 7 October; _ZZRB_, 1 September 1957.

12. Thus, 320 incidents are said to have broken out in the suburb of Jiaozuo in spring 1957 (_DGB_, 5 August 1957). Also in the spring, three former landlords are said to have provoked a panic in Lucheng county by announcing the return of Chiang Kai-shek (_HNRB_, 15 August 1957). See also _LYRB_, 28 May; _HNRB_, 15 and 29 July, 11 August 1958.

13. _HNRB_, 11 August 1957. In Xincai an attempt was made to steal the register of individuals placed under surveillance (_HNRB_, 3 August 1957).

14. See for example _HNRB_, 2, 10, 15, and 28 August 1957. But the area actually seized back was small in the sole case known in detail: just a little over one hectare in the whole of Minquan county (_HNRB_, 11 August 1958). Among the 9,159 families of landlords and rich peasants in Linxian (which had some 110,000 households), 20 percent misbehaved in the summer of 1957, as did 71 percent of the 263 families of "counterrevolutionaries" and 22 percent of the 22,990 families of well-off middle peasants (_HNRB_, 29 August 1957).

15. _RMRB_, 18 October 1957. In a model cooperative in Lushan, 45 percent of peasants said they were dissatisfied with cooperatives and the unified purchase and supply system (_HNRB_, 26 September 1957).

16. In one cooperative in the suburbs of Zhengzhou, the "peasants' representatives" were brutally convinced by cadres to ask for the suppression of private plots (_HNRB_, 8 June 1957).

17. _HNRB_, 3 and 10 November, 8 December; _LYRB_, 20 and 28 May; _RMRB_, 25 April 1957.

18. See in particular _LYRB_, 23 and 28 May; _HNRB_, 2 June, 17 August, 15, 17, and 28 September; _ZZRB_, 10 October; _HNRB_, 16 October, 30 November, 8 December 1957.

19. _DGB_, 8 August; _HNRB_, 15, 17, and 28 September, 16 October 1957.

20. _HNRB_, 8 December 1957.

21. _HNRB_, 18 November 1956, 12 January, 11 July, 6 August 1957, 15 July 1958; _RMRB_, 22 October 1958.

22. _DGB_, 23 April; _HNRB_, 24 August 1957.

23. _HNRB_, 24 October, 11 December 1956, 31 July, 4, 7, 10, 11, 13, 15, 18, 20, 25, and 27 August 1957.

24. _DGB_, 1 March, 18 November 1957; _HNRB_, 11 October 1956, 15 August, 22 September 1957.

25. _RMRB_, 7 August 1957.

26. _HNRB_, 27 November 1956, 31 December 1957.

27. The reappearance of usury (or rather its spread) is something that definitely happened, but little is known about it. In one township in Huixian, the rise in the number of private loans was such as to precipitate the collapse of the credit cooperative (_DGB_, 13 November 1957). Numerous peasants borrowed at the official rate in order to lend out at a higher rate (_HNRB_, 4 September 1957). See also _ZZRB_, 30 September 1957.

28. _Quanmian dayuejin zhongde liangshi gongzuo_ (Grain work during the total Great Leap Forward) Zhengzhou, Henan renmin chubanshe (Henan People's Publishing House), 1958, pp. 60–62. For similar individual cases, see _HNRB_, 11 January, 18 September 1957.

29. It must be remembered that the occupation of cadre must be seen as an urban one. A young schoolboy in Luoyang special region said: "I shall never return to the village, not even to die there" (_LYRB_, 29 May 1957).

30. *HNRB*, 1 October 1956, 4 August 1957; *LYRB*, 10, 29, and 30 May 1957; *ZZRB*, 16 November 1957.

31. Available sources certainly do not provide any figures comparable in terms of number and importance to those reproduced by Christopher Howe (*Employment and Economic Growth in Urban China*, Cambridge, U.K., Cambridge University Press, 1971, 170 pp.) and, for Canton, Ezra Vogel (*Canton Under Communism*, pp. 66–67, 72, 187, 213, 220).

32. *HNRB*, 25 September 1957.

33. *LYRB*, 17 May 1957; *ZZRB*, 15 September 1956.

34. On supply problems in Henan villages, see in particular *DGB*, 20 February 1957; *HNRB*, 16 July, 16 August, 15 and 21 September, 31 October, 26 November 1956; *LYRB*, 17 and 28 May, 7 June 1957; *ZZRB*, 7 and 15 September 1956, 18 July, 29 October 1957.

35. On accommodation problems in Henan cities, see *HNRB*, 4 September 1956, 4 August, 18 October 1957; *ZZRB*, 4 June, 18 July 1956, 16 July, 23 October, 10 November 1957; *LYRB*, 25, 28, and 29 May, 7 June 1957.

36. Thus, in June 1957, forty-four families were occupying uncompleted buildings of the Zhengzhou engineering factory (*ZZRB*, 16 July 1957) and several dozen families of railway workers transferred from Xuchang were camping in the corridors of housing for workers at the Zhengzhou freight station (*ZZRB*, 23 October 1957).

37. There were three per room in a big store in Zhengzhou (*HNRB*, 14 July 1957); two doctors or four nurses in a Luoyang hospital (*LYRB*, 27 May 1957).

38. In 1949, the floor area occupied per person is said to have been 2.9 square metres (*ZZRB*, 7 July 1957).

39. A report by the president of the province's supreme court is the most detailed source available (*HNRB*, 25 August 1957). See also *HNRB*, 4 September 1957.

40. *HNRB*, 4 July 1958.

41. See, for example, *ZZRB*, 23 October 1957.

42. *HNRB*, 10 December; *LYRB*, 25 May; *ZZRB*, 10 and 16 October 1957.

43. "Meetingitis" is a national calamity in China. Between January and July 1956, Sheng Wan, a famous model worker in Zhengzhou, spent 120 whole days in meetings (*HNRB*, 14 October 1956). On this excess of bureaucratic obligations, see also *ZZRB*, 26 September, 24 and 25 November; *HNRB*, 6 October 1956.

44. In the mines at Hebi, sixty-one workers were punished with imprisonment between spring 1955 and summer 1956. See also *HNRB*, 26 May 1957.

45. In summer 1957, to prove that a rightist had intentionally made his mistakes, it was explained that he had used this conjunction six times in the same speech (*HNRB*, 21 June 1957).

46. In autumn 1956, 5,769 probationary members of the Party, 10 percent of the total in Luoyang special region, were waiting to be confirmed (*HNRB*, 25 October 1956). The need to wait long years before being admitted to the Party led to an ageing of members of the Youth League; in Zhoukou, over 30 percent of its members were over the age limit (*HNRB*, 13 November 1956).

47. Among the 265 demobilised soldiers who settled in Yichuan county during the first half of 1957, 245 married or remarried with the help of the authorities (*HNRB*, 6 August 1957). See also *HNRB*, 6 and 17 June 1956, 9 June, 6 August 1957; *LYRB*, 31 May; *ZZRB*, 13, 18, and 31 July 1957. In Zhengzhou, 8,500 demobilised soldiers were settled between 1952 and 1957.

48. See, for example, *HNRB*, 21 August 1956, 9 August 1957.

49. The main issue was transport and overseas residence allowances, which might be as high as 40 yuan per month for an assistant bureau head—which actually seems rather moderate (*HNRB*, 5 June 1957).

50. The incompetence, pretentiousness, and spitefulness of wives of cadres were violently criticised during the Hundred Flowers campaign (*HNRB*, 2 and 4 June; *ZZRB*, 4 October 1957). On influence-peddling among cadres, see also *HNRB*, 5 and 8 June; *ZZRB*, 5 October 1957. On their legendary love of official cars, and failing these, bicycles, see *HNRB*, 8, 16, and 17 August; *LYRB*, 17 May; *RMRB*, 27 August 1957.

51. *LYRB*, 6 June 1957. See also *LYRB*, 27 and 29 May, 7 June 1957.

52. *HNRB*, 2 June 1957. His luxurious habits did not hurt him: He was promoted to head of Changge county in December 1957 (*HNRB*, 25 December 1957).

53. *LYRB*, 6 June 1957. These criticisms (and many others that were made of him in spring 1957) did not prevent Wang Tianduo from subsequently being promoted to city secretary (*RMRB*, 20 October 1958).

54. *LYRB*, 23 May 1957. At that time, only 300,000 copies of *Reference News*, reserved for the apparatus, were published for the whole of China, and they were only available above the county level (*HNRB*, 24 May 1957).

55. *HNRB*, 24 May; *LYRB*, 6 June 1957.

56. In the textile industry, a worker received on average 70 yuan per month in the first year. But in basic construction, the monthly wage after four years of seniority did not exceed 50–60 yuan.

57. In Zhengzhou, industrial accidents increased by 250 percent during the first half of 1956 (*ZZRB*, 8 July 1956). See also *LYRB*, 7 June; *ZZRB*, 20 July 1957.

58. *LYRB*, 1 May; *ZZRB*, 15 September 1957.

59. Over a thousand work-hours were lost in unjustified absences in the Zhengzhou engineering factory in the first half of 1957 (*ZZRB*, 21 September 1957), which seems on the low side if European management criteria are used. See also *HNRB*, 12 and 14 May, and in the 31 August 1957 issue, a very sombre picture of the situation in the Jiaozuo mines.

60. In some cases, disenchantment with trade unions was almost total. In a factory in Luoyang, 95 percent of trade union dues remained unpaid (*LYRB*, 31 May 1957).

61. *HNRB*, 11 September 1957. For a similar example, see *HNRB*, 13 July 1957. Information on workers transferred will be found in *DGB*, 3 February; *LYRB*, 24 May; *ZZRB*, 28 October 1957.

62. *HNRB*, 15 June, 15 November 1956. In spring 1957, morale was bad in the big stores in Luoyang (*LYRB*, 7 June 1957).

63. Temporary workers found it relatively easy to regularise their position at the time of the big works in 1956, but it later became extremely difficult and three workers guilty of having requested it were even dubbed "counterrevolutionaries" (*ZZRB*, 21 May 1957). See also *HNRB*, 31 May 1957.

64. *ZZRB*, 10 and 22 July 1956; *LYRB*, 28 May 1957.

65. *LYRB*, 30 May 1957. In the Dafeng factory in Zhengzhou, an assistant secretary of the municipal committee of the CCP had to intervene to restore order (*HNRB*, 24 May 1957). For a similar example, see also *ZZRB*, 21 September 1957. On apprentices, see *ZZRB*, 22 May; *LYRB*, 22 and 31 May 1957.

66. Such was the case with 42 percent of parents of Lankao secondary school students (*Renmin jiaoyu* [Popular education], 9, 1957, pp. 27–29). On these educational problems,

see *HNRB*, 3 August, 13 and 18 September, 30 November 1956, 24 September 1957; *LYRB*, 14, 17, 22, and 31 May 1957; *ZZRB*, 19 July 1956, 13 July 1957.

67. *HNRB*, 18 October 1956; *LYRB*, 29 and 31 May 1957; (*Renmin jiaoyu* [Popular education]), 5, 1957, pp. 15–16, and 9, pp. 27–29.

68. On the malaise in the world of medicine, see in particular *LYRB*, 24, 27, and 30 May, 6 and 7 June; *ZZRB*, 22 May 1957.

69. There were a total of only 1,600 actual withdrawals in the whole province (chiefly former small proprietors, according to the press, but in Zhengzhou the number of individual craftsworkers was nine times higher; see *ZZRB*, 29 October 1957).

70. *ZZRB*, 30 November 1957. One of the "black enterprises" had ten workers and capital of 2,000 yuan (*ZZRB*, 7 September 1957). See also *ZZRB*, 25 September, 11 and 24 October 1957.

71. *ZZRB*, 19 November 1957.

72. *DGB*, 5 August 1957. In Zhengzhou, some small businessowners specialised in buying sewing machines sold cheap by crafts cooperatives on their way out, and then selling them at high prices (*ZZRB*, 14 September 1957). On all this petty trafficking, see in particular *LYRB*, 23 May, *ZZRB*, 21 September, 24 October, 14 November 1957.

73. Proportionally the Moslems had almost as many Party members (4,700) and cadres (2,000) as the rest of the population (*HNRB*, 28 December 1957); but to take only one example, the 7 February district in Zhengzhou, which included over 4,000 Moslem households, did not have a single minority cadre (*HNRB*, 6 June 1957). On the national minorities in Henan, see Zhengzhou shifan xueyuan dilixi (Department of Geography of the Zhengzhou Teacher Training School), *Henan dili* (Geography of Henan), Beijing, Shangwu yinshuguan (Commercial Publishing House), 1959, p. 82; *HNRB*, 17 July 1956, 6 June, 24 August 1957; *LYRB*, 29 May 1957.

74. It did so using a vocabulary full of references to the fate of Christians under Nero (*RMRB*, 9 August 1957). See *HNRB*, 17 May, 6 June 1957; *XXRB*, 20 April 1958).

75. This is the proportion of inhabitants deprived of their civic rights in nine cities and seven rural counties by autumn 1956 (*HNRB*, 29 November 1956).

76. Such was the case of the father of a leading "democratic personality" in the province, Zhang Yunchuan, who owned one hectare in eastern Anhui and died of the violence he suffered after the agrarian reform (*RMRB*, 7 July 1957).

77. *HNRB*, 16 July 1956, 29 August, 30 November 1957; *ZZRB*, 11 September, 27 November 1957.

78. *HNRB*, 6 June 1957.

79. *ZZRB*, 21 May; *LYRB*, 23 and 30 May, 7 and 12 June 1957.

80. *LYRB*, 10 May; *ZZRB*, 16 November 1957.

81. *ZZRB*, 4 October 1956.

82. *HNRB*, 11 January; *LYRB*, 29 May 1957.

83. See for example *ZZRB*, 21 November 1956.

84. On the street disorders in Luoyang, there is a colourful account in *LYRB*, 8 May 1957.

85. For the month of July 1956 alone, see *ZZRB*, 1, 4, 5, 12, and 21 July.

86. But other features would make it possible to distinguish amongst the various social crises: How closely, at a given point in time, the regime was sticking to its own objectives of transformation; the sociological makeup of the opposition; its ideological objectives; the nature and seriousness of the difficulties that precipitated the social crisis. On the

confrontation that arose in winter 1978 and how it relates to earlier examples, see the article by G. Padoul, "A propos de la contestation", *Projet,* February 1979, pp. 159–169.

87. The most serious criticism to be made of the otherwise excellent work by Roderick MacFarquhar, *The Origins of the Cultural Revolution,* is that it is almost exclusively concerned with factional struggles at the top. And it is the chief merit of Siwitt Aray's little book *Les Cent Fleurs,* Paris, Flammarion, 1973) to have brought out the relationship between social and political phenomena.

Chapter 3

1. Sources are fewer than for the second half of 1956 and the months of May to October 1957, as the collection of the *Henan Daily* is very incomplete and no local newspaper is available. I therefore mainly rely on the information published in the central press or subsequently disseminated in the provincial and local press.

2. This is clearly shown in the speech made in March 1957 by Liu Hongwen, head of the United Front Department of the provincial committee (*RMRB,* 10 March 1957).

3. Thus, the notes taken by Xu Deheng, an old democrat in Beijing, circulated in some circles; two Henan democrats, Zhang Yunchuan and Wang Yizhai, distributed among their associates a number of rather doubting comments by the chairman about the role of the Party in schools (*HNRB,* 29 June, 13 July, 31 August, 13 September 1957).

4. This is according to the later account by Zhao Wenfu (*HNRB,* 17 November 1957).

5. According to later accusations, between January and June 1957, Wang Tingdong, a Pan Fusheng loyalist, ran an internal publication *Gongzuo dongtai* (Situation of our work) in which he accused basic-level cadres of blocking implementation of rural policy (*HNRB,* 28 August 1958).

6. For a more detailed analysis of this directive, see Roderick MacFarquhar, *The Origins of the Cultural Revolution, 1. Contradictions Among the People 1956–1957,* Oxford, U.K., Oxford University Press, 1974, pp. 210–217.

7. *RMRB,* 4 May 1957.

8. *LYRB,* 16 May; *HNRB,* 17 May 1957.

9. *RMRB,* 10 May 1957.

10. On the organisation of the rectification campaign in Luoyang, see *LYRB,* 8, 13, 15, 18, and 21 May 1957. One secondary school teacher would later observe that "the spring wind has difficulty crossing the Luoyang pass" (*LYRB,* 29 May 1957).

11. *HNRB,* 24 May 1957.

12. *HNRB,* 17 May; *LYRB,* 18 May; *HNRB,* 19 May 1957.

13. *LYRB,* 3 May 1957. The same Wang, at a recent congress of municipal trade unions, had argued from the Maoist theory of contradictions to ask for a reassertion of control over the working class (*LYRB,* 1 May 1957).

14. *HNRB,* 29 August 1957.

15. *HNRB,* 26 May; *LYRB,* 24 and 28 May, 6 June 1957; *ZZRB,* 23 May 1957. In some schools in Luoyang, cadres continued calmly to require students to study *More Reflections on the Historical Experience of the Dictatorship of the Proletariat,* a text published in . . . December 1956!

16. To print a criticism of a leading cadre above the county level, permission had to be obtained from the provincial committee (*HNRB,* 26 May 1957). On several occasions

newspapers had to publish corrections sent in by speakers (see, for example, *LYRB*, 6 June 1957).

17. *HNRB*, 5 and 8 June; *LYRB*, 6 June 1957.

18. *LYRB*, 21 May, 7 June 1957.

19. A Party member complained in June that Henan was "behind other provinces in everything . . . . Whereas they had already launched the rectification campaign, we were just beginning it, and the guilty were being rounded up straightaway" (*HNRB*, 16 October 1957).

20. *LYRB*, 7 June; *HNRB*, 8 June 1957.

21. These ten contradictions are: (1) the inadequate supply of firewood and cereals, (2) natural calamities, (3) disputes over water use, (4) the insufficiency of draught cattle, (5) the unified purchase and supply system, (6) the lack of places in schools, (7) inequality between cities and countryside, (8) national minorities, (9) poor relations between Party members and nonmembers, and (10) excessive centralisation of power (*HNRB*, 4 July 1958). Pan Fusheng is also said to have stated that "antagonistic contradictions have diminished, contradictions amongst the people have become the most important ones, and the class struggle is finished" (ibid.).

22. *HNRB*, 24 May 1957.

23. *HNRB*, 26 May, 1 June 1957. The plenum concluded that "within the Party too, many comrades want to bloom and contend; it is the new development of the rectification campaign".

24. But Pan Fusheng did not miss an opportunity to let it be known that for his part he was an advocate of "tearing down the wall" between the Party and the people (see, for example, the colourful interview he gave to the *Henan Daily* on 17 May, when he had just been to work on a site in a great fanfare of publicity; *HNRB*, 19 May 1957).

25. *HNRB*, 4 July 1958.

26. What they asserted was that (1) the fight against flooding, on which the most costly investments had been focused, wrongly privileged show projects, was incomplete (since it neglected small water courses), was too costly, was dangerous (because of soil salinity), and above all, was less urgent than the fight against drought; the digging of the many vitally needed wells would cost less and could be partly delegated to cooperatives; and (2) to fight against both drought and floods, it was not enough to concentrate on a few show projects, but big projects must be integrated into an overall framework that would be mainly made up of many small local works; without a coordinated effort at soil control, the Sanmen complex would not last thirty years (*HNRB*, 4 June 1957).

27. *HNRB*, 5 June 1957.

28. It is worth noting that this did not occur in the Rural Work Department that Pan Fusheng's initiatives were aimed at.

29. These two figures were accused of having misused their official car. Both nevertheless were to continue their career normally, notably Shi Desheng, then head of the Civil Affairs Office, whom Mao Zedong himself was to invite to dinner on 14 June 1958 to congratulate him for his good leadership of the fight against Yellow River flooding (*RMRB*, 1 July 1958).

30. It was actually in this issue of the provincial newspaper that the famous editorial in the *People's Daily* marking the sudden ending of the rectification campaign was published. Reports of the proceedings of the various meetings mentioned above will be found in *HNRB*, 7, 9, and 12 June 1957.

31. *HNRB*, 2, 6, 7, and 8 June 1957. Note that Xuchang special region remained very quiet all through this period.

32. See, for example, *HNRB*, 4 June 1957.

33. *HNRB*, 6, 26, and 27 August, 11 September 1957.

34. The journalist Li Qing added ironically: "With or without the leadership of the Communist Party, China will continue to exist" (*HNRB*, 31 August 1957). See *HNRB*, 4 June, 3 August; *ZZRB*, 23 July 1957.

35. The brutality shown towards press photographers by this assistant to the minister of Agriculture had led to almost unanimous protests in central and provincial newspapers (*RMRB*, 10 May; *DGB*, 14 August; *HNRB*, 4 September 1957).

36. *HNRB*, 7 August, 21 September 1957. The situation at the *Zhengzhou Daily* is described in *ZZRB*, 20 September 1957.

37. The provincial leaders most often attacked by name seem to have been the officials of Cultural Affairs departments: Zhang Baiyuan, head of the Cultural Affairs Department of the provincial committee, and Chen Jianping and Feng Jihan, director and assistant director, respectively, of the Cultural Affairs Office of the provincial government.

38. *HNRB*, 4 June, 20 August, 14, 17, and 26 September; *LYRB*, 30 May; *ZZRB*, 4, 11, and 20 September 1957.

39. *HNRB*, 4 and 30 June, 30 July, 2 and 3 August 1957.

40. One of them contained the names of students who had expressed criticisms of *More Reflections on the Historical Experience of the Dictatorship of the Proletariat* (*HNRB*, 4 June, 12 September 1957).

41. *HNRB*, 17 and 30 July 1957.

42. The same day or the next they daubed vengeful slogans on the cars of officials of the Education Office of the provincial government (*HNRB*, 16 October 1957). These events at the Zhengzhou Specialised Teacher Training School have been pieced together from information in *HNRB*, 25 and 29 June, 3 and 10 September, 16 October 1957.

43. A "propaganda movement" orchestrated discussion meetings in the suburbs of Luoyang (*LYRB*, 9, 14, and 23 May 1957). In *HNRB*, 16 June 1957, there is a letter from a cooperative cadre regretting that the *zhengfeng* was not formally extended to the countryside.

44. For a case that occurred in Miyang, see *MYRB*, 20 January 1958.

45. In one case at least, in Zhengzhou, the workers launched the slogan to destroy personal files (*ZZRB*, 18 September 1957). See also *LYRB*, 10, 13, 18, 21, and 25 May; *ZZRB*, 19 July 1957.

46. *HNRB*, 17 November 1957.

47. *HNRB*, 17 November; *ZZRB*, 28 November 1957.

48. *LYRB*, 21 and 27 May 1957.

49. But only 60 percent of members of ten "rightist cliques" in Luoyang special region were of bad origin (*HNRB*, 15 September 1957); the proportion (probably exaggerated by the official press) was lower and it would be satisfying to have the necessary information to verify the existence of numerous rightists amongst the "purest" social strata.

50. In the meetings held in Luoyang, a good half of the speakers seem to have been teachers and artists.

51. On Wang Yizhai, see in particular *Changjiang ribao* (Yangtze Daily), 14 July 1952; *XHBYK*, 1, 1957, pp. 121–123; *HNRB*, 1, 3, 4, 9, and 15 August 1957.

52. Of the eleven leading rightists, two were criticised at the time of the agrarian reform

and three during the Sufan. Of the thirty-four other rightists, two experienced problems during the agrarian reform, six during the Sanfan, five during the Sufan, and the last on another occasion. The family of eleven rightists was decimated, which drove them to use extremely violent language (see *HNRB*, 10, 16, 27, 28, and 29 August, 2, 12, 15, and 20 September; *ZZRB*, 1 and 7 September 1957).

53. "We are all overseas Chinese", said an engineer (*HNRB*, 2 August). See also *LYRB*, 29 May 1957.

54. For example, one complained of having to ask for permission to make a long-distance telephone call and another reported that he had been forbidden any contact with his workers (*ZZRB*, 21 May; *LYRB*, 3 June 1957).

55. *HNRB*, 2, 6, and 9 June 1957. They complained, for example, of being reimbursed only 30 percent of medical expenses by the health insurance, whereas workers had their full bills paid.

56. See, for example, in *LYRB*, 31 May 1957, the violent protest by an actor in Luoyang.

57. Notably teachers wanted a school programme in line with children's intellectual possibilities and the teaching of civic education, which clashed with a general contempt for serving others and manual labour (*LYRB*, 28 and 29 May 1957).

58. *HNRB*, 8 June; *LYRB*, 23 May 1957.

59. *HNRB*, 8 June; *LYRB*, 25 May 1957.

60. *HNRB*, 23 June; *ZZRB*, 21 May 1957.

61. The poet Ma Changfeng declared to applause: "To write, you need an artistic feeling, and to observe life, you need to use an artistic eye; political enthusiasm is not enough" (*ZZRB*, 23 July 1957).

62. *HNRB*, 30 June, 20 August; *LYRB*, 6 June; *ZZRB*, 24 September 1957. There were complaints, for example, that the government of Anyang county had met only four times in the whole of 1956 (*HNRB*, 17 May 1957).

63. *LYRB*, 27, 29, and 31 May 1957.

64. *LYRB*, 31 May 1957.

65. *HNRB*, 11 June, 6 September; *LYRB*, 21 May, 6 and 7 June 1957.

66. *HNRB*, 8 June, 25 August 1957. But Zhang Yunchuan and Wang Yizhai would be criticised for circulating texts by Lin Xiling in their circle (*XHBYK*, 18, 1957, pp. 68–69).

67. *HNRB*, 7 July, 28 August; *ZZRB*, 21 May, 18 September 1957.

68. *HNRB*, 21 August; *ZZRB*, 11 September 1957. But these attacks, though sometimes brutal (Wang Yizhai compared reform through labor to ancient slavery), were rare (see, for example, *HNRB*, 12 July; *ZZRB*, 1 September 1957); it was all as if such things were too dangerous to be talked about by anyone who did not have serious protection. This relative discretion about horrors that were known about is one more sign of the enormous distance between the two weeks of controlled freedom in 1957 in China and a true uprising.

69. *HNRB*, 22 June 1957. See also *HNRB*, 11, 21, and 30 June, 9, 21, and 30 July, 25 August 1957.

70. *DGB*, 12 August 1957. Another said: "In my home village, everyone is against the Party." See also *HNRB*, 24 May; *LYRB*, 7 June; *ZZRB*, 30 July, 1 September 1957.

71. For example, a Party member declared: "At each turning point, Zhou Enlai makes mistakes; Peng Dehuai is an old fool, he too does nothing but commit blunders" (*HNRB*, 21 August 1957). Wang Yizhai compared Mao to Stalin and sharply criticised a speech by Liu Shaoqi in Zhengzhou (*HNRB*, 1 August 1957). See also *HNRB*, 18 August, 6, 22, and 24 September 1957.

72. *HNRB,* 25 July, 10 and 28 August, 4 September 1957. See also *HNRB,* 24 May, 8 June, 13 July, 6 September; *LYRB,* 25 and 28 May; *ZZRB,* 15 September 1957.

73. *HNRB,* 31 August 1957. For several speakers, ideological orthodoxy may have changed content, but it still fulfilled the same police function: "Under the Qing, there was the prison of language; today, it is with words like 'liberalism' and 'small clique' that thought is enclosed" (*HNRB,* 16 August 1957).

74. Siwitt Aray, *Les Cent Fleurs,* Paris, Flammarion, 1973, pp. 90–107.

75. Four members of each of these two organisations are to be found on the list of leading rightists in the province. Of thirty-one other rightists, twenty-one had a political affiliation: three in the Chinese People's Political Consultative Conference, three in the Democratic Construction League, five in the Guomindang Revolutionary Committee, six in the Democratic League—and four in the CCP.

76. *HNRB,* 8 and 17 August 1957.

77. On these various individuals, see *HNRB,* 6, 17, 20, and 26 July 1957 (Luan Xing); 3 and 15 September, 16 October 1957 (Zhang Shumin); and 20 August 1957 (Deng Zhailin).

78. That is Wang Yizhai, Liu Jixue, Luo Shengwu, and Liu Xicheng. At least twenty-one cases are documented of liberals leaving the Party (*HNRB,* 10, 13, 21, and 29 August, 3, 4, and 22 September, 6 October 1957).

79. See, for example, *HNRB,* 2 and 11 September 1957. On Zhang Qingheng, see in particular *HNRB,* 1, 14, and 27 September 1957.

80. *HNRB,* 4 July 1958. The list of ten contradictions in Henan, compiled by Pan Fusheng (see above, note 21), is good evidence of his rural concerns.

Chapter 4

1. See in particular *HNRB,* 13, 15, 16, and 22 June 1957.

2. The regime would treat these activists with striking ingratitude; not one of them would ever reach a position of real power.

3. *HNRB,* 14 June 1957.

4. See, for example, *HNRB,* 11, 14, and 15 June 1957. The minutes of the discussions that had taken place 1–6 June at the United Front Department were only published on 16 June, in a way that emphasised the aggressive speeches by the rightist Li Qingzhi.

5. See in particular *HNRB,* 15, 22, and 28 June 1957.

6. A typical speech by Hou is to be found in *HNRB,* 15 June 1957.

7. See, for example, the speeches by Li Qingzhi and Wang Yizhai (*HNRB,* 14, 16, and 18 June 1957).

8. *HNRB,* 4 July 1958.

9. See Mao Zedong, *Selected Works,* vol. 5, Beijing, Foreign Languages Press, 1977, pp. 417–457.

10. His stress on the need to persuade rather than crush nevertheless seems strange. One may see it as a last attempt by Pan Fusheng to slow down the movement by insisting on "discussion".

11. *HNRB,* 3 and 11 September, 16 October 1957. Unfortunately no detailed description is available of how these interviews were carried out.

12. On all these revelations, see *HNRB,* 30 July, 11 August, 4 and 6 September 1957.

13. *HNRB,* 26 September 1957. There is a contrary example of astute firmness in the "self-criticism" by Zhang Yunchuan before the National Assembly (*XHBYK,* 8, 1957, pp. 108–109).

14. See the editorials in *HNRB,* 5, 10, 12, and 13 July; *ZZRB,* 2, 5, 6, 7, 9, 17, and 19 July 1957.

15. Falls in yield were recorded in Boai, Wenxian, and Yuanyang, for example. On the summer 1957 harvest, see in particular *HNRB,* 20 June, 18 July, 30 August 1957; *RMRB,* 22 October 1958.

16. See, for example, the editorials in *HNRB,* 13 June, 12 July 1957.

17. *HNRB,* 26 June 1957.

18. On the July 1957 floods in Henan, see in particular *HNRB,* 18, 25, and 31 July, 25 August; *ZZRB,* 26 July 1957.

19. For the situation a year later, see *HNRB,* 10, 14, 15, 17, 20, and 25 July, 4, 7, and 11 August 1958.

20. The file on this affair is reproduced in *HNRB,* 4 July 1958.

Chapter 5

1. On this meeting, see Roderick MacFarquhar, *The Origins of the Cultural Revolution, 1. Contradictions Among the People 1956–1957,* Oxford, U.K., Oxford University Press, 1979, pp. 285–289; and Parris H. Chang, *Patterns and Processes of Policy Making in Communist China, 1955–1965: Three Case Studies,* New York, Columbia University Press, 1969, pp. 69–76. "Central work meetings", although nonstatutory, have played a considerable role in the political history of the PRC, to prepare for regular meetings of the Central Committee and the Politburo and even to replace them.

2. *Selected Works,* vol. 5, Beijing, Foreign Languages Press, 1977, pp. 514–524.

3. *HNRB,* 4 July 1958.

4. *HNRB,* 6 August 1957, 4 July 1958.

5. *HNRB,* 13, 25, and 30 July, 2 and 3 August 1957.

6. *HNRB,* 10 August 1957.

7. *HNRB,* 16 August 1957.

8. The former would even step up his activity and be given major responsibilities at the time of the launch of the Great Leap Forward, either as a reward or to compromise him in the new course.

9. *HNRB,* 4 July 1958.

10. Wu was mentioned six times by the press and Pan four times between mid-August and the end of September, generally obliquely (see, for example, *HNRB,* 8 September 1957).

11. *HNRB,* 24, 25, and 27 August 1957. Pan Fusheng was not mentioned once in the accounts of this meeting.

12. *HNRB,* 4 and 8 September 1957.

13. *HNRB,* 24 September, 1 October 1957.

14. On all these threats, see in particular *HNRB,* 10 and 16 August, 15 September, 20 October, 30 November 1957.

15. On these punishments and the apportionment of blame, see *HNRB,* 17, 21, and 29 August, 4 September 1957, 10, 15, and 25 July, 7 and 11 August 1958. Some cadres previously

punished for having opposed the rightwards shift in the rural areas were rehabilitated at this time (*HNRB*, 15, 17, and 25 July 1958).

16. *HNRB*, 4 September 1957.

17. On the other provincial purges of 1957–1958, see the article by Frederick C. Teiwes, "The Purge of Provincial Leaders, 1957–1958", *China Quarterly*, July-September 1966, pp. 14–32.

18. *HNRB*, 10, 11, 15, 18, and 28 August, 11 and 20 September, 28 December 1957.

19. *ZZRB*, 5 and 14 September 1957. Of those arrested, one petty malefactor already incarcerated three times had robbed thirty travellers on 27 August in the middle of the railway station (*ZZRB*, 11 September 1957). On the raids, see also *ZZRB*, 15 September. On the sects and pseudo-parties, see *HNRB*, 9 and 15 August, 8 and 11 September; *ZZRB*, 4 September, 22 November 1957.

20. *HNRB*, 29 September 1957. On 26 November, in Zhengzhou, seven "criminals" were executed by shooting before a crowd of 10,000 people: a recidivist thief, a murderer, a former member of the Guomindang, an agitator, and three members of traditional sects (*HNRB*, 30 November 1957). For a general discussion of the repression of the "rightists", see my *Chine, l'archipel oublié*, Paris, Fayard, 1992, pp. 126–134.

21. On the unfolding of the Socialist Education Movement in the Countryside, see *HNRB*, 6, 13, 17, and 29 August, 15 September, 20 October; *ZZRB*, 8 September, 11 October 1957. See also *Quanmian dayuejin zhongde liangshi gongzuo*, (Grain work during the total Great Leap Forward), Zhengzhou, Henan renmin chubanshe (Henan People's Publishing House), 1958, which is wholly devoted to the problem.

22. See inter alia *HNRB*, 6 September, 11 December 1957.

23. See, for example, the speeches by Zhao Wenfu and other officials in charge of the provincial economy in *HNRB*, 24 August, 1 September 1957.

24. *HNRB*, 4, 7, 8, 13, 15, 20, and 25 August, 11 September 1957.

25. For Zhengzhou, see *ZZRB*, 21 September, 19 November 1957.

26. *HNRB*, 2, 4, and 18 September, 20 October 1957.

27. *HNRB*, 8 and 15 September 1957.

28. *ZZRB*, 5 October 1957. The assistant in charge of public security in Zhengzhou was transferred to run a secondary school (*ZZRB*, 29 October 1957). See also *HNRB*, 5 and 27 September, 19 November, 29 December 1957.

29. At the Zhengzhou Specialised Teacher Training School, the Party eventually "convinced" 92 percent of the teachers to volunteer to go to the countryside (*HNRB*, 29 December 1957).

30. *DGB*, 22 October; *ZZRB*, 7 and 25 September, 11, 23, and 24 October 1957.

31. *HNRB*, 9 and 18 August 6, 14, 21, and 22 September; *ZZRB*, 2, 8, 15, 18, and 21 September 1957.

32. *HNRB*, 28 and 29 September; *ZZRB*, 18 and 21 September, 22 October 1957.

33. *HNRB*, 3 and 13 August, 14 November; *ZZRB*, 2 and 14 September 1957.

34. It has not been easy to assess the actual results of this savings campaign. A savings of 685 metric tons of grain was announced for September in Zhengzhou (*ZZRB*, 8 October 1957), where the grain ration of inhabitants was in future to include 20 percent sweet potatoes (*ZZRB*, 12 November 1957). But there are examples of low or zero savings in an area of Luoyang (*RMRB*, 5 November 1957) and a street in Zhengzhou (*ZZRB*, 29 October 1957). A plausible hypothesis is that the savings actually achieved was due to a reduction by fiat of rations in enterprises rather than a cut in consumption by households.

35. In the last days of August the departure of seventy-nine children of provincial leaders was celebrated—but they were only going as far as the suburbs of Zhengzhou (*HNRB*, 28 August 1957). See also *HNRB*, 4, 16, and 19 August, 6 and 24 September 1957.

36. *HNRB*, 19 September, 19 October, 30 November; *ZZRB*, 4, 6, 9, 10, and 13 October 1957. It seems that Personnel departments, where many cadres' wives worked, were particularly affected by these measures—a posthumous (and short-lived) victory of the rightists.

37. *HNRB*, 29 September 1957. This was another posthumous victory for those liberal functionaries who had dared to criticise Soviet-type growth.

38. *DGB*, 24 September; *HNRB*, 16 June, 26 September 1957.

Chapter 6

1. *RMRB*, 31 March 1958; Zhengzhou shitan xueyuan dilixi (Department of Geography of the Zhengzhou Teacher Training School), *Henan dili* (Geography of Henan), Beijing, Shangwu yinshuguan (Commercial Publishing House), 1959, p. 106. The share of industry in overall agricultural and industrial output is said to have risen from 20 percent in 1956 to 26.1 percent or 28.4 percent in 1957, according to equally unreliable sources (*HNRB*, 24 August 1957; *RMRB*, 7 January, 1 October 1959). The 1990 Sun Jingzhi, *Huabei jingji dili* (Economic geography of North China), Beijing, Kexue chubanshe (Scientific Publishing House), 1957, p. 529, provides higher figures, but they show a slightly lower rise: 1.61 and 1.66 billion yuan.

2. *Henan dili*, p. 107.

3. *HNRB*, 12 August, 31 December 1957; *Henan dili*, p. 90; Guojia tongji ju zonghe si (State Statistics Bureau General Company), *Quanguo gesheng, zizhiqu, zhihaishi lishi tongji ziliao huibian (1949–1989)* (Collection of historical statistical materials in all the provinces, autonomous regions, and directly administered cities), Beijing, Zhongguo tongji chubanshe (China Statistical Publishing House), 1990, p. 158.

4. *RMRB*, 22 October 1958; *Henan dili*, p. 88. The cereal yield rose by 3.8 percent (*HNRB*, 29 November 1957). The 1990 *Quanguo gesheng*, p. 534, gives a slightly different figure (11.8 million metric tons), which marks a small decline compared to 1956 (12.1 million metric tons). If this figure is right, it partly invalidates my argument. Conversely, the advances in cotton and pig-raising (but not cattle-raising) are confirmed. Was there an improvement or simply a stabilisation of the agricultural situation in Henan in autumn 1957? The question awaits an answer.

5. Around 1.15 million metric tons (*HNRB*, 10 February 1958). For the production of Xinyang special region, see *HNRB*, 11 February 1958.

6. In 1955, 1956, and 1957, areas sown to cotton were 730,000, 860,000, and 800,000 hectares, respectively, and production reached 170,000, 150,000, and 170,000 or 185,000 metric tons (depending on the sources). See *RMRB*, 5 October 1955; *HNRB*, 11 September 1956; *RMRB*, 21 July 1956; *HNRB*, 12 January 1957; *HNRB*, 17 November, 29 and 31 December 1957.

7. *RMRB*, 22 October; *DGB*, 21 November; *HNRB*, 14 December; *HNRB*, 27 November 1957; *Henan dili*, p. 99.

8. *DGB*, 7 December 1957. Strict limits on distribution to individuals and home weaving made it possible to collect 150,000 metric tons of cotton in the end, instead of the 135,000

planned (*DGB*, 15 November; *HNRB*, 6 December 1957), each peasant being entitled to only 1 kilogram for personal use (*DGB*, 6 October 1957). Tobacco and oilseed were delivered with the same speed. The 1990 *Quanguo gesheng* confirms the improvement in the situation in this respect.

9. *HNRB*, 8 December 1957.

10. On this plenum of the Central Committee, see Roderick MacFarquhar, *The Origins of the Cultural Revolution, 1. Contradictions Among the People 1956–1957*, Oxford, U.K., Oxford University Press, 1974, pp. 301–310; Parris H. Chang, *Patterns and Processes of Policy Making in Communist China, 1955–1962: Three Case Studies*, New York, Columbia University Press, 1969, pp. 69–76; and the text of Mao's speech in *Selected Works*, vol. 5, Beijing, Foreign Languages Press, 1977, pp. 525–539.

11. *HNRB*, 22 October 1957.

12. *ZZRB*, 15 November; *HNRB*, 16 and 19 November 1957; *XHBYK*, 21, 1957, pp. 160–162.

13. *XHBYK*, 23, 1957, pp. 168–169. The model in this area must have been the plan to control the Shaling River, a tributary of the Huai, that was drawn up by a meeting held by the same Tan Zhenlin, from 10 to 15 December 1957, in the presence of a vice-minister of Irrigation, Qian Zhengying (*HNRB*, 17 and 29 December 1957).

14. Miyang county's plenum, was held in January 1958 (*MYRB*, 25 January 1958) and the city of Xinxiang's in March–April 1958 (*XXRB*, 1 April 1958).

15. On the second plenum of the first congress of the Henan CCP, see *ZZRB*, 14 November; *HNRB*, 16, 17, and 19 November; *ZZRB*, 20 November; *HNRB*, 27, 28, and 30 November, 1 and 4 December; *RMRB*, 5 December; *HNRB*, 8 December; *RMRB*, 16 December 1957.

16. *HQ*, 8, 1958, pp. 5–12; *HNRB*, 27 November 1957, 12 May 1958; *Zenyang ban renmin gongshe* (How to set up people's communes), Hangzhou, Zhejiang renmin chubanshe (Zhejiang People's Publishing House), 1958, p. 53. It seems, however, that the pattern varied from one part of the province to another.

17. Townships fell from thirty-three to twenty in Changge between June 1957 and June 1958, and from twenty-one to twelve in Lushan (*HNRB*, 21 June 1957; Zhonggong henansheng changgexian weiyuanhui (Changge County CCP Committee), *Changge shuili jianshe* (Irrigation construction in Changge), Beijing, Nongye chubanshe (Agricultural Publishing House), 1958, p. 9; *ZGNB*, 7 July 1958).

18. *Henan dili*, p. 6.

19. The number of people's communes in Henan fell from 1,350 at the beginning of September 1958 (*DGB*, 27 December 1958) to 1,209 in December; the number of counties fell from 115 in 1957 to 107 in summer 1959 (*RMRB*, 7 August 1959); after Anyang, Shangqiu special region was to be suppressed in December 1958 (*RMRB*, 16 February 1959).

20. In Dengfeng, a meeting was held on the literacy campaign; in Yanshi, a conference on wheat growing; in Xinyang, a study session on rice growing (*HNRB*, 13 April, 14 May 1958). See also *HNRB*, 11, 15, and 16 February 1958.

21. This amounts to more than one cadre in every three (*HNRB*, 31 December 1957). But many were in the inner suburbs of cities. See also *XXRB*, 11 April, 14 May 1958.

22. On Miao Huaming, see *HNRB*, 15 August 1956, 6 January, 11 August 1958; on Zhao Guang, *HNRB*, 28 June 1957, 17 August 1958.

23. There is still very little known about this movement. One would like to be able to give a precise list of its victims (I only know of a single case, that of seventy-three "rightists" criticised in Buyang county; see *HNRB*, 26 January 1958). See *HNRB*, 29 December 1957, 10, 17, and 26 January; *MYRB*, 15 January, 26 February, 9 March 1958.

24. *HNRB,* 27 and 30 November, 7 December 1957.

25. And the *Henan Daily,* until then practically silent on the question, suddenly revealed on 25 December 1957 that 826,000 diaphragms had been distributed in the province during the past year (as against 140,000 in 1956) and 11,000 condoms (as against 1,370).

26. *HNRB,* 7 and 24 December 1957; *RMRB,* 5 January; *HNRB,* 19 March 1958.

27. See in particular *HNRB,* 21 March, 29 May 1958.

28. One of the significant factors in the launch of the Great Leap Forward, about which unfortunately too little is known, was the transfer of Statistical departments into the hands of Propaganda departments (see, for Henan, *Tongji gongzuo* (Statistical work), 14, 1958, pp. 15–18, and 18, pp. 2–4.

29. The target for the whole country was still only 6 million hectares, and Henan was far ahead of Hebei (0.8 million hectares).

30. In fact, according to the newspapers of the time, what Mao said to Wu Zhipu exactly was: "Secretary Wu, there is hope! If the whole of Henan is like this commune, then everything is fine. . . . If there exists one people's commune like that one, then there can be many communes." (*RMRB,* 12 August 1958). See also *RMRB,* 16 June, 1 July 1958.

31. All the tracts glorifying the people's communes that flourished from summer 1958 onwards devote considerable space to the Henan models, for example, the collection *Lun renmin gongshe* (On people's communes), Beijing, Zhongguo qingnian chubanshe (China Youth Publishing House), 1958, which devotes 80 pages out of 190 to them.

32. *Zhongguo shuili* (Chinese irrigation), 8, 1958, pp. 13–17; *RMRB,* 20 July, 16 August 1959.

33. On the 1959–1961 drought in Henan, see above all *RMRB,* 7 and 8 August, 7 October 1959, 10 February, 14 March, 14 and 28 April, 27 July 1960, 15 February, 15 April, 3 May, 21 June, 22 December 1961, 19 April 1962; *XHYB,* 8, 1960, pp. 44–45, and *Dili* (Geography), 4, 1961, pp. 190–191.

34. Notably by leading to rises in salt that sterilised the soil. See *Dilizhishi* (Geographical knowledge), 2, 1965, pp. 50–56, and 5, pp. 239–241; *RMRB,* 28 May 1971.

35. *PI,* 9 October 1972, 11 August 1975. In four of the seven counties for which figures are available, the wheat yields announced in 1958 were of the same order as cereal yields (that is, including a second harvest) in 1973–1975! Those counties are Changge, Mengxian, Xiangcheng, and Yanshi.

36. Thus, in Xinyang special region, production in 1957–1958 was supposedly 7 percent higher than average production for 1953–1957, according to a source that may be serious because it is later (*RMRB,* 11 December 1962). The 1990 *Quanguo gesheng* confirms this hypothesis by giving the figure of 12.6 million metric tons as against 11.8 million metric tons in 1957.

37. *GMRB,* 18 April 1973. The 1990 *Quanguo gesheng* also offers support for this hypothesis with the following production figures: 9.7 million tons in 1959, 8.8 million in 1960, 6.8 million in 1961, 9 million in 1962, 7.8 million in 1963, 9.5 million in 1964, and 11.6 million in 1965. In this series, the novel figure is that for 1963, which marks a significant setback in the cereal situation. The agricultural crisis appears to have been not only more acute but also longer than elsewhere in Henan. I have analysed interviews about the disturbances that occurred between 1958 and 1963 in my article: "Chine, la victoire ambiguë du vieil homme", *Revue française de science politique,* June 1985, pp. 384–401.

38. Sources: *RMRB,* 14 March 1960, 11 December 1962, 2 April 1962, 26 February 1962; *Dilizhishi* (Geographical knowledge), 2, 1966, pp. 50–56; *Dilixuebao* (Geography courier),

1, 1966, pp. 41–42; James C. Cheng (ed.), *Kung-ts'o tung-hsün: The Politics of the Chinese Red Army*, Stanford, Stanford University Press, 1966, pp. 117–122, 209–213 and 566–572.

39. *XXRB*, 6, 9, and 29 May 1958; *Renmin gongshe de caizheng he caiwu* (Financial policy and resources of people's communes), Beijing, Caizheng chubanshe (Financial Publishing House), 1958, pp. 24–26.

40. See, for example, *HNRB*, 11 July 1958; *HQ*, 10, 1958; *ZGNB*, 7 July 1958.

41. A particularly clear example will be found in the work compiled by the Financial and Commercial Work Department of the Henan provincial committee: *Renmin gongshehua hou de caimao gongzuo* (Financial and commercial work after communisation), Zhengzhou, Henan renmin chubanshe (Henan People's Publishing House), 1958, pp. 26–28 and 116–117; in the Sputnik commune itself, over half the cadres expressed concern about their status.

42. *JJYJ*, 5, 1958, pp. 16–18.

43. These visits are confirmed respectively by *HQ*, 7, 1958, p. 22; *HNRB*, 16 April; *RMRB*, 24 April 1958; *Renmin gongshe hao* (People's commune is good), Beijing, Nongye chubanshe (Agricultural Press), 1973, pp. 118 and 120; *HNRB*, 8 August; *RMRB*, 12 August, 11 October, 24 September, 27 October 1958.

44. Like the three previous counties, Jiyuan was liberated early and implemented an agrarian reform well before others. The Linxian secretary, Yang Gui, was to become vice-minister of Public Security in 1975–1976 in the last days of Maoism.

45. *RMRB*, 23 October 1958; *JJYJ*, 11, 1958, pp. 16–23.

46. On the political rise of Xinyang special region, see *HNRB*, 20 September, 28 December 1956, 3, 8, and 9 August, 4 September 1957, 30 August 1957, 4 and 11 February 1958; *RMRB*, 13 March 1958.

47. On this model commune, see in particular *RMRB*, 18 August 1958; *HQ*, 7, 1958, pp. 16–22; *GMRB*, 11 September 1958.

48. According to refugee accounts, the failure of the Great Leap Forward earned them violent criticisms, and one of them was even shot.

49. He had informers, certainly, but not protectors. On this point, there is no certainty, but it is tempting to contrast the incomplete character of Wu's first victory over Pan in summer 1954, and the slowness of his return to power in 1957–1958, with the stunning speed of Pan Fusheng's victories in 1953 and spring 1957 and also his rise from nowhere in winter 1966–1967. It all makes it seem that Pan Fusheng had better connections in the centre than Wu Zhipu, but with which faction?

50. *Miscellany of Mao Tse-tung Thought*, Joint Publications Research Service (hereafter *JPRS*), 20 February 1974, vol. 1, pp. 114-115.

51. This was at the Lushan conference in 1959, when the Great Leap policy was being dissected. See *The Case of Peng Teh-huai, 1959–1968*, Hong Kong, Union Research Institute, 1968, p. 23.

52. Wu Zhipu wrote no fewer than six articles in favour of the Great Leap and Maoism, after the Lushan conference (*RMRB*, 2 October 1959, 1 January 1960; *HQ*, 1, 1960, pp. 14–21; *Zhongguo qingnian* (China youth), 11, 1960, pp. 9–11; *Xinjianshe* (New construction), June 1960, pp. 1–6; *HQ*, 18, 1960, pp. 1–6).

53. See in particular *JPRS*, vol. 1, pp. 166–167 and pp. 214–215.

54. Wu Zhipu was criticised in veiled terms by an editorial in the *Henan Daily*, 26 August 1961, and shortly afterwards was demoted to the rank of provincial second secretary (*RMRB*, 11 October 1961) and then transferred in autumn 1962 to a post as secretary of the Central-South office where he appears to have laid rather low.

55. *JPRS,* vol. 2, p. 412. Wu apparently died in autumn 1967. As for Pan Fusheng, he resurfaced in the leadership of one of the first provincial revolutionary committees, in Heilongjiang, and wrote two triumphant articles in *HQ* in May and June 1967. But he was shunted aside in 1970.

56. Sources: *HQ,* 8, 1958, pp. 5–12; *HNRB,* 7 January 1960; *JJYJ,* 9, 1958, pp. 40–46; *RMRB,* 18 August 1958; *Lishi yanjiu* (Historical studies), 1, 1974, pp. 158–168.

57. Sources: *RMRB,* 18 August 1958, 23 February 1960; *JJYJ,* 9, 1958, pp. 40–43.

58. They appeared, for example, in Xiuwu and Fengqiu counties. Xinxiang county decided to make them universal on 11 July, and Qiliying *dashe* was founded on 18 July 1958 (*JJYJ,* 11, 1958, pp. 16–23; *RMRB,* 26 January 1960; *Lishi yanjiu* [Historical studies], 1, 1974, pp. 158–168).

59. An article in *HNRB,* 21 August 1973, reported the presence of Chen Boda in Suiping in summer 1958. The accusations made on numerous occasions (and in vaguer terms) against Chen Boda seem very likely true—provided that Mao Zedong is not relieved of responsibility, for he encouraged the excesses of summer 1958, especially in Henan.

60. By founding the model commune at Yingju, the leaders of Fengqiu were returning a compliment to the chairman, who had cited them as an example in his article for the first issue of *Red Flag.* By creating a county commune, the leaders of Xiuwu were erasing the memory of their recent rightist past (*JJYJ,* 11, 1958, pp. 24–28). The first secretary of Xinxiang county was an opponent, and it seems, a personal enemy of Pan Fusheng (*HNRB,* 4 July 1958).

61. *Lishi yanjiu* (Historical studies), 1, 1974, pp. 158–168.

Conclusion

1. In the same way, from autumn 1959 to 1961, Wu Zhipu vainly endeavoured in Henan to hold back the ultimately victorious rightward drift of rural policy. He then found in none other than Ji Dengkui, his faithful ally in Xuchang special region who had just been appointed to head Luoyang special region, a vigorous adversary whom the centre, now under the influence of Liu Shaoqi, would appoint to work alongside his successor Liu Jianxun (see the Hong Kong journal *Qi yi* [The seven arts], number 4, February 1977, pp. 45–49; and the Taibei journal *Zhongguo yanjiu,* [Studies on Chinese communism], 11, 1971, pp. 8–12).

2. Victor C. Falkenheim, *Provincial Administration in Fukien,* New York, Columbia University Press, 1972; Donald H. MacMillen, *Chinese Communist Power and Policy in Xinjiang, 1949–1977,* Boulder, Westview Press, 1979.

3. Ezra Vogel, *Canton Under Communism: Programs and Politics in a Provincial Capital,* Cambridge, Mass., Harvard University Press, 1969, pp. 116–124 and 211–216.

4. A study of Sichuan in the early 1960s shows in any case the existence of a provincial conflict between Li Jingquan and a small group of cadres who were defending the Great Leap Forward line, and whose fate was to parallel the twists and turns of central policy right up to autumn 1976 (see Thomas Jay Mathews, *The Cultural Revolution in the Provinces,* Harvard East Asian Monographs, Cambridge, Mass., Harvard East Asian Research Center, 1971, pp. 94–146).

5. The decision to remove 143,000 Henan peasants to Hubei and 65,000 to Gansu-Ningxia was taken in November 1957 (*HNRB,* 7 and 24 December 1957).

Bibliography

1. The main Chinese works consulted have been cited in the notes. The central, and above all, local press is the most useful source. The almost complete runs of the *Henan Daily* from April to December 1956 and June 1957 to August 1958 make up for the small number of local newspapers available. Its tone is not fundamentally different from that of the central dailies—like them, its chief aim is to inform cadres—but its content is more concrete, more diverse, and more intelligible.

2. Also in the notes will be found details of the books and articles in Western languages that have been consulted. Here I list only the most general ones and the ones most important for my purpose.

Aray, Siwitt. *Les Cent Fleurs*. Paris: Flammarion, 1973. 186 pp.

Barnett, A. Doak. *Cadres, Bureaucracy and Political Power in Communist China*. New York: Columbia University Press, 1967. 563 pp.

Bernstein, Thomas, P. "Keeping the Revolution Going: Problems of Village Leadership After the Land Reform". In John W. Lewis (ed.), *Party Leadership and Revolutionary Power in China*. Cambridge, U.K.: Cambridge University Press, 1970, pp. 239–267.

———."Leadership and Mobilisation in the Soviet and Chinese Collectivisation Campaigns of 1929–1930 and 1955–1956: A Comparison", *China Quarterly*, number 31, July-September 1967, pp. 1–47.

Chang, Parris H. *Patterns and Processes of Policy Making in Communist China, 1955–1962: Three Case Studies*. New York: Columbia University Press, 1969. 378 pp.

Ch'en Ho-chia, and Domenach, Jean-Luc. *Une ténébreuse affaire: le faux rapport de production de Lushan*. Paris: Publications orientalistes de France, 1978. 172 pp.

Doolin, Dennis. *Communist China: The Politics of the Student Opposition*. Palo Alto, Calif.: Stanford University Press, 1964. 70 pp.

Fainsod, Merle. *Smolensk Under Soviet Rule*. Cambridge, Mass.: Harvard University Press, 1958. 484 pp.

Falkenheim, Victor C. *Provincial Administration in Fukien*. New York: Columbia University Press, 1972. 387 pp.

Guillermaz, Jacques. *Le Parti Communiste au pouvoir*. Paris: Payot, 1973, 549 pp. (Tr. by A. Destenay, *The Chinese Communist Party in Power, 1969–1976*. Boulder, Colo.: Westview, 1976. 614 pp.)

Hofheinz, Roy. "Rural Administration in Communist China", *China Quarterly*, number 11, July-September 1962, pp. 140–160.

Lieberthal, Kenneth Guy. "Reconstruction and Revolution in a Chinese City: The Case of Tientsin, 1949–1953". Ph.D. thesis, Columbia University, New York, 1972.

MacFarquhar, Roderick. *The Origins of the Cultural Revolution, 1. Contradictions Among the People 1956–1957?* Oxford, U.K.: Oxford University Press, 1974. 439 pp.

Teiwes, Frederick C. "Provincial Politics in China". In John Lindbeck (ed.), *China: Management of a Revolutionary Society.* Seattle: University of Washington Press, 1971, pp. 116–189.

————."The Purge of Provincial Leaders, 1957–1958", *China Quarterly,* number 27, July-September 1966, pp. 14–32.

Vogel, Ezra. *Canton Under Communism: Programs and Politics in a Provincial Capital.* Cambridge, Mass.: Harvard University Press, 1969. 450 pp.

About the Book
and Author

The first major study of the Great Leap Forward, this seminal volume has now been translated into English for a wider audience. Like no other work, it suggests compelling political and social answers to questions that have long plagued scholars: How could a party with such a successful rural base launch a movement so divorced from reality—especially in the countryside? Why was the movement pressed to the point of social chaos and economic collapse, giving rise to arguably the greatest famine in human history?

Utilizing a wealth of primary material, Jean-Luc Domenach focuses on the central China province of Henan, which emerged as a national model of the Great Leap and was one of the most devastated by its failure. The author's documentary sources enable him to illuminate the development of provincial and local political life as well as to gauge popular reactions to the dictates of the center. Domenach presents a lucid analysis of the setbacks in agriculture in 1956 and 1957, the rise of economic corruption, and the launch of the CCP rectification campaign in 1957.

Despite the enormous impact of the Great Leap on Chinese politics and economics in the decades that followed, it has proven immensely difficult to research. Domenach's contribution thus stands out as an original and important work on the period.

Jean-Luc Domenach is director of the Centre d'Études et de Recherches Internationales in Paris and the author of a number of books and articles on the PRC, including *Forgotten Gulag: China's Hidden Prison Camps*.

Index

Public enterprises, 12–13, 28, 133, 135
Public health, 76
Public Security Bureau, 78, 128–129
Purges, 128. *See also* Repression

Qiliying, 40, 154, 155, 178(n21)
    commune, 144, 154, 195(n30), 197(n58)
Qingdao central work conference, 123
Qingfeng county, 43
Qi Wenjian, 32
Qixian county, 26
Qu, 26, 41

Radio, 12
Railways, 5, 138
Rainfall, 5, 43, 46
Rao Shushi, 37
Rationing, 126
Rectification campaign, 68, 72, 81, 83, 85, 87–88
    aftermath, 98–99, 108, 110, 111. *See also*
        Antirightist campaign
    alleged anti-party plot of, 95–96
    criticism of CCP, 88, 91, 96, 102–107, 189(nn
        68, 71), 190(n73)
    criticism within CCP, 92, 94, 95, 100, 187(n23),
        190(n75)
    disturbances during, 96–98
    issues of, 91, 187(n21)
    local implementation of, 87, 88–90, 91, 92, 99,
        188(n43)
    meetings, 89–90, 91–92, 93–96, 99, 187(n19),
        188(n34)
    party resistance to, 48, 87, 88, 89
    protesters, and demands of, 99–108
    rural, 142–143, 194(n23)
Red Flag, 144, 153, 197(n60)
Reference News, 184(n54)
Relief operations, 44, 45–46, 117, 134
Religious minorities, 77
Repression, 104
    during antirightist campaign, 112, 113, 114, 115
    1949–1955, 27–28, 29
    1955–1957, 37–39, 49, 77–78, 177(n4)
    during socialist campaign and Great Leap
        Forward, 124, 128–129, 142–143, 192(nn 19,
        20)
Reservoirs, 8. *See also* Sanmen, hydroelectric
    project
Rice, 20, 42, 138, 194
"Rightist conservatism," 47, 48

"Rightists," 135, 193(nn 36, 37)
    and antirightist campaign, 112, 127
    and rectification campaign, 98, 99–100, 104,
        105, 107, 109, 188(n52), 190(nn 75, 78)
    See also "Democratic figures"; Intellectuals;
        Liberals; Non-Communists
River control projects, 8–10. *See also* Irrigation
Roads, 8, 9(table), 14
Runan county, 63, 149(table)
Rural areas, 4, 8, 21, 25, 26, 27, 28
Rural policy
    1949–1955, 29–34. *See also* Agrarian reform
        movement
    1956–1957, 41–48, 50, 51–53, 55, 57, 58, 59–61,
        87, 116–119, 138, 178(n23)
    during rectification and antirightist
        campaigns, 91, 92, 99, 104–105, 109, 118–119,
        186(n5), 187(n21), 188(n43)
    during socialist campaign, 124, 128, 130–132
    See also Agriculture; Cooperatives; Peasants;
        Private enterprise
Rural Work Department, 109, 187(n28)

Safety, 72, 184(n57)
Sanfan, 188(n52)
Sanmen, 9, 11, 25, 175(n53)
    hydroelectric project, 9–10, 20, 138, 172(n5),
        187(n26)
Schools, 5, 50, 74, 102, 132–133
"Secondary activities," 43, 46–47, 52–53, 58, 116,
    117
Secret societies, 59–60
Sectarianism, 103
Seed selection, 18
Service sector, 73, 184(n62)
Shaanxian, 59
Shaling River, 194(n13)
Shangcheng county, 60, 62, 154, 178(n26)
Shangqiu county, 144
Shangqiu special region, 44, 62, 63, 77, 135, 143,
    174(n42), 180(n64), 194(n19)
Shangshui county, 179(n35)
Shengchan, 31
Sheng Wan, 183(n43)
Shen Xiaozhang, 63–64
Shi Desheng, 187(n29)
Shi Shaoju, 50
Small business, 28, 76–77, 78, 100
Social benefits, 28, 50, 72, 133
Social change, 20–22
Social crisis, 80, 81, 82, 83, 185(n86)

**Library and Learning
Resources Center
Bergen Community College**
400 Paramus Road
Paramus, N.J. 07652-1595

Return Postage Guaranteed